Tribes of Arunachal Pradesh

Encyclopaedia of Indian Tribes Series

Tribes of Arunachal Pradesh

Dr. S.S. Shashi

ANMOL PUBLICATIONS PVT. LTD.
NEW DELHI - 110 002 (INDIA)

ANMOL PUBLICATIONS PVT. LTD.
Regd. Office: 4360/4, Ansari Road, Daryaganj,
New Delhi-110002 (India)
Tel.: 23278000, 23261597, 23286875, 23255577
Fax: 91-11-23280289
Email: anmolpub@gmail.com
Visit us at: www.anmolpublications.com

Branch Office: No. 1015, Ist Main Road, BSK IIIrd Stage
IIIrd Phase, IIIrd Block, Bengaluru-560 085 (India)
Tel.: 080-41723429 • Fax: 080-26723604
Email: anmolpublicationsbangalore@gmail.com

Tribes of Arunachal Pradesh

First Edition, 1995

Reprint, 2004, 2014

ISBN 81-7488-012-7

PRINTED IN INDIA

Printed at Balaji Offset, Delhi.

Preface

The word "tribe" would seem to be one of the most glaring anachronisms of our time. In a world which is so often described as a global village, applying the term "tribe" and its adjective "tribal" to a particular kind of ethnic and social groups of people who are distinguished by their way of life and existence remote from the beaten paths of "civilisation", seems an error of visual acuity. When ways of life, as people of the so-called civilised world know it, are being questioned and all right-thinking people of this world harbour the yearning to return to nature and simplicity, surely the tribal folks all over the world may appear to be far more wise and sagacious in their defying and suspecting access to the many "benefits" that the civilised world is all too willing to confer on them.

It was Mr. W.R.H. Rivers who gave to anthropological literature the most popular definition of "tribe": a social group of a simple kind, the members of which speak a common dialiect, have a single government and act together for such common purposes as war. Other characteristics of a tribe have been listed as a common name, contriguous territory, a relatively uniform culture or way of life and a trace of common descent. However, these traits could be only superficially relevant. One tribe can in fact comprise many communities of neighbourhoods and villages. Many enthropologists have preferred to study them as what they refer to as "clusters of a higher order". They have also called them nations. The unfortunate aspect is that due to historical reasons tribes as such have been associated with incessant and relentless hostility, aversion to change of the most elementary kind and a ferocity which would appear to have blocked most do-gooders' intentions of bringing light into the life of these "children of lesser gods". The most fortunate aspect of the social history of mankind is that there have been true pioneers, full of empathy and a profoundly human concern for the tribal peoples of the world. In this hall of fame are such illustrious personae as Margartet Meade, Sir John Frazer, Verrier Elwin, Christoph von Furer Haimendorf, and William Crook and, among our own fellowmen, D N Mazumdar, S C Roy, L P Vidyarthi and Basu Deve Sharma. Together, their works constitute a body of knowledge which throws open magic windows onio the fascinating, sometimes disturbing but always revealing world of people who are after all our own fellow-beings.

India has the largest concentration of tribal population in the world, numbering almost 54 million in 1981. There are roughly 360 tribes all over the country, with four times as many sub-tribes spread over 24 States and three Union Territories. Arunachal Pradesh, Dadra and Nagar Haveli, Lakshadweep, Meghalaya, Mizoram and Nagaland have an average of 80 per cent of tribal population (as proportion of total population of the State/ Union Territory); Madhya Pradesh, Manipur, Orissa, Sikkim and Tripura have about 26 per cent; Andaman and Nicobar Islands, Assam, Daman and Diu, Gujarat and Rajasthan have about 12 per cent, while Andhra Pradesh, Himachal Pradesh, Karnataka, Kerala, Maharashtra, Tamil Nadu and West Bengal account for about 7 per cent. Uttar Pradesh has the lowest percentage of tribal population, 0.2 per cent. Of the total tribal population, about 86 per cent is concentrated in the eight States of central India, namely, Andhra Pradesh, Bihar, Gujarat, Madhya Pradesh, Maharashtra, Orissa, Rajasthan and West Bengal. To protect the interests of the tribal peoples in the matter of social and economic justice, Articles 330, 332 and 334 of the Indian Constitution provide for reservation of seats in Parliament for the Scheduled Castes and Scheduled Tribes in proportion to their population in their respective States and union Territories. However, there is no provision for reserved seats for tribal representatives in the Rajya Sabha, but in view of the consideration shown to them, there are always some Scheduled Tribe Members in the Rajya Sabha too.

One interesting feature of tribal history in India is the number of revolts and uprisings that have taken place as a result of the tribal peoples' attempts to fight injustice, oppression and exploitation. There have been as many as 65 uprisings by tribal communities all over the country, from as far back as the mid-eighteenth century when the British were first consolidating their presence in India. And, even after Independence, there have been over a dozen major uprisings since 1956. The most recent are the continuing Naga insurgency, the Bodo problem in Assam and the tribal violence in Tripura. Several sociological problems have been exploited by politicians to give them political overtones. It is evident that the great Indian tribal communities are being exploited even today, by a different set of people and with a different kind of tool. Dr. S. Radhakrishnan, the great Indian statesman and philosopher, once President of the Republic, said: "We must approach the tribal people with affection and friendship and not with condescension or contempt." That, in the end analysis, holds good even today. We must give the hostile tribals too a chance.

It is with such thoughts and a more than academic interest, even empathetic understanding, that I have endeavoured to bring together readable as well as useful material in this collection. The purpose is to present, in these companion volumes, a more than fleeting glimpse of the ways of the tribal peoples of this country. The attempt has been to stress the human aspect rather than the academic. This has necessitated tapping a vast range of sources: Central and State Government libraries and information centres, universities and other higher institutions, departments, agencies, autonomous bodies, research organisations and voluntary bodies. A vast amount of material had to be seen and sifted and the articles, papers, excerpts, notes and commentaries had to be placed in composite wholes in order to make the volumes an asset not only collectively but also individually. It is hoped that this effort has borne fruit.

I am grateful to a large number of scholars, students and welfare agencies for having provided copies of much of the material in this compilation. I owe a special word of thanks to the information centres of Andhra Pradesh, Assam, Mizoram, Meghalaya, Nagaland, Kerala and Orissa for their excellent response to request for material. The World Telugu Conference, Hyderabad, the Tribal Development Department, Government of Orissa, the Information Department of the Government of Himachal Pradesh, and the Research and Information Wing of the Government of Arunachal Pradesh have been equally forthcoming with a vast range of material. My student friends from Nagaland, Mizoram, Arunachal Pradesh and Bihar have been most helpful, as usual. I thank them all.

Editor

Contents

1

INTRODUCTION

Arunachal Pradesh was known as the North-East Frontier Agency (NEFA) till 1972. It was directly administered by the Ministry of External Affairs. On 20th January, 1972, the area was renamed as 'Arunachal Pradesh'. In the same year, it was declared as a full-fledged Union Territory. Because of this step, this territory attracted the attention of the Central Government and started its slow and arduous journey towards socio-economic and political development, as a distinctive entity in the geo-political framework of the Union of India. It was declared a State in 1987.

Arunachal Pradesh has an area of 83,578 sq, kms. with a population of 6,31,839. Of this population, 4,41,167 people belong to Scheduled Tribes. The territory is in the extreme north-eastern part of India, lying between 26.28' and 29.31' north latitudes and 90.31' and 97.30 east longitudes. The area is bound by China and Tibet in the North, Burma in the east, Bhutan in the west and Nagaland and Assam states in the south. The total length of its International border is about 1,628 kms. At present it has ten districts: 1. West Kameng. 2. East Kameng. 3. Lower Subansiri, 4. Upper Subansiri, 5. West Siang, 6. East Siang, 7. Dibang Valley, 8. Lohit, 9. Tirap, and 10. Tawang. The region is farely rich in natural potential, viz, forest products, minerals (coal, gas and petroleum) and hydel power. There are 24 major and 86 sub-tribes residing in different places of the area. All of them speak Tibeto-Burman languages. Some dialects are mutually understandable but at the same time some other dialects are so varied that communication between different groups is difficult.

Despite its gradual development during 36 years of independence of the country, the socio-economic development of Arunachal trails far behind in comparison to that of the rest of the country. Its infrastructural facilities are negligible. There are few roads and these too connect only district headquarters, generally constructed by and serving the Defence Services. The Border Roads Organization (code name 'Tusker') was set up primarily to construct roads in the far-flung frontier to meet the logistics of India's strengthened frontier defences in the face of China's mounting hostile attitude towards India.

In the field of education, the state has the lowest literacy rate in the country. While the all-India average literacy rate is 36.17 per cent, Arunachal's literacy rate is only 20.09 per cent. It has also the lowest density of population per square kilometre: only against the rest of the country's 221. However, every effort is being made to provide necessary impetus for development to the extent that it can match up with the standard of developmental activities of the rest of the country.

The tribal societies of the different parts of the country, particularly Arunachal Pradesh, are undergoing a process of transformation from their erstwhile seclusion and backwardness in many respects of modernity and development in social, cultural, political and economic spheres.

Development and Change

At present it seems that the system of development and occupational activities of the people are far wider than they were in the past three decades. Road and building construction, enlargement of electric power network, setting up of new administrative centres and opening of new schools mark the pace of development taking place in the area. These activities are exerting an inevitable influence on the life-styles, the attitudes and the standards of the tribal people. As a result, a surge of economic, social and political transformation is sweeping over the area. However, even at the accelerated pace of development, the concerned authorities have taken infinite care to avoid interven- tion in the local traditions and folk ways; the more cloistered people, like tribals, are therefore, content with the ways of civilisation and development. Pandit Jawaharlal Nehru said that " The Nagas vary greatly in education and general intelligence. Many of the Nagas are, I think, better material then most non-tribal people in India. At the same time, they are much tougher and they will not easily put up with impositions. Some of the Nagas are much more backward in this respect. Apart from the Nagas, many of the tribes in the NEFA are very backward indeed. All these factors have to be kept in view and we should not try to apply some rigid uniform rule to everybody regardless of circumstances." Hence, the imposition of any rigid rule may hamper their all-round development.

One of the great problems is how to evolve and effect the synthesis, how to bring about the development of modern political awareness, how to provide economic development with modern science and technology and education to them without eliminating the rare and precious values of tribal traditions and customs. For adopting this policy, steps have been taken to preserve tribal identity and they have been allowed to develop in their own way without any outside interference. However, there is controversy over this issue and the problem of the best way of administering the so-called tribal population has been debated for many years. Of these, isolation vs. integration is and interesting and well-known point of debate. Though some social anthropologists have contradictory views on the integration policy, we have observed that achievement of set objectives through this policy has had positive results in Arunachal Pradesh and Nagaland. The 'Inner-Line' policy which was introduced by the British Government and later followed by the Indian Government, played a major role in making this a big success. However, the 'Inner-Line' policy of colonial rule was constituted by the British for their own benefit, i.e., to exploit the rich forest resources of the area without carrying out its development in any real sense.

The vested interest of the British colonialists was evident from the very early years of the advent of the mechanics of exploitations in those areas. British officers were interested in discovering new areas and bring them under control, an accepted historical trait of any colonial rule. Second, the colonial rulers restricted entry into these areas only to certain class of British subjects. This 'Inner line' policy was not only to protect tribal people from outside exploitation but also for their own benefits. The British were aware that it was in their own interests and the interest of "Empire" to remove all possibility of exposing the susceptible tribal people to other political influences. It also prohibited businessmen from the hill areas, so that they could not be involved in commercial activities. Their involvement could have benefited the tribals, too, who are not as gullible as they are made out to be. However, the British writ prevailed. It is evident that all business was excluded from the area in order to leave the British free to exploit the rich forest wealth.

Third, the hill areas were isolated to keep away the tribals from joining hands with the National Movement for freedom which was then at its peak. The 'inner line' was an artificial barrier between tribal and non-tribal peoples. The colonial rulers were sure that any revolt by the tribals would be difficult for them to control inside the deep forest.

Mackenzie's writing and the 'inner line' rules are self- explanatory to these arguments. The 'inner line' regulation was implemented in 1872-73, under statutes 32 and 33 vic, cap 3, which gives the power of summary legislation for backward tracts to the executive government, was to be extended to Assam. It was found necessary to bring the commercial relations of hill tribes under control. According to 'inner line' rule, no British subject of certain classes or foreign residents can enter on transit without a licence. The pass or licence when given could be subjected to such conditions as may have appeared necessary. Specific rules were laid down on trade, the possession of land beyond the line, preservation of, elephants, etc., this also authorised government to lay down rules for their capture. These were made for their own interest.

Major Tribal Groups and Development

Therefore, it is very important to see how these developments, based on 'inner line' policies, are effectively taking place in different tribal groups of Arunachal Pradesh even at present. Now we shall discuss the major aspects of these developments in some of the major tribal groups of Arunachal Pradesh with special emphasis on Apatanis, Gallongs, Minyongs, Hill Miris, Sherdukpens, Khamtis, Wanchos, Noctes, etc. The study will also touch briefly upon the history and habitats of these tribes.

The Apatanis live in Ziro, the headquarters of Lower Subansiri district. They are occupying about 26 sq. kms., of very fertile land at a height of 5754 feet from sea level. Their present population is about 16,335. Before Haimendorf's visit to the Apatani country, there was a great confusion over the nomenclature of the tribe. Dalton writes that "to the North-West of the Hill Miri country we hear of a tribe called Anka Miris by the Assamese, who never visit the plains, but who, from the accounts we have received of them, must be very superior to the tribes of this family that we are acquainted with, resembling the Padam in their polity and customs. Surrounded by lofty hills, the country which they inhabit is an intensive valley, represented as being quite level and watered by a branch or perhaps the prinicipal stream of the Sundri river, and richly cultivated."

Thus from this we can safely assume that they have well organized polity and well established cultivation for ling period. However, we do not have correct historical accounts regarding the evolution of these aspects. The Apatanis are one of the most advanced tribes in the area, even well known to outsiders.

Including Minyong and Gallong from the Adis group, most of the tribes of the East Siang and the West Siang districts were known as 'Abor' in the recent past. The term 'Abor' signifies 'barbaric and independent' to the Assamese. They like to call themselves Adis which means 'hillmen'. At present the Adis comprise two broad divisions. The first constitutes of Padams, Minyongs, Pasis, Shimons, Boris, Ashings and Tangam and in the second category are the Gallongs, Romos, Bokars and Pailibos.

The Gallongs live in West Siang, East Siang and Upper Subansiri districts. Mainly they are concentrated in Along areas of West Siang district headquarter. Their present population would be approximately 48,000.

The Minyongs inhabit the Pasighat area, the headquarters of the East Siang district. Their present population would be about 27,000. The customs and traditions and the dialects of Minyong and Gallong are almost similar. But the Minyong dialect is closer to that of the Hill Miris and the Nishis of both the Lower and Upper Subansiri districts.

The Hill Miris occupy both the banks of the Kamala river to the north-east of Apatani plateau and the east of the Nishis, with a population of about 10,000. Their customs are a blend of Adis and Nishis.

The Khamtis immigrated from Assam in the last quarter of the nineteenth century. During that time the Khamti chiefs were acknowledged by the Assam ruler and subsequently by the British. In 1794, they overthrew the Ahom Viceroy of Sadiya who was known as Sadiya Khowa Gohain. In 1839 the Khamtis rebelled against the British and were expelled from Sadiya. It shows that they were a powerful tribe during those days. Now they live in Lohit district of Arunachal Pradesh and in some parts of Assam,. The Khamti population of Arunachal Pradesh is about 6,000. They belong to Hinayana Buddhist sect and are considered to be one of the most advanced tribes of Arunachal Pradesh. Khamti society is well organized with defined code of conduct and is economically very sound.

The Sherdukpens are also a major tribe of the area, even though their population is only about 2,000. They are concentrated mainly in the three important villages of Rupa, Jigaon and Shergaon of the south-west of West Kameng district. Their religion is a curious blend of Mahayana Buddhism and local belief.

The Wanchos inhabit the south-western part of the Tirap district with a population of about 23,000. Their social organization is different from the tribes of western parts of Arunachal. There is a chief in each village who controls the village affairs. In fact there are 36 villages which formed into 11 confederacies. They call it Jan and people of each group of confederacy are generally known by the distinctive name of the Jan.

The Noctes occupy the central part of the Tirap district to the north-east of the Wanchos. Their concentration is in Khonsa area of the district headquarter, and Borduria and Namsang are the two important villages. The chiefs of the abovementioned two villages are the most important and influential among the Nocte chiefs. Their present population would be approximately 23,000.

These tribes are passing through a period of great transition. Political and economic transformation is inevitable from traditionality to modernity due to the pace of fast development of science and technology in the country.

Therefore, the traditional political organization, the village council to the Legislative Assembly in the territory and the reaction of the people would comprise an interesting aspect of studies. The traditional village council had a three-fold function – judicial, administrative and developmental. After the introduction of governmental adminis- tration the area, the political system has branched off in different directions. The beginning of the administration of the territory, which was earlier known as the North-East Frontier Agency, may be traced back to the formation of the Government of India,

Foreign and Political Department, Notification of 1914. This was promulgated as the Assam Frontier Tracts regulations of 1880.

On the economic front, development has been very noteworthy since Independence, though the pace of development is unable, due to obvious reasons, to match up with that of the rest of the country. Only a few decades back the money economy was unknown to the people; barter was the only means of exchange. Thus, there was problem in valuation of goods which in turn limited the scope of trade and commerce. Agriculture, hunting and fishing were the main occupations of people.

In the Apatanis' traditional political system, Buliang is an important political institution. The Buliang or village council consists of members who are selected for their individual character and ability. Generally members are drawn from rich families of prominent lineages, noted for their wealth, traditional status and intelligence. However, few buliang members are chosen on account of their personal standing in society. Although Apatani society has no centralised authority, some minimum power required to run the local administration has been granted to members of the Buliang. Village affairs are managed by an informal procedure implemented through buliang.

There are three categories of Buliang, viz., 1. akha-buliang, 2. ajang-buliang, 3. vapa-buliang. Akha-buliang is chosen from elders, while vapa-buliang and ajang-buliang are chosen from middle-aged men and youths respectively. Only males can become members of buliang. This means that women have no political rights in this society. This old tradition went through many changes. But with the introduction of Panchayati Raj System in the area, women's political right was accepted and they were selected as Panchayat members. The emergence of democratic systems of government in the village and in the district council, i.e., Gram Panchayat and Zila Parishad (whose members are elected by adult franchise), enable members of the lower class of the society named as "guchi" to attain position of responsibility in the social hierarchy.

The Kebang of Adi is similar to the Apatanis' buliang. The members of the Kebangs are selected from clan members. There are others who do not have any particular clan but are selected on account of their personal influence and power of oration. A kebang has jurisdiction over its own village. Kebung-abus or elder members of the village council are usually senior men having long experience and have enough knowledge of the tribal lore. The younger Kebung-obus are given the necessary training. Usually each clan having more than one or none, are also not uncommon. Inter-village or Inter-bango disputes are settled by a superior body called bogun-bokang which is introduced by administration.

Dormitory System

In Adi society, there is a dormitory system like "morung"of Nagas which is called "moshup". This dormitory came into existence for the purpose of successful hunting or for provision of training in the science of the chase and for propitiation of the hunting gods. Dormitory is also used as the meeting place of the youth of a village and deliberation of Kebang. Thus, the place of moshup in the social organization of the Adis has great importance; young men sleep in the moshup until they marry. This institution is known by different names among different sections of Adis. Minyongs call it "dere", while Padam call it "moshup". The other allied groups term it "ngaptek", Boris and Ashings call it "byango." Girls dormitory is called "rasheng." Moshup boys help the elders by passing messages informing the village members about the decisions of the Kebang.

The Hill Miri's traditional political system was previously somewhat different from the Apatanis or the Adis. A few years ago, there was no specific political institution such as buliang or kebang. In fact, this society does not have a constituted central authority. Yet the Hill Miri society cannot be termed as an amorphous mass of people all pulling in opposite directions. Their informal code of conduct is clearly determined and may be accepted as binding. The Hill Miri society also does not have a formal council of elders which other tribal groups in the area possess. However, heads of families in a village do meet whenever circumstances demand. This meeting place is called "lopu". Their political and judicial systems are very similar to that of Mishis, and like them they rely considerably on "gindung" or intermediaries in decision of disputes.

However, at present the Hill Miris are moving towards a regular organization. In this new development there is a provision that there should be a bango council system consisting of village elders as members. This system is basically adapted from the political system of the Adis.

The Sherdukpen society is also basically a democratic one. There is a village council called 'jung' in each important village which is presided over by the village headman known as 'thikakhao' or 'gaonbura'. Village council members are called 'jung me', 'kechung' and chowkidar. Usually they are the elders elected by the villagers. The primary duty of kechung is to keep members informed of the place and the time of the council's meeting and also to act as messengers in all important matters. The function of kechung can be compared with the vapa-buliang of the Apatanis. There may be more than one kechung depending upon the magnitude of a village. Earlier there were dzong-pan appointed by the Tibetans who supervised the collection of revenue which was given to the Tawang Monastery in the form of grain.

Unlike the Apatanis, Adis and Hill Miris, the Khamtis have a different type of political system. They have a chief in the village aggairs. However, gaonburas or Keman assist the chief in discharging his duties. In a Khamti village there may be a hereditary king who is honoured by all the villagers. Next in social hierarchy is the Keman and then pathak. Keman has to perform his duties in consultation with the king and pathak acts as a guide in all religious activities. Next to pathak are free men who form the bulk of the population. The slaves of the past are at the bottom of the social hierarchy.

The assembly of the village elders congregates in the chief's house and settles all disputes.

The Khamtis are followers of Hinayana Buddhism. The monkhood amongst the Khamti is different from the priesthood because his role is basically not that of a priest. They are men of letters and well-versed in religious texts. They are influential and command high respect from the people. They live in a monastery which is known as 'chong' or 'kyong'.

In Wancho society both the chieftainship and the democratic village council had started functioning after introduction of the administration in the area. The society is divided into four classes according to the order of social status. Thus, according to this social hierarchy the chiefs are at the top who constitute the class of wanghams. Wangshas are next to wanghams who are offsprings of

Wangham father and Mangpan mother. Wangsus come in third category and are born of Wangsha father and Wangpan mother. Wangpans belongs to the lowest rung in the social hierarchy. Wangham post is hereditary.

The political organisation of the Wanchos is well defined and in each village the council functions as a centralised body. Every village has a council of elders known as Wangchu-Wangcha presided over by the chief. The sessions of the council members and their designations vary from village to village according to the nature of their functioning.

Both the Wangcho and the Wangcha are also called 'Khonsais' who act as ministers. Before giving a decision on any matter the chief consults the khonsais. The Wangcham acts as messenger and informs members and the village in general about the commencing of meeting and requests the members to attend the meeting. They too have a morung system like Adis.

The political structure in the Nocte tribe is almost similar to that of the Wanchos. They also have a chief and village as is found in Wanchos society. The council is constituted of the members with their power and functions as follows:

1. *Pan-bang* or chief of the village is also in charge of education and financial matters, and procuring of seeds, tools etc.
2. *Wangsai* or old chief, looks after the local festivals and ceremonies.
3. *Rangman* or senior chief is in charge of agriculture, orchard plantations, wet rice cultivation and terracing etc.
4. *Nok-bang* or junior chief looks after all engineering activities such as construction of buildings, bridges, paths etc.
5. *Somnai-Khonsai* is the Nok-bong's assistant.
6. *Tale* or Gaonbura of Chanmu is in charge of transport, kitchen garden, construction of water sheds, etc.
7. *Nomu* or sister of the chief who is given a post as an organiser among the women for poultry keeping, weaving, sanitation hygience.

A council elder is called *ngothun*, *ngothun* and *ngongthun*, and *ngongthin* among different sections of the Noctes. They too have a typical council where the ordinary members represent each clan comprising several officials. Their chief is called *lowang* who presides over the council. The functionary officials in the council are *ngongba, ramba* and *tanba.* Its members are called *noktang* or *kampa*. Ngongba is also popularly known as handique who acts as a minister to the chief and consults him or every important matter. He enjoys a position next to chief. Ngongba looks after all the rituals and cummunity festivals. Ramba keeps liaison with public as in the holding of council and its decisions. Tanba is the chief's messenger and is enjoined to inform the village of any matter related to the village council and also other villages representing on behalf of the chief. Other elderly persons who are called *noktang* or *kampa* are selected from each clan. They advise the council according to their knowledge and experience. Nowadays gaonbura is also a member of the council. Normally he acts as the official representative of the administration.

The post of the chief is hereditary and the eldest son from the first wife called Wangsadong is the heir-apparent. Wangsadong or the first wife must be a daughter of a chief of another village. Lowang remains as chief till his death, when the mantle of authority falls on the son. The succeding chief has to perform a rite called Panzbem thrice in his lifetime.

The Noctes also have the morung system known as Pang. It serves as an institution for the transmission of cultural heritage and the learning of civic duties. Informal education, such as training in cottage industries, is also provided to youths. Thus, the dormitory in Noctes has not much political significance, but it does serve as an important political institution in Adi society. However, this system has undergone a number of changes in Arunachal Pradesh. The gaonburas, who in the new system are appointed in the council by government, are provided with a red coat which distinguishes them from the common man. But they are not entitled to any salary or allowances. As a result of this there are two types of members in the tribal councils. Besides this there are two major different political organisations among the tribal groups of the territory, i.e., democratic type of village council and chieftainship system.

Village Councils

The buliang of the Apatanis and the kebang of the Adis are the model of a democratic village council in the area. Their members are chosen by the people, while in the chieftainship system the members are basically hereditary and appointed by the chief (who is the head of the village). However, there are some similarities in style relating to the functioning of the members of buliang or kebang and the Wanchos Wangchu-Wangcha. For example, vapa-buliang of the Apatanis and the Wangchams of the Wanchos are quite similar. The major differences among them are about the election of the council members and recognition of the chief in the council. While the council members are chosen from among men of high status, personal standing in the society and intelligence among Adis, Apatanis and Hill Miris, the member of Wangchu-Wancha and ngothun of the Wanchos and the Noctes society, usually come from among the chief's relatives. The chiefs of the villages whose post is hereditary, preside over the council meeting. But Buliang or Kebang membership is neither hereditary nor as powerful as that of the chief of a Noctes or Wanchos. Normally any of the council member is asked to initiate the discussion and the decision will have to be declared jointly on the basis of majority opinion. There are no divisions of power and function. Members are jointly responsible for any act of commitment of the council. Thus any arbitrary decision is not possible since all the members have equal rights and privileges in the council. On the other hand, any member of the village can take part in the deliberations of the council and the good points raised by them may always be noted down by the council members. But in those societies where the chief is the head of the village, there is considerable likelihood of improper judgement on any matter because of his unchallengeable power. Even the chief's relatives (who have a higher standing in the social hierarchy) have more weight in their voice. Owing to these powers and privilleges the chief and his relatives are always in an advantageous position and the common people are subjected to their mercy. Therefore, the procedure of the buliang or kebang is a comparatively simpler system, having an edge over the chieftainship system.

Equity and Social Order

There is no caste system among the tribal people of Arunachal Pradesh. But there are classes in society. Thus, there is no politics of caste in the territory which the other parts of the country are suffering grieviously from. Besides, there are no village slums or segregation of living residences on caste basis and the economic differences between the poor and rich are negligible. Hence, there is no evidence of marked social stratification.

In spite of the non-existence of a caste system, different classes can be witnesses in some tribal groups of Arunachal Pradesh. Among the Apatani community there are two distinct classes. Guth or Mittie are patricians and guchi or mura are commoners. In the past the commoners were dominated by the patricians and they were kept away from all political activities. In Adi society there were slaves who were deprived of political and economic rights. However, this system was abolished a few years back. Now they are free men and enjoing equally all the facilities available to them. Among the Khamtis, Wanchos and Noctes, the chief is the highest in the social hierarchy and next to him are his relatives whose functions we have already discussed. Hereditary classes can be witnessed among many tribal groups of the area under study. But among the Nishis it depends upon the economic status of the person. If a slave or nyria can accumulate property, after repaying his debt he may become a free man and can acquire the status of those of other freemen. It he becomes rich or accumulates more wealth he can have in turn his own slaves. But among the Apatanis, guchi can never become a guth because of his economic status. A similar system prevails in Wancho and Nocte societies.

Regarding the class system of the Apatanis, Wanchos and Noctes, Haimendorf has rightly observed that "despite the fact that the great chiefs of Wanchos had much more power and prestige than even the richest Apatani patricians, there is yet a certain conceptual similarity between the class system of the Apatanis who frown on inter-marriage between guth and guchi, girls of upper class may have premarital love affairs with guchi boys. The Wancho too have a custom which seems to make nonsense of the great chief's claim to the "purity of their line". Such rules are also prevailing among Sherdukpens and Monpas. However, among the Monpas there are simple divisions of status which Apatanis maintain.

The role of democratic village-government is very progressive as it functions according to the people's opinion.

The Apatanis' traditional system of social control was based on the general recognition that there cannot be the existence of central authority capable of laying down the law and in the last resort may enforce compliance with a code on conduct by the exercise of irresistible force. Buliang as the leading men of individual clans may debate and counsel it, they are all agreed on a course of action. But unanimity was not easily attained because powerful groups, each represented by a set of buliang, adamantly opposed each other. Resort to such devices as gambu with the charitable use of a measure of crude force was the only way out of such an impasse. In this regard the pressures of expediency overruled any call for impartial justice. Generally, the device of gambu is forced when dispute occurs between persons belonging to different villages or dispute is between two strong persons who have high status and influence in society. In either case the disputes are settled by the village buliang and by the elders of the village. Haimendorf reiterates that "though the buliang were collectively the upholders of tribal custom, they acted primarily as the spokesmen of their own clans and not as village headman with clearly defined functions. Their duties were those of arbiters rather than judges, and they usually did not take action unless a dispute had become a public issue which had to be dealt with by the community as a whole, be it by mediation or the use of force." Thus, according to him, council's functions are democratic in the sense that the opinion of the people are taken into account.

There is also a unique procedure of challenging the opponents in Apatani society, which is called "lisudu." Lisudu involves the ritual destruction of wealth. This is similar to the potlatch rites of the north-west American Indians. A man who challenged a co-villager to lisudu competition started by killing one or several of his mithun in front of his opponent's house and leaving the meat for distribution. In this system relatives of the participants who played a role and their social status is affected. The debt of a particular individual if borne by his relatives could only repaid if his opponent's relatives are capable of supporting him in the payment. This has a social binding as well on the relatives of both the parties. In this procedure sometimes added to the holocaust were certain valuable items like Tibetan bells, bronze plates, elephant tusks and swords. These items were smashed so that they could not be used again. Even though there was certain coercion in a lisudu, it was of moral and not of physical kind. The challenger destroys his own property and forces opponents to undertake such destructions if he wants to maintain his prestige. Such acts are generally performed by wealthy people. Some time the lisudu served a positive social purpose by curbing the accumulation of wealth in few hands and thus lessoing the pride and influence of a few prominent men competing for a dominant position in the village. But such a challenger is always a loser on the economic front. The relatives of both parties suffer from economic loss.

In the Apatani community there is another political systems which is called Dapo. Dapo is a formal treaty of friendship which assures peace and harmony. This system also prevails among the Hill Miris and Nishis of Subansiri district. Dapo is made between different tribes also, for example between the Apatanis, Hill Miris and Nishis. When these pacts are settled, certain rules and norms are laid down. These rules and norms may be extended to other willing villages or tribes. Violation or breaking down of dapo may result in severing of relationship and disputes may arise in this situation. Generally dapo pacts are broken or violated when there are certain disputes which could not be settled under the guideline of dapo. The dapo pact is almost similar to the present international law of agreement. There are no objections to consideration of a new dapo pact of agreement if both the parties are willing. Generally, it takes several years to reconcile with a village which has already violated a dapo.

About dapo Furer-Haimendorf rightly pointed out that "the dafla" have developed the forging of ceremonial friendships to a fine art and as those sharing a village side without forming a real community are under no obligation to afford each other mutual protection, it is only the web of specific alliances which gives a Dafla any sense of security. Individual trade relations between Dafla (or Miris) and Apatanis are less formal, and it is very occasionally that an Apatanis enters into a friendship pact with a Dafla by an exchange of mithun, known as gyotu-rako-sudu." However, there is a difference between dapo and gyotu-rako-Dapo pacts arise out of certain disputes between the villages and community as a whole and gyotu is initiated by the individual members of a village of community in times of peace and harmony as a precaution against conflict in near future. Furer-Haimendorf also asserts that "Apa Tani villages, moreover, conclude treaties (dapo) with the men of neighbouring Dafla villages in order to safeguard as far as possible the safety of the men and women visiting such villages in the pursuance of trade."

The system is similar to the Adis' bogung bokang which settled inter-bango disputes. Like buliang of the Apatanis, the kebang is the main functionary body in the villages. It has its juridiction over a village. All the disputes of the village settled by the kebang. The settlement procedure is similar to that of the buliang of Apatanis. Decisions of the councils are supposed to come from the people. The gams of headmen help only to enforce it. This injunction is associated with the latter, because they have profound respect for their customs and traditional law. This procedure seems to be a true democratic system.

Right from the beginning, Adis, Apatanis, Hill Miris and Nishis have never recognised the chieftainship system in the villages. The wealthiest and the most influential persons of the village often acted as leaders in all activities. Their word and orders were given due weightage and obeyed because of their privileged position in society. But he could never go against the wishes of the people. The leader did not rise to his position by election, nor in any case was the post hereditary.

Those who became despotic and tyrant leaders were thrown into the background and were forced to give opportunity to other influential and wealthy persons to assume such authority. At a later stage this led to the kebang system.

This shows that the political career of the people is characterized by the traditional procedure and the internal organization of an individual village and its relation with neighbours. The political structure of the societies of Adis, Apatanis, Hill Miris and Nishis are essentially democratic. Autocracy and oligarchy in any form are not known to them. The organization was very simple and effective.

Economic Activities

The traditional economy of the tribes of Arunachal Pradesh, with the excellent exception of Apatanis, is based on a type of agriculture known as shifting or slash-and-burn cultivation. This is one of the archaic forms of tillage. The economic variations and different patterns of agriculture are due to the nature of the terrain each tribe has occupied from time immemorial. Another type of economy is hunting and fishing as a means of processing food, domestication of animals, gathering of wild fruits and roots from the forest. This may, therefore, be described as fostering of animals food with progress in domestication of animals, hunting and fishing which which gradually changed from a means of livelihood to a form of entertainment. This obvious indication of the transformation of subsistence economy to the economy of surplus and larger communities based on assured means of production. Besides agricultural activities even today some tribal groups of area practise hunting and fishing from childhood. The elders teach youngsters how to use various types of weapons whenever, they get an opportunity.

Before the advent of the post-independence administration, another type of the livelihood was earned by posa collection. However, some scholars describe it as raiding. Adis, Nishis and Akas were the tribes who raided occasionally in the plains. However, it was not a raid but a tribal attack on the plains people when the latter failed to make posa payment. Before the British introduced posa system in the area, the tribal people collected tax from the plains people who used their land for agricultural purposes.

Sherdukpens used to get tribute from the Kacharis of Assam who live in the foothills. This tribute, according to some writers, was paid to get relief from such raids under pressure. The Adis were also occasional raiders. Two hundred and thirty-eight gams of the Adi clans were posa holder. They were paid a sum of Rs. 2,543 that time which they equally distributed among them. Adis, Nishis, Hill Miris and Sherdukpens chiefs claimed sovereignty over the Miris in the foothills and over fish and gold mine in the rivers that flowed down from their hills. Because of fear and interest the Behea gold washers inhabiting the west of Dibong and between the rivers Brahmaputra and the Bururisuti entertained the Adis with hospitality and occasional payment of the tax when the chiefs visited the lowlands. But the situation altered after British occupation in the area and when the Miris moved themselves to another area under the protection of the government, away from Adi (Abor) masters, the gold washers too withdrew themselves from their original homes, though they continued to frequent for golddust.

It is evident that the tribal people collected posa as a tax from the plains people who used their ancestral lands for cultivation in the Brahmaputra Valley. The Hill Miris who inhabited south of the Kamala river used to be semi-nomads. In the spring and summer months they cultivated their fields in the hills and during the winter they moved to the plains where each clan hunted and fished within the borders of its own clan's territories between the foothills and the

Brahmaputra Valley. When Assamese peasants first settled in those areas, the traditional owners demanded and received rent from the new settlers for the use of their clan lands.

With the establishment of administrative centres in the area and the development of roads and communications, ample opportunity is being offered to the hitherto primitive economy for adopting scientific technology and machinery and tools of modern age. Therefore, construction of roads is playing a significant role in socio-economic development of Arunachal Pradesh. However, the tpographical situation of Arunachal Pradesh is a distinct challenge to any activity of economic development. Education of tribal people is also playing an important role in socio-economic development.

The government's education policy is not only on the expansion of the literacy rate but more on its reorientation to meet the specific requirements of the economy, because without proper education primitive people may not be able to understand the developmental programmes and volunteer co-operation. Thus education has to be conceived as an integral part of the development scheme to bring the people in the area to accept progressive change in their social and economic life. This change requires to be promoted by imparting scientific knowledge and technology. Actually, the human factor itself needs more development in Arunachal Pradesh than in other parts of the country for which proper education is unavoidably essential.

Thereafter, the establishment of administrative centres, educational institutions, new technology for agricultural production, and development of co-operative societies in the area were the first steps to modernize the socio-economic development of Arunachal Pradesh. Priority was given for the establishment of consumers co-operative societies and to encourage trade and commerce to eliminate the middlemen and outsiders in economic policy. It was a successful policy. In 1960-61, there were only 28 co-operative societies and in 1979-80 their number increased to 114. This shows the increasing tendency, though development is slow and steady because the average annual growth rate in 20 years is only 1.54 per cent.

In the field of agriculture, substantial development has been achieved in over 40 years of independence. There are about 34,007 square kilometers land under the land development programmes for permanent cultivation. Out of total 1,453 square kilometers of cultivated land, about 1,268 sq. kms., is under the jhum cultivation, i.e., 87.35 per cent of the total cultivated land is under jhuming which shows underdeveloped cultivation in the area. Forest and occupies about 51,540 sq. kms., of 83,578 sq. kms. of the total area. Therefore, the agricultural activities in the area need priority for accelerating economic development.

Horticulture is new to Arunachal Pradesh, having been started in 1974-75. Now about 60 hectares of land are under horticulture. The terrain which is not suitable for agricultural cultivation is conductive to horticulture and the climate too is suitable in many places. Therefore, at present, the government has taken various steps to develop horticulture in the territory on a large scale.

In Arunachal Pradesh 72.29 per cent of the total population is cultivators, 2.45 per cent engaged as agricultural labourers and 25.26 per cent is engaged as other workers. If we compare figures for the last two decades, only 0.58 per cent of the total population was cultivators in 1961 and it increased to 78.34 per cent in 1971. This shows that in 1961 there were only few cultivators and 99.38 per cent of the population was engaged in hunting, fishing, and food-gatering activities. Due to modernization of agriculture and development in the area, cultivators increased to 76.34 per cent at the annual average growth rate of 134.07 per cent in 1971. The decrease in the number of cultivators to 0.05 per cent in 1981 from 1971 is due to increase in other occupations, such trade and commerce and the employment of the educated people in white-collar jobs. There are more than 4,542 persons of Scheduled Tribes in the territory who are employed in government jobs.

Besides agricultural development many economic development avenues have been established as a source of income in the area. Forest contributes a good amount to the territorial income. In 1979-80 it contributed Rs. 426.62 lakhs. Raw cane, bamboo, timber and plywood are the major export items to neighbouring States.

In Arunachal Pradesh, according to the Geological Survey of India, about 7,500 sq. kms. of area comes under geological map of the area in different districts. The geological information obtained so far has led to the deciphering of various geological aspects. These are structural, tectonic and geomorphic in broad patterns and helping in establishing and exploiting the mineral potentialities of the territory.

Coal and oil have been discovered in Miao in Tirup district. Polymetallic sulphide ore, limestone and dolomite, marble, graphite, rock phosphate, saline springs and afforescence thermal springs are available in different places in the area.

Arunachal Pradesh has innumerable river streams many of which cascade from 150 to 250 metres. The hydel potential of those streams ultimately emptying themselves into the Bhahmaputra accounts for an astronomical 20,000 megawatt. Theoretically it can produce 50 per cent of hydel potential of the rest of India. The local requirement of electric power is extremely limited because of paucity of industries in the area. Fully utilised, this hydel potential can earn Arunachal a net income of about Rs. 150 crore per year which will be enough to finance all its developmental progammes. In order to develop this potential Five Year Plan allocations can play a significant role.

The rate of economic development in Arunachal Pradesh is not so rapid as it seems from outside. The majority of the people in area are still living hand to mouth, particularly in the far flung and interior areas where road communication has not yet penetrated. This could be revealed from the standard of living in those areas. Essential commodities like rice, salt, wheat pulses, etc., are not available those areas. Foodgrains are supplied by air-dropping which is a very costly affair and involves considerable wastage due to obvious wear and tear. Commodities are lifted from Assam. In order to avoid these difficulties, therfore, the road construction in those areas is of the utmost necessity. Although this too is a very costly affair, road construction will be a permanent solution. It will also be very helpful in the overall socio-economic developmental activities in the area.

Although the territory claims self-sufficiency in foodgrains production, practically it has to get supplies from the neighbouring State of Assam. Thus, it is essential to ensure that self-sufficiency leads to surplus productions in the areas. Though it is not possible to produce surplus in all the agricultural productions, it has to produce surplus in some items and specialize in it. This will enable the territory to earn more revenue and become self-reliant. Therefore, suitable agricultrural items can be identified which can be produced in the area. It is also necessary as about 95 per cent of the total population of the area depend of agriculture. It is also important to invest a large amount of the plan allocation for agricultural production, with thrust areas in land development, irrigation, fertilisers, livestock, fisheries etc. Tribal people will derive maximum benefit out of this.

At present, Arunachal produces 162,116 metric tonnes of foodgrains and 8,121 metric tonnes of oil seeds. Of these, lower Subansiri district produces the maximum of foodgrains with 37,553 metric tonnes and Tirap district leads in oil seed production with 2,239 metric tonnes. The irrigation facilities in the area are also not significant. Above 6,383 hectares of land is under channel irrigation and 357 hectares of land is irrigated by other sources. West Siang and Tirap districts have the most of irrigation facilities, with each district having more than 1,000 hectares of irrigated land. West Kameng, Lower Subansiri and Lohit districts are having minimum irrigation facilities, with 250 hectares each. Thus, it is necessary to improve the irrigation facilities in the area particularly in low-lying areas and valleys where such facilities are possible.

In the field of horticulture and fruit-growing the area has started planting apple and pear trees in Tawang, Lower Subansiri and West Kameng districts. This cultivation is encouraging and West Kameng has started surplus apple production. The area is more suitable for horticulture than any other cultivation due to its hilly and terraced nature of land. In this field Himachal Pradesh and Jammu and Kashmir have set a good example. Vast areas of Arunachal Pradesh can be very well utilized for this purpose. The experiment of horticulture is successful in many areas. Unused and abandoned jhum land can be easily adopted for this purpose. Horticulture also helps in maintaining the ecological balance, adversely affected by deforestation due to the process of jhuming. At present only 1,010 hectares land is under horticulture which is negligible in such a vast area. Of these, about 100 hectares of land has been brought under the horticulture in the districts of West Kameng, West Siang, Lohit and Tirap. West Kameng district produces surplus apple and is creating a market in the neighbouring states. The level of horticulture production in the territory for the year 1984-85 was 6,390 tonnes of apple, 5,270 tonnes pineapple, 1,450 tonnes of bananas and 9,60 tonnes of orange. This shows the increasing horticulture potentialities in the area. Thus improvement of horticulture will also improve the lot of many Arunachal tribal people and fetch good revenue for the territory.

In the field of industry also no significant development has been made so far in the area. Till today there is no major industry in the State. There are about 784 villages and small-scale industries, only 6 medium industries and 40 weaving units in the area. Of these 254 villages and small-scale industries are located in Siang district, 5 medium industries in Tirap and 1 in Lohit district. Of the 40 weaving units 12 are established in Tirap district. Tawang and Subansiri district have 9 and 12 units respectively.

The outline above reveals that Arunachal is still backward in many socio-economic developmental aspects. The fund allocation on priority basis must benefit larger sections of the society and also accelerate the economic growth in the area. It is to be noted that the rich are becoming richer and the poor are becoming poorer. For instance, the so-called contractors are lining their pockets by foul means and fair. Only rich men are involved in such works as they have money to invest. The poor, obviously not in a position to take up sudh works due to lack of capital, end up working on sites as daily-wage labourers. On the other hand, there are non-tribal contractors who make huge profits and are draining the region's wealth. Therefore, in the matter of public works like road contracts, if the allotment is made on a co-operative basis or to willing and able tribal groups, the benefit derived from such projects will be distributed in the local society and the exploitation of labour class will be minimised. Thus, it is very important that planners bear in mind that the fund allocation is made to benefit the larger sections of the society, particularly needy and poor people. To achieve this and accelerate economic growth at par with the national level, the people of the area have to work hard with sincerity.

2

TANGAMS OF SIANG DISTRICT

Cultural History

The Tangams are a branch of the Adi tribe of Siang District and they trace their origin from Pedong Nane, the mythical mother of all beings. After a long stay in the beginning at Luku Tirang, they wandered for some time along the Siang till they come at last to their present habitat.

Originally they had eight clans viz. Tamut, Daji, Doron, Mudo, Judo, Kondo, Ngakki and Ngakko. Of these the Ngakko have completely died out and the Mudo, Jodo and the Kondo have each but one family left.

In the beginning they were distributed 25 villages scattered over a large area running for about 90 kilometres along the Nigong from the Siang in the east. These villages were Mayung, Kopu, Jido, Ngaming, Kindo, Kuging, Nyering, Adun-Moyi, Demi-Tengen, Yoying, Yeng Jinging, Gedok, Tore, Peying, Tore-Baying, Turing, Gunggong, Teyi, Joso-Tirang, Chuji, Tanging, Lodi, Gelling and Korbo. Of these Kindo, Tore-Baying, Mayung, Ngaming, inhabited by the Jodos, Tamuts, Dorons and Mudos, were the largest with more than 100 houses each.

Kindo no longer exists. It was destroyed long ago in one of the numerous internecine feuds that these settlements frequently were engaged. Only a few sago palms and groves of bamboo and cultivated trees stand as melancholy witnesses to what flourishing village it used to be.

Some of these disastrous wars still live in the memory of the people. Once a family quarrel over the betrothal of a girl of the Tamut clan involved them and the Tore, the Mudo and the Doron in a regular war. The Tore proved more than a match for the other three arrayed against them. The latter looked around for help. Secret emissaries sped along the *Lenging bedang* to Robok where they crossed the Siang to Bomdo. They succeeded in winning over that village to their side. The Bomdos marched to Gete Lempi and from there delivered a swift and sudden attack on the Tore. Unprepared and taken unawares the Tore were over whelmed; many of them were killed and their village was destroyed. Only a few survivors managed to run away to Oran in Pemako beyond the high hills.-

A mistake involved the village of Adun Moying in a war with the Idus. The country of the Idus was separated from the Tangams by the high range of Abroka. Once the villagers of Kuging and Kindo went to these hills to hunt *takin*. They built a hunting shed and left the small boys who were with them behind in it as they went out to hunt. When they returned they found the children missing but some strange people in the shed whose language they did not understand. They were Idus. The Idus tried to explain to them by gestures that the children had left the place and they did not know where they had gone. But the Tangams believed that the Idus wanted to kidnap the children they kept them hidden somewhere. So they fell upon them and killed nine of them. One managed to escape and carried the news of the massacre to his village. The Idus were furious and vengeance was speedy. In the darkness of the night they fell upon the village of Adun Moyi and slaughtered all on whom they could lay their hands. The children in meantime, weary of waiting for their elders returned from the forest but only to discover the horrible tragedy on their account.

Biangog, a rich man of kindo, who originally belonged to Tore had an only son Ngolling.One day he went to a pool Busho Sitong in Tore Baying. After a little of fishing he was resting in a shed near the pool when the Idus returning from Adun Moyi came upon him. They seized Biangong, tied his hands and took him up a high cliff called Uro-Moning. There they speared him and threw him down. Two Tangam youngmen were hunting in the forest nearby and they saw all this and rushed to the village to inform his son Ngolling. The village rallied at once and went after the Idus. From the top of Abroka they saw an Idu village. The pursuers wanted to attack immediately. But Ngolling thought that if they attacked, some of their own men were likely to get killed in the fight and then their clansmen would demand compensation from him which would be enormous. So, he planned to stop them from attacking, and said that he had dreamt that his father had turned into a bird and was living on a tree near the village. His father's soul had also become one with his and if they attacked the village they were sure to lose in the battle. The Tangams believed in what he said and reluctantly returned to their village. After a few days Ngolling told his wife to make some rice cakes for him and gave out that he was going to the hills to lay traps for game. But instead he secretly went to the Idu village across the Abroka and hid near the water point. A woman in an advanced stage of pregnancy came to draw water and he killed her with a single stroke of his dao. The impact of his stroke was so great that the woman delivered a still-born child. Ngolling took the palms of the woman back to his village and showed them to all as a proof that he had avenged his father's death.

The Idus when they discovered this murder raised a war cry and marched against the Tangams. They came upon Ato Koniong an old man of the village and tried to seize him. But Ato Koniong fled before the Idus could detach their quivers from their back to shoot at him. The Idus considered it unwise to attack the village after this incident as the old man must have alerted the people and so they turned back. But the Tangams followed them caught up with them and succeeded in killing one of them.

Once there was a war between the Padams and Shimongs in which many Shimongs died. The Tangams took pity on them and helped them in the construction of their damaged houses and the *byango*. On another occasion the Tangams sided with the Shimongs in a war with Membas. Some Tangam elders had gone to the Memba country and found to their surprise that the Membas were preparing for war against them. They did not know the reason but asked the Membas for a peaceful settlement of any dispute that there might be. The Membas made a show of agreeing to their proposal and treated them to copious drink and when they were drunk they beheaded them. The news reached the Tangams and combined columns of the Tangams and the Shimongs attacked the Memba village and killed all the people. Other Memba villages prepared to retaliate and secretly pushed two columns, one to Kongkangong and other to Ruskin. The Tangams had also placed patrols against surpirse attacks. Three members of one such patrol, Kabeng, Tani and Yeapo by name, fell in the hands of one of the columns. Two of them, however, managed to escape and alert the people of Kindo. The Kindo people, were not prepared to face an immediate attack and fled across the Nigong. When the Membas reached Kindo, they found it deserted. They got busy with pillage in the course of which one of them found a paper on the rack of the house of one Begong. This was an order from Kanam Deva of Taro forbidding the Membas to attack the Tangams and warned that if they disobeyed the order they would be visited with severe punishment. This frightened them and they immediately withdrew. On their way back they met Tangam stragglers and asked them to go back to their village as they were going back in peace.

But this friendly relation between the Tangams and the Shimongs did not last ling. An unhappy and thoughtless incident caused a war between them which was the ruin of the Tangams for all time to come. This was the famous Shimong Tangam war. Pasu Chuchik, a dwarf from Karko on the other bank of the Siang opposite the village of Shimong, was seized with a thirst for travel. He followed the course of the Siang and came to the villange of Rigu-Rirang. There was a place Yaro Bongo near the village from where he got a grand view of broad valley of the Nigong and decided to go there. The villagers told him that the land was unknown and nobody knew the tracks, and so he should not undertake the risk of going there. But he persisted in his desire, crossed the Siang by the Cane suspension bridge 'Ladum' and came to the first Tangam village of Jido. The people received him well and treated him to good cheer and drink. This reception encouraged him to proceed further and he came to Kindo where also he was received kindly and well. A *kebang* was called in the byango in his honour and the villagers gathered there to hear from him abount his land and people. Unfortunately some wages in the gathering were amused with his small size and thought of playing practical jokes with him. First they lifted him up and put him on the *kumbang* below the ceiling. Next they took him down and tossed him from shoulder to shoulder. This amused the gathering and all lauged merrily.

Pasu Chuchik felt insulted and flushed with anger leapt down from the *byango* platform and walked away in huff. The elders realized at once that the joke had gone too far and set after him. They caught up with him, begged him not to take any offence and to forget about it, and presented him with a felling axe as a sign of their friendship. Pasu accepted the felling axe but did not forgive the wrong. He said nothing and went back to Shimong by a different route to throw the Tangams out scent. He had *kebang* called in the village and addressed the gathering, "Oh my Shimong brothers, if there be big trees in the field left standing they cast their shadows on the growing crops and do not let them grow. You have to cut the trees if you want the crops grow. But this simple thing I find you neglect. In your fields I found many of such obstructive trees. I call your attention to this and it is your concern whether you would have your *kebang* be strong and resolute enough to remove these trees. For me I now go to my own village to warn them of the same negligence." So saying Pasu Chuchik left for Karko.

The Tangams heard of this and they sensed danger. A deputation of their leaders went to Likor, one of the big settlements of the Shimongs. The people there assured them not to worry as they would blunt their spears on stones and break their arrows even if others decided on war. In return for their neutrality, however, they demanded a *danki* and the Tangams got one from Ato Doni Yong of the Jodo clan who was one of the richest man of the time and gave it to the Likor people. The latter, however, did not keep it themselves but passed it on to the Shimong village, probably to intimate that the Tangams had bought peace. From Shimong danki found its way to karko and fell in Pasu Chuchik's hand. He planned to use this symbol of peace for his own purpose. He strapped the danki on the back, fastened the axe to his side and went to a Memba village on the bank of the Siang. There he told the Membas that the Tangams had given him the vessel and the telling axe and had commissioned him to chop of the heads of all the Membas with the axe and cook them in the pot. Naturally this enraged the Membas and they decided to punish the Tangams for their audacity. The news of this development reached the Tangams too late for negotiation and they prepared for defence. They cut the suspension bridge over the Siang to disrupt the line of communication of the Membas.

Pasu Chuchik was not idle all this time. He came once again to the village of Shimong and repeated the false story there. As he was thought to have come straight from the Tangam country his story was believed. There was great anger and a big *kebang* was called at Likor. The meeting however, was divided in opinion till and old man respected for his wisdom supported war to drive away the Tangams from the Nigong valley. Immediately preparations were set a foot but with such secrecy as no news of it leaked to the Tangams.

On the appointed day a strong Shimong detachment marched against Jido at the confluence of the Nigong and the siang. The movement was swift and efficiently executed and the Tangams were absolutely in the dark about it.

The Bomdos, however, on the other bank of the Siang were on friendly terms with the Tangams. When they saw the Shimong warriors marching they wanted to help the Tangams and came upto Rigu Rirang. This village unfortunately was on good terms with the other Shimongs and stopped the Bomdos from further progress by cutting down the Ladum bridge near their village. The Bomdos waited for five days on the other bank and shouted to the Tangams on the other bank to alert them of the danger and to make rafts for them cross.

But as providence would have it, the Tangams did not hear the call for a long time and when they did and understood the message and set to make rafts burriedly it was late. The Shimongs had already crossed the Nigong. They had sent a detachment by another route which came down from the Abroka via the Dadogong hill near the present Tasigong village and caught Jido in a pincer drive. There was hardly any opposition and all were massacred. The invaders advanced attacking and taking village after village burning them and killing men, and women and children without mercy. A few miserable survivors managed with great difficulty to escape by different routes to Pemako across the mountains and went as far as Rashing. Shimongs too followed them and came to Po which was then governed by the Taro Deba Jipon Deman wang. He had taken the Tangams under his protection. The Deba told the Shimongs to go back but the Shimongs insisted on surrender of their victims. The Deba thereupon thought of a plan to impress the Shimongs with his prowess. He had three long stout bamboos placed side by side and invited some one from the Shimongs to cut the three with a single stroke of the dao. If any one could do it he would let them to do whatever they liked with the Tangams. Many a Shimong tried but not one could do it. After the Shimongs gave up the Deba drew out his own big sword and accomplished the féat with great ease. He next had an egg placed on the head of one his men and from a distance shot at it and hit it without as much as touching a hair of the head. The Shimongs were fully demoralized with these two demonstrations of strength and skill and so when he ordered them to go back and threatended them with dire consequences if they dared molest the Tangams now in his protection they left quietly without any protest. Back in their country they held a *kebang* and the *kebang* agreed that the war was a great mistake on their part. It had done them no good but on the contrary had made them kill their own kith and kin. It was decided to send emissaries to the Taro country to persuade the Tangams to come back. At first only a few of the Tangams could be induced to return and live in the Shimong village. They too found the life of refugees depending on charity very unpleasent. They had no right of their own on the land and rivers and had to depend solely on what their hosts gave them out of pity. So they decided to go back to their own land at Kuging and Nyering. Some of the Shimongs had settled in these places soon after the flight of the Tangams but they had to come back out of fear of the Idus who had occupied the upper Nigong valley deserted after the war. The idea of Tangams settling in that unsafe region which would serve as a buffer between them and the Idu appealed to Shimongs and they willingly allowed the Tangams to resettle in their village. The Tangams on their side felt more secure when they got assurance of protection from Kanan Deba of Taro. Thus, Kuging, Nyering and Mayum were resettled by the Tangams and the others who has stayed back in po gradually returned.

Their descendants now live in those villages in two of which Nyering and Mayum they are gradually merging with the Ashings, and in no distant future may lose their identity.

A legend later grew up among the Tangams introducing supernatural element as the cause of the war. A big *bine* snake used to come to the *byango* of Kindo every day and lie on the main beam below the ceiling with its tail hanging down. The children of the village once saw it and started playing with the tail pulling it from one corner of the byango to the other. The sanke liked it. So taken up with the game were the children that they forgot to go home for lunch. The elders did not know of this absence at meal times because they were out in the fields in the day. When, however, they came to know it, they were very much intrigued with the strange behaviour of the children. They asked them why they did not come home for food. The children told them of the game with the snake. The parents did not believe the story and while going to the field next day asked one of the old men to stay back in the village and look into it. The man went to the *byango* and saw the snake glide up the beam and the children catching hold of its tail and playing with it. He ran to the fields and told the people of what he had seen. They did not believe him and decided to check up with story. The next day they did not go to the fields and waited for the snake to come. But it did not come that day. They thought that the snake perhaps had come to know of their presence and so did not turn up. They, therefore, secretly left ten warriors behind when they went to the fields next day. These warriors hid in the jungle near the *byango* and waited. They saw the snake come and sprang at it from thier hiding with bows, arrows and daos to kill it. But to their astonishment the snake just vanished and was nowhere to be seen.

It is only after a few days of this incident that Shimongs attacked and the war started. The Tangams believe that the snake was a *wiyu* of the Shimongs and it set Shimong to punish them for their unprovoked attack on it.

Language

Tangams speak the Adi language with dialectical variations. It is a little more removed from the Padam than Shimong. Among differences in pronounciation, the preference of 'r' is very marked.

The speech has not been written down as yet. The Tangam have no knowledge of use of paper inspite of close association with the Membas and Khambas of the Yang Sang Chu valley. Yet they have a rich literature which has been handed down generation by oral transmission. It is mostly poetical and recited and sung on festive and religious occasions.

Village

Tangam villages are perched on narrow spurs between 2000 to 3000 ft. Such sites are considered healthy being open to fresh breeze. Security from surprise attacks by enemies is also greater in such places. Closeness to water sources does not seem to have as much weight as the other two. In all the three Tangam villages water is to be brought by bamboo pipe lines over considerable distances.

The fields generally lie close to the village, usually within a radius of five or six miles.

Houses are built on level grounds wherever possible otherwise on gentle slopes. No definite plan is followed in the lay out of the village.

Distances between the houses and their facings are determined by the lie of the ground. The general pattern, however, differs from that of the Shimongs. In a Tangam village houses are not huddled together as with the Shimongs. The advantage is that in case of fire only single house affected and not the whole village. Unlike the other sections of the Adis, the *byango* also is built in one side of the village and not in a centre; and the granaries lie scattered about within the village and near the houses of the owners and not in a separate place all together.

The *rasheng* or the girls' dormitory stands in the centre of the village. It is a dying institution as the girls nowadays have started preferring to stay in their own homes. Here the older girls taught the younger the art of weaving, folktales and folk-songs and it served as a place of relaxation after a hard day's labour. The boys of the *byango* used to visit the girls here to make friends and to woo for marriage. No girl was allowed to pass the night in the *byango*. Bachelors of the village slept in it and mount guard. All social functions and important *kebangs* were held in it. This system of *mekudura* has died out as with the cessation of feuds vigilance bacame unnecessary. Remains of defence constructions of the older days may still be seen in an old village like Kuging; stone walls and stone chutes guarding the main approaches to the village. *Tengi* a species of plant which never dies reinforced the walls. This plant had a psychological significance also. It symbolized the spirit that never dies and its flame-coloured flowers inflamed the fiery ordour of the braves. The tree blooms in the month of Biro (March) and proclaims the advent of the new year and for preparation of the land for cultivation. Tangam houses are of the common Adi type and structure, with locally found materials such as bamboo, stone and wood.

Blacksmithy must have been once a common craft with the Tangams but later the art declined among them against the competition of the Membas and the Khambas who were superior to them in technical competency. Nowadays it is more or less dead. There used to be one blacksmith in Mayum—but recently he too has given up the profession.

The Tangams now use a few metal articles of iron, brass and bellmetal but most of these used to be of Tibetan manufacture. The most important of these are:

Hangu	– A bellmetal cauldron
Tali	– A large brass plate
Tashi Merang	– A large brass bowl
Mera	– A medium sized brass bowl
Ledo Peki	– A brass cooking vessel
Lenkit	– A three-legged iron stand which is placed over the fire to support cooking vessels.

Of these, the first four are considered to be valuable, costing from a pig to a mithun according to the size.

Stone as a material for domestic articles is rare. The only instance of its use is a vessel shaped out of solid stone. This type of stone work is not indigenous. It is a Khampa art and such vessels are obtained from them.

Dress

The Tangam man wears a long blue full-sleeved coat reaching down to the kness, usually woolen in the winter. When out hunting or treking he puts on along black coarse woolen piece known as *payong* with a hole in the middle to slip in the head and with the sides unsewn and the two ends hanging loose in the front and the back. The loin cloth called *Hapung* is very small just on the extreme verge of the modesty. On the head they wear stong finely woven cane hats *(lugiyum)*. If it has a brim, it is called *beji lugiyum* and if none, *yokkut lugiyum*. A piece of black cotton cloth (goying kirak) is tied round the waist along with a cane belt fitted with *tilus* which are made of shells.

Tilus are costly and two rows in a belt is equivalent to a small mithun in value. The legs from the knees to the ankles are covered with two cotton strips (leyi and ambiyok) in puttee fashion. These are meant to keep the muscles stout and to protect the legs from insect bites. The men do not wear beads everyday. These are stored away to be worn on special occasions. The pongku, *podat, tarbun and duleng* are the costliest valued at a full grown mithun each, while the cheap not costing more than a small pig are the *ipong* and *kyami.* Bead necklaces for the men are called *tabiyap.* Its price depends on the kinds of beads used and that depends in its turn on the pocket and status of the wearer.

The dress for the woman comprises *jabin,* a blue coarse wrapper of cotton or wool held in place by a cane string passing over the head, *abc,* a skirt of maroon colour either plain or with light chocolate horizontal stripes reaching upto the knees and a *latu* a woolen coat blue or white. *Bayin* a cloth of cotton or the fibre of the *tamak* tree is worn like a belt round the waist. Young girls from three years age till puberty wear beniyops which are cane belts with three four metal discs. When very young these belts are the only dress they wear. It is going out of fashion.

Ginchaks or white cylindrical shells are worn in belts around their waist over the skirts. These are costly. Forty such cylinders may cost a small mithun. On the ear the men wear parang blue earings suspended from the tube. *Gibung* and *Alu Yami* are tight-fitting brass wristlets. Tangam men can hardly be said to have a hair style. They just let it grow and wear it unkempt. When inconveniently long they just clip it in the front and the back.

The women wear blue beads known as *parang* and *patok dumpi* in their earnings. Each earning has a number of them ten or more. There are two kinds of *patok dumpi,* the *miling* and *milun.* Beads for necklaces are different. *Doppun, dange and kilun* are the costliar and *punni, gunning, kiku* and *kili* the cheaper varieties. Three large mithuns are paid for one of former, while one of latter may be had in exchange of a fowl. *Legam* is a wristlet for women, but worn only on festive occassion. It is belived to have come from Bisi Ado the Vulcan of the Adi Mythology. *Gange* is the wristlet for everyday wear.

Tangam women let their hair grow and plait it into pigtails which are passed over the head and tied into a fine knot. These are decorated with beads.

They wear flowers in the ear. Young maidens prepare a kind of rouge with the red juice of a plant and paint their cheeks with it. This is a fashion learnt from the Khambas. Oil obtained from a fruit called *temin* is used for the hair. The ripe fruits are gathered and allowed to rot. The outer coating is then peeled off and stones inside and dried in the sun. These are then crushed on stones, pounded in a morter, fried and pressed with an wooden block on a cane basket. The oil that comes out, is collected in a bowl and is used for the hair. Mython butter is also used sometimes for it.

Weaving:

Tangam women are good weavers as all Adi women and meet all their family needs with their portable loin loom. Locally grown cotton, wool and fibres of some plants supply them with the yarn. Cotton grown by them is a short staple variety and the wool they get from the sheep they rear. Ginning is done with the help of hand operated wooden tools. Spinning is an occupation for the leisure hours. The yarn spun is made into balls. The Tangam Textiles are not very rich in patterns and designs. Maroon skirts with black borders are universal. Departures are rare.

Dyes are obtained from plants. Blue dye is obtained from *angot* a small herb. These are collected and allowed to rot in water. The dye is extracted only in winter as at that time only one gets really fast colour. The yarns are dipped in the colour and dried. The *temen* creeper gives them the red dye. It is crushed in morter after being cut into pieces and dried in the sun. It is then boiled in water and the yarn is dyed in it. The green dye comes from a small ginger like plant called *gamba.* The seeds of this plant are crushed and boiled. All these dyes are fast and do not fade even after constant use of several years.

For washing clothes they use the runner of a plant known as *dopiyang tehat.* These are dug up, washed, crushed and then rubbed in the cloth. The cloth then is threshed on a stone or beaten with a flail and washed in clean water.

Domestic Animals:

The Tangams rear mithuns (*Bos frontalis*) pigs, cows, fowls and dogs. Of these the Mythun is the most important because of its place in the socio-economic life of the people. The status of a man is judged by the heads of mithun he owns. It is the highest sacrifice, most acceptable to the deities in religious rites and to the people in social festivals. So mithun is always in high demand. It is kept in a semi-domesticated state being allowed most of the time to stay free in the Jungle. The only link that ties it to the house is the occasional visit it pays for salt. There are also salt-licks in the jungle known as *doyit* and if the owner wants his mithun at any other time he goes to them. Every mithun has got its ear punched with special marks indicating the village and the owner, so if it strays beyond the village boundaries, it is not difficult to identify it. It is not easy to steal a mithun. The theft would be easily found out. Still in early days mithun has caused many a feud. Even nowadays disputes over mithun are very frequent though instead of feuds these are settled in the village councils or in the village councils or in the courts of law.

Pigs are reared a large number. They stay around the house specially under the platforms. A few hogs are castrated to make them fat and tasty. Every village has got persons who know the surgery. A hog is castrated when three months old with a sharp knife and the *oil of layer* fruits is applied to the wound to keep away maggots and to heal it. One day of taboo follows the castration. After castration the hog is put into the latrine where it acts as a scavenger as well it fattens. This is again followed by a light taboo in which husking, milling and brewing are forbidden but not cultivation.

Other pigs live on the kitchen refuge scattered over the yard. A special pig feed (*ayik doke*) is made from the *aha* plant. Its bark is cut into pieces and soaked in water for a few days.

Then the pieces are scrapped with dao and given to pigs. This is supposed to fatten their body and put additional meat.

Remains of beer known as apopopi also given in large quantity with left over food.

Fowls also reared in great number because of its importance in religious rites.

Dog is another valuable animal. Without dog a Tangam family is incomplete. Dog is used as a watcher, scavenger, hunting guide and for religious rites. Tangam Adi loves his dog and never wilfuly kill it except during religious sacrifice.

Ordinary dog however, not well looked after and allowed to gather its food from scraps. But hunting dog known as KIMON is a valuable asset to family. This type of dog have a special aptitude to smell the animal trail and lead the hunter to the den of animal. If the animal is hunted its stomach and blood is given to the dog. If the dog dies it is given a ceremonial burrial. If it dies in jungle then a hole is dug in the ground and leaves are spread on the bottom so that it gets a bed. Ten or such number of poisoned arrows are put in the grave. The arrows are provided by each member of the Party. The idea is to furnish the soul of the dog with weapons to bring down any game it might meet on its way to the other world. If the death happens to take place within the village graveyard ordinary and poisoned arrows and bow are placed in it but no superstructure is raised. The Carcasses of other dogs are just thrown away. But if it happens to be a special favourite, the body is hung on a tree. The death of a hunting dog is a great loss to the family and is mourned as death of a family member. The hunting dog does not differ from the ordinary in anything else except its special knack for tracking down animals. It is never trained to do so but develops it as a natural gift. Many with this quality are not be found and hunting dog, therfore treated as Prized possession. Dogs when they go mad are not killed. For madness is caused by the spirit (ILITAGON) and killing his victim may displease him. It is rather the spirit propitiated with the sacrifice of a big red cock on the village road on a bundle of ferns (TATENG). If the rite is performed in the correct way the bite of a mad dog which usually turns into painful swell heals within 15 or 20 days. A day of taboo follows the rite.

On some special religious ceremonies and to cure some diseases, dogs are sacrificed to the spirits.

Dogs have free access to the house and can move about freely.

Pigs on the otherhand are uncommon visitors to the house. Yet some people have special attachment on a pig and allow its entrance to the house. Such pig develops a keen sense of observation and respond to the call of its master and obey his command. It sleeps in the house by the side of his master and both develop love and affection. Author has seen an incident when people forced a man to part with his deer pig for religious sacrifice and the man burst in loud yell and did not take meal for two days.'

Goats and cows are not so common. They are reared only for meat. Tangams donot take milk and they do not milk their cows. But recently a few have started in imitation of the Khambas.

The Tangams have their own ways of ceremonial killing of animals. For a mithun a wooden structure in the shape of an inverted V, with horizontal bars tied in the fashion of the rungs of a ladder is erected. The victim is tied to it with a long strong rope round it neck. The free end of the rope is passed over the structure to the other side and a large number of men pull it from the end and the mithun is also pulled up the structure till throttled to death. This method of killing by strangulation is peculiar to the Adis and is said to be better than butchering because the blood is not wasted in this.

A pig is also sacrificed by throttling it between two bamboos. The head of a chicken is simply wrung off. In a few rites only where the blood has to be sprinkled it is cut off and the blood is allowed to flow out. A dog is killed with a blow on the head with a stout stick or with a dao when the blood has to be let out.

SOCIAL LIFE

Family and Household:

A village consists of a number of households. Each of a family consisting of a man, his wife or wives, sons and unmarried daughters. A daughter continues to stay with her parents even after marriage till the birth of the first child. During this period the son-in-law visits her regularly. In rare cases he joins the household as its member. A married son lives in the same house with his parents. Where, however, there are many brothers to share the accommodation, some of them separate and set up their own establishments.

Sons and Daughters:

A son is more important than a dauthter because it is through him the line continues and the property goes down to the descendants. A man without a son is unhappy and tries all means to have one. The means are mainly spiritual propitiation of spirits who are suspected to have denied one. Even if this fails, a man ultimately adopts a boy from the family of his clans relations. Fear of childlessness has genuine reasons, for, fertility among the Tangams is low. Families with more than one child are not many.

Girls are, on the other hand are economic assets. They constitute the major labour in cultivation, the principal means of subsistence. It is they who feed the family and keep it going with their hard labour in the field and at home. So, though lower than boys in the social scale. They are nonetheless welcome in a family: a female child is after all better than none.

Marriage:

When a son is to be married the parents seek the approbation of their choice of the girl from the members of the class. After they approve, two of them are entrusted with the negotiation. They call upon the parents of the girl with a present of a beer. If the proposal finds favour with them the present is accepted and the boy and the girl are considered to be engaged from then on. A period of courtship follows, the boy starts visiting the girl and takes care to keep his parents-in-law, regularly supplied with small games such as squirrels and rats and present them with the choicest portions of bigger game bagged by him. Sometimes, the groom moves to the place of the bride and lives there to win the consent of her parents by service. This probation is known as *"Mabo gira."* When the parents of the boy think that the boy had served long enough they go the girl's with meat and fish, two baskets of rice and two tubes of beer, to fetch her home. The presents are accepted and distributed to the members of the girl's clan by her parents. When the girl sets out with her husband she receives as parting presents from her parents-beads (*tadok*), a pair of bracelets (*konge and legan*) earrings (*pareng*) and sets of dress. She may go on alone but usually her parents, relatives and friends go with her. Her coming to her husband's is celebrated in a grand feast with the members of her clan. If there is any suspicion that the girl has not been happy over the marriage and is unwilling to come to live with her husband, a pig is sacrificed to the spirits for a change of her heart. If, however the charm fails and girl ultimately deserts her husband and returns to per parents they to pay a fine. The amount depends on expenses of the marriage. Usually, it is equivalent to a Mithun in value. If it can be established that the girl did so to escape ill treatment by her husband of his parents the amount is adjusted according to the gravity of the charges. Sometimes an unwilling daugher-in-law is subjected to beating to make her stick to the marriage tie. If the girl dies in consequences of such corporal inflictions, her parents extract a heavy compensation according to their status in the society.

The son-in-law has certain obligations towards his parent-in-law, even after he has taken his bride home. He is to help them a new house to be built by them. The best portions of the animal he hunts have to come to them.

Sometimes, there are marriages by exchange. The boy and the girl of one family are married to a girl or a boy of another family. Their consent in such marriages is essential becaue it involves payment of bride price and adjustment of relations between the two families. Elopment is rare. There has been no such case within the knowledge of the present generation. Though marriage is restricted within the tribe as a rule there have been a few with the Khambas and Membas in the villages of Mayung and Nyereng.

Polygamy is allowed. However; one takes second wife only if the first turns out to be barren. An additional wife is additional help in cultivation and domestic chores yet she may distrub the domestic peace. It may be due to this that there are not may cases of polygany. A most interesting incident of matriarchal arrangement is the sharing of one wife by two brothers. The father has of children born of such marriage is determined by the wife. As the husbands are brothers inherritance and domestic problems do not lead to any complications. The wife exerted great control over the husbands and strange as it may appear the arrangement works.

Within the domestic sphere woman enjoys great authority. All domestic matters are controlled and decided by her. If there are two wives the senior has the charge of the key and allots tasks to the other. The granary also is in her charge. The husband usually does not interfere in the domestic affairs, but rather tries to toe the line of his wife's wishes and accepts her management. This convention is usually honoured and encroachment on each other's preserves is rare. A woman never enters into her man's affairs and the man always allows the woman to rule the hearth. Woman does not inherit property, except her personal ornaments such as highly prized beads which she received from her mother as gift. The quality and quantity of such gifts depend on the affection between the mother and the daughter. A woman's position in the house be it her parents' or her husband's depends more or her capacity to influence than on any wealth or ornaments she possesses. She is welcome in her birth place and treated as sons. After all her contribution to day household works not at all Negligible and she is more an asset than liability.

A woman does not return to her parents on her husband's death, though she may go there to spend a few days after the bereavement. She belongs to the family of her husband and stays there till her death. In rare cases if there are disputes and consequent doemestic troubles her parents or brothers construct for her a separate house in her husband's village. Her children, on the other hand, may be taken charge of by her parents or brothers and live with them as member of the adopting family. Brothers are specially responsible in respect of their nephews. A maternal uncle has got specially important position in the family of his nephew. In serious illness for instance, it is the maternal uncle who should tie the charm bead on a child's neck to counteract the influence of evil spirits. Generally maternal uncles are affectionate to the nephews and treat them as their own children.

Pregnancy is attended by a number of taboos. In this period a woman refrains from eating hornbill or monkey. If she does so the child might it is believed be born as bird or the ape. The father does not lend his smoking pipe, knife, dao and flint to others. At the time of delivery fish, rats and birds are trapped and beer is prepared in large quantities to feast the relatives and friends. The delivery is followed by a taboo of five days for a male child and three for a female child. Milling, husking, mowing, weaving, ginning, gathering of firewood and work in the field are not done. No dry or smoked meat or fish nor any bulb or tubers are taken.

The umbilical cord is cut with the sharpened bamboo preferably by the father.

There is belief that a child born with its head pointing towards the door does not live long. It dies in youth if not earlier. If on the other hand the head points opposite the door it lives long and attains a very old age. It is also supposed that evil spirits always are on the look out at the place of delivery and try to get the child named after one of them by any strategy. If this happens it is extremely unlucky for the infant. In order to forestall such a mishap the child is given a name by the parents directly when it is born. The name is usually derived from the father's the second syllable of his name, being the first of child's. Sometimes however, it is named after the patal under tillage at that time or after some of the benevolent spirits of the *byango'*. The more common method of naming is the first. It is as shown below:

Et-tor– (grand-father's name)

Tor-bing– (father's name)

Bing-gon – (the child's name)

The same method is followed as fancy in naming after a patat. Supposing the name of the patat is Bango the child would be called go meng. The name of the byango spirit is given if the mijik or priest finds that the soul of the child has been brought by it. If it is not named after the spirit in return of his good service it might take back the soul and child die. Such a name would be Guming-ke Pajir-ke Gir-jong-or Guming-ke Tari-Yumuk.

A rite known as Nite podung is performed to try difficult delivery attended with one day of abstention and sacrifice of a pig or fowl near the front ladder leading up to the floor of the house.

Nipon is the dreaded evil spirit that obstructs delivey and causes still birth and death in child-bed. She is propitiated in a rite called Nipo-mopak by the side of a small stream or in a gejong or deep pit in the jungle. For this a conical basket is made of wild banana bark with a skirt of leaves of same plant over it. Preferably a black pig and if that be not available a black cock is sacrificed and the head is put into the basket. If this rite does not answered and the pain is unbearable a black dog or a black pig is sacrificed and the blood is allowed to trickle on the body of the couchane. In the event of the death of the mother in child-bed her body is buried by the husband out side the village precincts. In his absence his brother or father or son does it. A very simple and unostentatious structure of bamboo is built over the grave and the clothes and personal possessions of the deceased are hung on it. In the night following the burial the youngmen of the village first gather at the byango and from there proceed to the house of death and surround it. They pelt stones on the roof with loud shouts of ho, ho. From there they go to the grave destroy the bamboo structure and scatter the grave articles all round. This is alone to scare Nipong from the village. All work stops for five days with two days gap in between with the usual abstentions. A still born child or one dead son after birth is burried out side the village to keep away the wrath of Nipong.

Nipong is the most obnoxious of all the evil spirits that haunt the Tangam country. Woman is her main target but she does not spare man either. A man attacked by her has an acute pain in the lower abdomen and in serious cases the victim dies with dilated eyes and fingers clawing. She haunts small trees, and gejongs in the jungle and lives on tall banana plants known as korung. These plants are on that account avoided and never cut or even touched.

Barrenness in the woman is caused by another evil spirit, UYU PIYONING. She is propitiated with a piece each of the beying belt. The abe (petticoat) of the woman is put in a gourd vessel (apun) with a small hole at the bottom and a little beer and beads and ginger. A conical structure of banana known as kodok is built in an unfrequented place. A black dog and a black cock is sacrificed over it and placed over the epun. From that time this place becomes forbidden to woman. For a whole year fruits, tubers and jaggery are not taken by her. The usual genna lasts for five days during which not guest is allowed inside the house. In addition to this operation there is a protective measure as well. Nite is a benevolent spirit who blesses women with choldren. She is worshipped to cure barrenness. For her two bamboo poles are carefully scraped to have fibres hanging like a tussel at the top and fixed on the ground. A black pig is emolated by suffocation between these and a black fowl sacrificed by its side. A black dog is also killed near the pig. The dead body of the dog is thrown in a water channel. The rite ends with the usual genna.

POCHUMIRE is the spirit responsible for female disease of the general type. This spirit is propitiated in a rite near the granary. A banana stalk is shaped into a cone and the blood of a sacrificed black hen allowed to drop on it. It is then put up near the front door of the granary.

APON – ACHUNG – is another spirit who resides in the granary. Rite for her is done on the approach path of the door. Two bamboo tips crossing each other are planted on two side of a conical bamboo structure. Fine bamboo shavings and bamboo rings are tied on each. A pig or a cock is sacrificed and the head is put on the conical structure so that the blood trickles down it. It is then hung on the structure pointing out ward. Feathers are also tied to the bamboo tips. The granary is closed to outsiders during the five days genna that follows.

The spirits Dabo and Lechikomne (Rock spirit) cause muscular pain in the legs after heavy stain. They have to be propitiated for relief and cure. Two wood stumps of approx. 2 ft. height are scraped at two ends and set up on the two sides of a stone. An egg is placed on the top of it, Preferably a fowl also should be sacrificed. Fermented maize, ginger and little rice urapped in a canna leaf are placed on the ground near it. Three stumps are fixed at a slightly slanting angle.

Free mixing of unmarried boys and girls is common. If a girl conceives during this period she generally names the boy she holds responsible for it and her identification is accepted. If, however the boy refuges to accept the obligation, the parents of the girl may demand from him all the cost of the rites to be performed during pragency and at the time of the delivery. If she dies, the compensation is extremely heavier, generally ten mithuns. If the child born is a boy the man keeps him with him. A girl continues with the mother though she bears the clan name of the father.

After a divorce, a girl child may live with her mother but a boy must be in keeping of the father. He may continue with the mother only as long as he sucks. In any case, when he attains age he can live away from her and returns to the father.

If divorce is on mutual consent the birde price not be returned. If, however, woman goes away on her own accord without the consent of the husband, appropriate compensation is realized either from her parents or from her new husband if she married again. On the other hand, if the husband deserts or sounds away his wife she has a right to compensation known as 'ANINITAK' which varies with the period of her stay with him.

Adultery is liable for compensation generally equal to the cost of a small mithun. If the woman happens to be with child the fine is heavier, the price of a full grown mithun.

Incest between sisters and brothers is looked down upon with horror. The guilty pairs used to be banished from the village even killed in the past. This incest is known as MIPUNMIPAK and the entire village has to expiate for the pollution by a genna of five days and the sacrifice of a mithun in a rite called MIPUNDOJE.

A man can change his clan and join another by distributing the meat of a pig and beer to the members of his native clan. From that time on his rights and responsibilities are transferred to the adopted clan as if he was born in it. When he dies however all the members of the adopted clan attend the funeral with beer and food, and those of his native clan cut the Tabiyap or the string round the neck and the waist belt. After the burial both the clans take bath. The person who carries the corpse to the grave, digs the pit and has two costly beads (gunning) tied to the pigtail as his reward. After the bath both the parties gather in the house of the deceased and drink beer together. This is known as UGADONAM. If a man is buried by anybody other than his son or near relatives he receives usually a big mithun and a costly bead doppum abyi or articles equal in price to these two. This is known as "Sima ure".

Law and Order

In the indigenous system every Tangam village used to be a self-contained unit of administration, independent of any external authority. It was a village state by itself. The administration was democratic in form and spirit, in theory and practice. The *kebang* or the village council was the custodian of the unwritten customary law which governed the social conduct. It administered justice in cases of dispute, punished transgressions, maintained law and order and directed developmental activities within the village and decided external relations including war and peace with other villages and peace with other villages and tribes, and set up new villages for surplus populations of the old and settled outsiders in the village. Even matters of individual household which involved or were likely to involve financial, social and cultural life and harmony had to have its approval and decision. The old system still obtains modified to suit the modern present day conditions. For instance the external relations and heinous crimes are no longer triable by the village authorities whose jurisdiction and powers have been defined in the Assam Frontier (Admininstration of Justice) Regulation of 1945.

The council is led by elderly persons who have knowledge of the laws and customs of the community along with ability to expound them and to give impartial judgements. No formal election is held. Such persons get automatically inducted in the council. Such senior members were known as MILUN. There were junior members also, named TACHAK, who were so to say probationers in the art of government under the milums (seniors). Nowadays all the council members are known indiscriminately as GAM.

When a Kebang is in session every adult male is free to attend it and speak on the matter under consideration. Women normally do not take part in the deliberations unless they are a party in the dispute. In that case they have the same freedom of speech as the men.

When a dispute comes to the Kebang for adjudication, both the parties go to the *Kebang*, where they may be followed with their supporters. The leaders of their respective clans are expected to speak in their favour. After the case has been placed, the members deliberate on it until unanimity is reached. If unanimity is not possible majority decision is taken. The directives of the Kebang are consequently acceptable and so binding on both the parties. If, however, in extreme cases, either both of the contending parties refuse to come to an agreement or if the Kebang is equally divided, supernatural guidance is sought through ordeals.

The accused has to pass tests and if he comes out unhurt he is declared innocent. An ordeal is known as DAKKAHIRA and there are three kinds of this:

1. Two pieces of stone one black and one white indicating guilt and innocence respectively are in water in a metal vessel. The maternal relation of the accused collect the stones and water from a large river like the Nigong. The water is brought in bamboo tubes of equal size and capacity. The vessel is then put over fire and when the water boils each of the party is asked to dip his hand in the water and bring out one of the stones. Each one prays that truth prevail and brings out the stone. It is believed that the accused if guilty would bring out the black stone.

After the guilts that has been established two full grown mithuns are tied by each party to a post near the council hall. Both are killed and the meat taken by all the villagers.

The dispute is believed has been caused by an evil spirit and the mithuns are the cause. By eating the meat of the sacrificed mithuns the evil things of these spirits will be established and counter acted otherwise many may sustain damages of properties and crops.

The persons who are proved guilty pay heavy compensation, normally three big mithuns to his opponent. In case of theft of beads the culprit should retun all the beads in addition to the compensation of mithuns.

2. The second ordeal is by placing hot melted lead on the palm, and to let it remain there till it cools. Blisters appear immediately in the hand of the accused if he is guilty.

3. In the third ordeal, the accuser and the accused eat earth from each other's hand. At the time of taking it they take an oath in the name of DONYI-PORO. If swers a falsehood, he would die the next day. The guilty person would suffer a slow death and within a period of one year he would die.

These ordeals are no longer in vogue. When a Kebang is unable to come to a decision either of the parties is not satisfied with its verdict the dispute then referred generally to the Judicial authority of the Administration.

There is a special type of oath known as YALLA. It is secret. One has to keep it to oneself and never to divulge. If such an oath is broken it is punished by forfeiture of Mythons which were kept as surety.

Customary Laws

The customary laws which govern the Tangam society are known to the people, and have never been written down. Everybody obeys them and transgression only come to the Kebang. It is not possible to give a full account of all the laws. Only a few are noted below to give a general idea.

Stolen articles have to be returned. In case they have been transferred and destroyed mython or articles equal in value have to be paid to the aggrieved person.

A death resulting from an assult is to be compensated by 10 mithuns or their equivalent. Disability or causing grievous hurt in any part of the body is a serious offence. If a finger is chopped off or a tooth is knocked off the compensation is a small mithun.

Similar laws cover other offences, such as abstenation from community work, breaking of taboo etc. The compensation usually ranges from a basket of fermented millet to a pig. Where intention is absent such as accidental death or fire no punishment is imposed.

Byango boys implement the decisions of Kebang. If anyone refuses to pay compensation imposed on him the byango is authorised to seize articles of equal value and present them to the Kebang. The Kebang also look after the development work such as maintenance of tracks, brifges etc. Refusal to carry out the work is alsmost impossible for any one and such person is subjected to pay heavy fine.

3

TANGSA LIFE AND CUSTOMS

I. SOCIAL LIFE

Family

The Tangsas live in joint families. A common house is shared by a whole family, consisting of parents, married sons and daughters. Even after the death of the faather, the family does not break up as a general rule but continues to live in the same house as previously including the widow with her children. A single family sometimes may consist of more than twenty members.

In exceptional cases, the family breaks up, and unmarried sons then establish separate households, each with an elementary unit of family. This usually happens when a single household cannot accommodate an expanded family or some quarrel amongest the members disrupts its unity. Even then, the family tie never ceases to exist.

In the Tangsa joint family, each of the married couples occupies a separate cubicle in the house. All the members participate in joint efforts to earn their livelihood, and husbands wives have equal responsibilities. A single hearth cooks food for all of them.

Kinship

The Tangas reckon their relationship through the male lin. Their kinship terminoloogy may be called classificatory, as they use certain common terms of address, both for lineal relatives and certain category of collateral relatives.

Abi is used to address the father's mother, as well as the mother's mother, and all the grandmothers of both the father and the mother. Similarly *atai* or *ati* denotes the father's father and also the mother's father. In thc same way, the father's father's sister's husband (FFSH), the sister's husband's father (SHF), and the mother's brother (MB) have the same term of address *aghu*. *Aphu* applies to a person's own brother (elder) and also to his father's elder brother's son (FeBZ). Moreover, persons of the elder brother's age are all addressed as *aphu*. *Ano* is used for a person's own younger brother, his father's younger brother's son (FyBZ), and all persons of the younger brother's age. *Abang* means both the elder and younger brothers of the father. The sister's husband (SH) and the wife's brother (WB) are called *anung* . The common kinship terms found among the Tangsas are shown in the following list. These are terms of relationship as well as of address and reference.

Father	...Aba
Mohter	...Anyu
Grandfather (faher's father and mother's father)	...Atai
Grandmother(Father's mother and mother's mother)	...Abi
Son	...Asha
Grandson	...Ashaw
Father's elder brother	...Abang
Father's younger brother	...Abang
Father's elder brother's son	...Aphu
Father's younger brother's son	...Ano
Father's elder brother's son's wife	...Anyu
Father's elder brother's wife	...Ashoi
Father's younger brother's wife	...Ashoi
Grandfather's sister	...Angai
Gransfather's sister's husband	...Aghu
Grandfather's sister's son	...Anyung
Grandfather's sister's son's wife	...Asalnyu
Mother's brother	...Aghu
Sister's son	...Aghek
Sister's husband	...Anung
Wife's brother	...Anung
Sister's husband's father	...Aghu
Elder brother	...Aphu
Younger brother	...Ano
Son-in-law	...Kiba
Daughter-in-law	...Anamonyu
Sister-in-law	...Anyanuinu
Brother-in-law	...Anong
Husband	...Awasa
Wife	...Eshik

Clans

The Tangsa subtribes are divided into a number of exogamous clans. The existence of this institution is recognised only in the matter of regulation of marriage. Some of these clans are again sub-divided into a number of sub-clans which may be called lineage groups.

Amongst the Lungris, there are five recongnised exogamous clans. These are Kimthak, Sidia, Liche, Jochi and Riadia. These clans are divided into a number of sub-clans. The main clans and sub- clans of the Lungris are shown in the following table.

Tribe	Tangsa				
Sub-Tribe	Lungri				
Clans	Kimthak	Sidia	Liche	Jochi	Riadia
Sub-clan	Songli Riwabang Langkhang	Nil	Wakhat Gaptok	Khosia Ledoi Waknam Nulip Buduk	Nil

Mariage between the Sidia and Riadia clans is prohibited. Similarly the sub-clans are also exogamous. Within the sub-clans of a perticular clan, marriage is not permitted.

The Mosangs have eighteen clans. These are – Rangka, Jongkhung, Rongbang, Samphang, Kenglum, Sithan, Joka, Kengdap, Kengthum, Longtu, Wakput, Rankhap, Hipa, Rangsum, Wangrai, Samhang, Thukhang and Thamfang. Marriage is prohibited between Sithan and Joka,and also among the six clans, Rangbang, Kenglum, Rangsum, Samhang, Thukhang and Kengdap.

The Ron-Rangs are divided into the following five clans: Longti, Waiti, Lichi, Chombo and Chumbit. Among these clans, marriage is prohibited between Longti and Chumbit, and between Lichi and Chombo.

The Khemsings have got six clans: Latom, Senang, Mepok, Sejam, Cholum and Changso. Marriage is allowed among all these clans, ·except between Latom and Senang.

Amongst the Yoglis, a sort of moiety organisation is found. The whole tribe has two distinct groups. One group traces its origin from Khanlim, and the other from Khanham. The former group consists of four clans, Taikin, Kolhriyen, Tainan and Taikhan; and the latter of three, Jamjok, Korah and Khanga. Marraiage is allowed between the two groups, but not in the same group.

The Tangsa clans are all ancestral. They do not trace their origin from any totemic object.

The clan organization does not exert any influnece on the political life of the peoeple.

Life-Cycle

Like other hill peoples, the Tangsas have got a busy daily round of work. During the full working season, none,with the exception of old persons, invalids and children, remain idle in their houses.

Women play the major role in the daily life of the people. Early in the morning at cok-crow, the rhythnical sound of the rice- pounder reminds a weary traveller of the busy life of these hill women, Beginning with rice-pounding, they continue their work till late hours of the night. They work in the paddy-fields as well as in their houses. In the morning after having finished the pounding of rice, fetched water and cooked for the entire family, they hasten to the fields and return home in the evening, with basketfuls of vegetables, paddy and fuel. On reaching home, they feed the pigs and prepare the evening meal for the family. They spend a few hours in gossip round the fire-place, before retiring at about 11 o'clock at night. Unmarried young girls after their meal collect in the morning and spend the night there with their friends.

Generally, men rise later than the women. They go to the fields after their morning meal, and return in the evening along with the women. Men work harder during the time of jungle cutting and the clearing of fields. In the day time, a Tangsa village would appear to be deserted but for the young children.

Training and Education

The Tangsas are illiterate, but their amiable behaviour and manners speak of a high sense of discipline in them. They speak and understand Assamese and Hindi, especially the women, who regularly come down for marketing to Ledo and Marghertia. Some of them may even speak Nepali. A visitor to a Tangsa village, provided he knows any of these languages, will never find it difficult to make himself understood.

In recent years, the idea of school education has caught the imagination of the Tangsas. They are now keen on sending their children to school.

Dormitories

In the past, the morung organisation played an important in the political life of the Tangsas. They had well organized dormitories called *looppong* , which served the purpose of guard houses and of places of recreation for the bachelors. Each village had a *looppong*, constructed at the entrance to the village, as there was fear of frequent attacks from outside in those days. All the bachelors of the village used to sleep there. It was equipped with all kinds of arms for war, and a big log drum, similar to those found in the morungs of the Noctes. These *looppongs* are no longer in existence.

Girls' dormitories which are called *loops* or *likpyas* are still in existence in some villages. It is a centre of recreation and a sleeping-house for the young unmarried girls of the village. Young bachelors pass their evenings in these, gossiping with the girls.

Marriage

Roogun (Ron-Rang), *milam* (Mosang and Lungri), *jinlam* (Khemsing) and *mailam* (Yogli) are the different words for marriage among the different subtribes of the Tangsas. Marriages is the accepted form of union between a man and a woman in their society. An illegal and unrecognized union is never given social cognizance.

The Tangsas get married after attaining puberty. Boys usually marry between the ages of twenty-five and thirty, and girls between fifteen and twenty-five.

Types of marriage. Exogamy is the general rule that regulates the marriage system of the Tangsas.

Monogamy is the socially and legally recognized type of marriage. Generally, polygamy is not practised, but according to the Mosangs and the Lungris, a man can have more than one wife, provided the first wife is barren, or suffers from any prolonged disease, or otherwise cannot help her husband in agricultural activities.

Preferential marriages, such as cross-cousin marriage (MBD), levirate and sororate are also in vogue in their society.

In the cross-cousin marriage, the mother's brother's daughter (MBD) is considered to be the potential wife of the father's sister's son(FSZ). In the absence of the mother's brother's daughter or the father's sister's son, either party can take partners from outside, according to their choice. It is otherwise with the Lungris. Marriage with the father's soster's daughter is strictly prohibited. The Khemsings also consider this type of marriage a sin. A person, who marries his father's sister's daughter, is socially ostracized.

A person is allowed to marry the widow of his elder brother, but not that of the younger brother. Only among the Khemsings, can an elder brother marry the widow of his younger brother. In case of widow marriage, a nominal bride-price is paid to the parents of the widow by the new husband (yB or eB) in order to secure social recognition of the marriage. If the bride-price is not paid, the parents of the widow never visit the new couple's house. Amongst the Yoglis, the amount of bride-price in such marriages is generally fixed at thirty rupees. A widow having no children can marry a second husband of her choice, provided her deceased husband does not have a younger or elder brother. A person, after the death of his wife, can marry the sister of his deceased wife, on payment of the bride-price.

Marriage forms, bride-price and rituals. Marriage by negotiation between the parents of the two parties is a common and regular custom with the Tangsas. This type of marriage is called *ibbei milam* (Lungri). Generally, negotiations follows courtship. The boy sounds his parents about his matrimonial choice through some relatives or friends. The parents of the boy settle the bride-price after negotiations with the girl's parents. Marriage by negotiation involves a lengthy procedure with a number of formalities.

Marriage for love called *diara milam* (Lungri) is also recognized in Tangsa society. In a love marriage, the consent of the parents of the girl is essential. If the parents of the girl do not agree, the boy has to pay a heavy bride-price.

Marriage by elopement is very rare, but not unknown. This marriage takes place only when the lover fails to obtain the consent of the girl's parents. In such cases, the couple take shelter in some village other than their own. If, however, the boy is caught, he is made to pay a heavy fine by his fellow villagers. The parents of the girl usually demand a high bride-price.

In the old days, when there were well organized girls' dormitories, elopment was very common. It was due to the fact that the boys of different villages used to pay frequent visits to dormitories, and often eloped with the girls of their choice.

Bride-price. In Tangsa society, the possibility of a marriage is virtually determined by the amount of bride-price which is demanded by the parents of the girl. The rituals, performed in the marriage, appear to be of secondary importance. The price is the main factor, and a high price makes a Tangsa father proud of his daughter.

The Tangsa word for bride-price is *kare,* but they generally explain it to a foreigner by the Assamese word, *gadhon. Kare* or *gadhon* may be paid in cash or in kind. The latter includes live-stock, such as buffalo and pig.

The amount of bride-price varies according to the types of marriage. Normally, the bride-price is fixed at one hundred rupees and a buffalo. But in the cases of love marriage without a prior consent, the parents of the girl demand a higher bride-price which may rise from a hundred rupees to two hundred fifty, two baffaloes, and a bucket of rice-beer in addition. In cases of elopement, the demand may be exorbitant. The actual amount depends on the decision of the villagers.

Marriage procedure. The procedure of marriage differs in the different subtribes. The rituals generally extend over three days. The day of the marriage is fixed to suit the convenience of the two parties after the amount of the bride-price has been agreed upon.

The first day is called *milamwang* (Mosang), *gunlang* (Ron-Rang), *rogui* (Lungri), and so on. On this day, the bridegroom goes to the bride's house accopanied by his relatives and friends. He takes with him one pig and few chungas of *laho* to offer to the bride's parents. The bridegroom's party is entertained by the bride's parents with drinks and meat. The bride is taken to the bridegroom's house on the same day together with two girls of her family. A feast is arranged there. At night the bride sleeps with the two girls in a separate compartment.

The second day is called *khorosai* (Mosang) or *gunsa* (Ron-Rang). On this day, the bride-price is paid to the parents of the bride.

In the morning, the bridegroom's party along with the bride goes to the bride's house. The parents of the bridegroom also accompany the party on this day. On arrival the party is entertained with drinks and food. On this day, the marriage thread is tied on the left hand of each of the newly married couple. The signifies their eternal union. The father of the girl ties round the wrist of the boy and the girl a string made of the fibre of a plant called *raiban* (*riha* in Assamese.) On the string is tied the tip of the tail of the pig killed for that purpose and a bead. While tying the string, the father says *'Ahe mon nu wangla'* (meaning, from today my daughter will be your's). Amongst the Yoglis, this string is tied by the mother of the girl. This system of tying the marriage thread is called *ja-khak*. After this ceremony, the bridal party goes back to the bridegroom's house.

On the third day, which is called *khoiru khun* (Mosang) or *roo-gup* (Ron-Rang), the new couple comes together to the bride's house and stays there for the whole day. A feast is given at the bride's house in honour of the visit. On the same day, both of them go back to the bridegroom's house. The bride takes with her a dao, a spear, a piece of cloth, and a basket from her parent's house.

Amongst the Yoglis, the ceremony lasts for five days. On the first day, which is called *jamung-rangnai* , the bride comes to the bridegroom's house. She stays there the second day which is called langkhung-pero. On the third day, accompanied by the bridgeroom, the bride returns to her parent's house. On this day which is called *rong-hul-ban* the bride-price is paid by the bridegroom. A party, consisting of the brothers and sisters of the bridegroom and a few relatives, accompanies the couple to the bride's house and then, return to its village, leaving the couple there. In the evening of the fourth day, the bride and the bridegroom return to the bridegroom's house. On this day, the mother of the girl ties the marriage string on the newly married couple before they return. On the fifth day, they again go to the bride's parents' house, and return the same day. The bride, on this day, brings with her a few articles necessary for her use, from her parents' house.

This procedure is followed only in the cases of marriage by negotiation. In other cases, the ceremony ends with the payment of the bride-price only.

Divorce is not allowed in Tangsa society. Desertion of a wife is considered a crime.

Though pre-martial sexual experience are not normal, yet they are not uncommon among the young people. In case of conception during such adventures, the boy responsible for it is forced to marry the girl.

Inheritance

All properties, movable or immovable, are held jointly by the family. The head of the family, the father, exercises authority over the property, but he cannot sell or distribute the property without the consent of all the other members. In the event of the death of father, the eldest son inherits the authority. There is a feeling of oneness amongst the members of the family. The head of the family is obeyed and respected by all the members.

Apart from the jointly owned family property, the individual members can acquire personal property, which is confined to the personal requirements of the individual.

The female members of the family have got little or no authority over the family property. They are entitled only to make use of it.

II. POLITICAL LIFE

System of Government

The Tangsas used to have a well constituted council of elders variously called *Khaphua, Khapong, Khapo,* and so on, which consisted of a leader (*Lung Wang, Ngowa or Lowang)* and a few members (*Sangta, Kamba or Dedwa*)chosen by the villagers. The leader was selected from a particular clan, consideration being taken of his wealth and intelligence, while the members represented the various clans.

The council adjudicated all disputes and maintained law and order in the village. Its leader was very powerful and his verdict was considered to be final.

Each subtribe had its own council of elders. The Lungris had their well-organized village council, the *Khaphu,* consisting of a leader, the

Phulung Wang, selected from the Kimthak clan, and a few members, the *Sangta*, representing each clan. The Yogli term for the council of elders was the *Khapong*, the *Lung Wang* being the head of the council. The members were called *Kamba* or *Phunwa*. The Mosang village council was called *Khanpong* . The *Ngowa* was the head of it, and the members were called *Dedwa* or *Fonwa*. The *Khapo* was the term for the village council of the Khemsings; the leader was the *Lowang*, and the members, the *Powa*. The village council assembled at the house of the *Lowang* . There was no other particular place for this purposes. The Ron-Rangs also had a village council similar to that of the Khemsings.

Customary Law and Justice

The council of elders had no set code of laws to safeguards the rights of the people. But the decision given by the council of elders on any dispute was considered decisive, and was respected by all the members of the comunity. Theft, non-payment of the bride-price, and encroachment on others' lands were the major offences tried by the council. Disputes arising out of non-payment of the bride-price (*kare* continue for generations.

A dispute could be intra-village or inter-village. Intra-village disputes were settled by the council of elders of the particular village, while the inter-village disputes led to frequent raids and head-hunting.

Corporal punishment was not given. Fine, in cash or kind, was the only punishment imposed on an offender, and this varied according to the seriousness asa well as nature of the offence.

A guilty person, if he was unable to pay the fine, was kept in the custody of the head of the council. He could also be taken out on bail by his friends and relatives on assurance of payment of the fine within a definite period fixed by the council. A person, who could neither pay the fine nor had relatives to stand surety, was kept as a servant (*binasa*) of the village. The head of the council could engange such a person as his personal *binasa* on payment of the fine. Sometimes, such offenders were made the *binasa* of the person against whom the offence was committed. A *binasa* could marry and settle in that village, but in that case, he and his family remained as *binasa* for the rest of their lives. Should a daughter be born to the *binasa*, the bride-price obtained at the time of marriage of that daughter would belong to the master.

A thief was regarded as a stupid rather than a criminal person by the people.

III. DOMESTIC LIFE

Economic condition of the people . The Tangsa economy can broadly be termed as a growing agricultural economy. The people are primarily agriculturists and they give priority to their agricultural activities. During the period of clearing a new paddy-field, a Tangsa man cannot sit idle in his house. Their livelihood depends on the out turn of the field. The field products also earn wealth for them, and make all the difference to their life. They are prepared to exchange everything for a suitable plot of arable land.

It was in a Yogli village that I noticed a sense of competition in cultivation. When the Yoglis hear the sound of the felling of big trees in the paddy-fields of their Lungri neighbours, they feel envious and wonder how they can best compete with them.

Because of their keen interest in agriculture, the Tangsas are better-placed economically than their neighbouring hill brethren. Throughout the year, with the exception of a very few villages, the Tangsas live on their padddy and seldom substitute their diet with arum and other edible jungle products. The products of their fields very rarely fall short of their demand. The villages, especially those situated near the Patkoi Range, grow sufficient paddy and millet to get a surplus. Particularly this can be observed in Jotingkok and Ranghill villages.

Most of the villages are self-sufficient in food, excepting those that are helpless against damage done to the crops frequently by elephants and rats. The elephant is a constant menace to Tangsa cultivators in some areas.

Tangsas celebrate a number of soci-religious festivals centering round their agricultural activities which have the effect of inspiring them with renewed zeal in their work. It is also told by some of the Tangsas that, in the past, when they were in the habit of offering human sacrifice in the *Dawan and Khartang* festivals, they were economically far better off. Though they feel that the sudden stoping of the custom has brought sorrows and miseries in their life, yet they are comparatively leading a better economic life than others.

Apart from depending on agricultural products, they also earn some money by exporting their surplus field products and other articles of their own manufactures to the people across the Patkoi and to the plains.

They are good craftsmen. Their bamboo articles could bring them more money if there were suitable marketing facilities for them.

Mention has been made about the fine weaving by the Tangsa women. Their textile products are worthy of mention.

They are laborious and work hard for their livelihood. Begging brings disgrace upon a person.

The Tangsas enjoy comparative economic security and have relatively settled habits. This renders them receptive to new ideas. It is, therefore, to be expected that a little technical assistance will bring about a great improvement in their situation. But as it is, they are quite content with their simple way of life and their traditional method of struggle for existence.

Food

Rice is the staple food of the Tangsas. Their two major meals consist of rice and vegetables. Like other hill tribes, the Tangsas are also in the habit of taking early meals. They take their morning meal before six and the evening meal before sunset. In between these two major meals, they generally do not take rice but some boiled or broiled potato, maize, arum and sweet-potato. Tea is an ideal drink after the regular meal. They all relish fowl and pork. Meat of buffalo and monkey are also included in their diet.

Preparation of rice .Millet and ahu are the two common cereals. Rice is boiled in water. But occassionally it is cooked by a steaming process. In this process, two pans are used. One is the *munkha,* a barrel-shaped pan made of bamboo and the other is a saucepan.The *munkha* is placed over the saucepan in which a quantity of water is boiled. The vapour passing through the perforated base of the *munkha* boils the rice kept inside it. The open mouht of the *munkha* is firmly covered with a *kaupat.* Rice cooked by this process is very tasty. This process is very common in the plains of Assam. The individual share of rice is wrapped in a *kaupat* and kept in a basket called *lephun* The cooked rice is called *dung* or *cham.*

Preparation of vegetable curry. Sweet-potato, pumpkin, cucumber, white-goured, bottle-goured, brinjal, mustard-leaves, bamboo-shoot and plantain-suckers are used as vegetables. In addition, ridge- gourd, sponge- gourd, radish, potato and some other varities have recently been introduced into their diet.

The Tangsas are addicted to opium, and smoke it in a very methodical manner. They smoke from bamboo pipes and along with it, take sips of tea from bamboo-cups. Some of them cultivate opium also.

Tobacoo comes nexr to opium. Both men and women, except the young ones, are habituated to smoking tobacco. They do not always purchase tabacco from the market, but grow it in their own gardens. They use a particular varity of jungle leaf for rolling the tabacco. They also chew the tobacco leaf as others would chew betal nut. Vegetables are taken boiled but never fried in any oil, nor are any foreign ingredients added to them. In the preparation of vegetables, they add saltm chillies and a kind of chutney called *mihi* made of bamboo shoot. They have about a dozen local spices, *chuka chereng.* These spices are *khamka* (chilli), *ponchi* (jungle dhania), *sekut* (garlic), *mihi* (bamboo chutney), *bichana* (mint), *chinke* (ginger) and *komon* (turmeric). The curry is called *watchu.*

Preparation of meat curry. Meat is prepared in the same manner as vegetables. No oil or any fat is used in the preparation. They only add indigenous spices in lieu of condiments. Plantain-sucker or white-gourd is added to their meat dishes. Meat is not fully boiled or cooked. Meat curry is called *ngam chu.* Both fresh and dry meat form their menu.

Preparation of fish curry. Fish both fresh and dry is boiled in water with salt, chilies and chutney of bamboo shoots. No vegetables are mixed with fish. They are also accustomed to broiled fish. They prepare a kind of chutney with dry fish, adding such spices as *chinke, chukaut, khamka, ponchi, bichana* and salt, which is made into a paste with a bamboo mortar and pestle.

Other items of food . Tea is a favourite beverage among them. No Tangsa hearth is seem without a bamboo tea-tube and a bamboo tea-cup *(falap-kok)*. They drink tea as often as possible. Even after a meal in the morning, before they set out for work they take tea. Whenever a guest pays a visit, the first thing they offer is a cup of tea. Tea is the primary item with which they welcome a guest. It is a token of their hospitality. They do not add sugar or milk to their tea.

Rice-beer *(sai or suwe)* and spirits *(laho)* are the two important drinks next to tea. But these two drinks are not prepared very often. *Laho* is a little stronger than rice-beer.

Preparation of tea. The tea-leaves prepared locally are more delicious to the Tangsas than tea manufactured in factories. The people of this area have their indigenous way of producing tea. The Manmao area appears to be a major centre of tea production, just as Borduria in the Nocte area is known as the centre of salt production.

Each village in the Manmao area has a small tea garden with a small number of tea bushes. The young green leaves of tea are plucked and fried sufficiently on a pan over a fire. During the process, a little quantity of water is added. The fried leaves are then spread out over a bamboo tray*(wanku)*, and dried over the fire-place or in the sun. The dried leaves are then rubbed into dust between the palms. The tea dust is rammed into a green bamboo tube, about one foot in length and two inches in diameter. The tubė is put on the fire till the outer portion is burnt. It is then removed from the fire and allowed to cool down, when the burnt portion is peeled off and the tube is preserved over the drying racks of the hearth. When needed a portion of the tube is cut and tea is taken out. They boil tea and drink it raw without milk or sugar.

Distillation of liquor. Sai and *laho* are the two kinds of popular intoxicants prepared by the Tangsas. *Sai* is the rice-beer and *laho* is the distilled spirit.

Preparation of sai. Sai is prepared out of rice. Ordinarily it is boiled in a pan and the boiled rice is spread out over a banana leaf. When it cools a kinu of fermenting material called *pi* is thoroughly mixed with it, wrapped tightly in a banana leaf, and kept in this condition for about three days for fermentation. The fermented rice is then removed into a water-proof bamboo basket called *paku* and water is poured on it. It is then kept in this condition for another two or three days, with the mouth of the basket tightly covered with banana or some other leaves. After three days, it turns into rice-beer. When they need a drink, the rice-beer is strained through a bamboo strainer or a funnel-shaped cane strainer *(lilo or siam)* and served.

Preparation of laho. Laho is brewed from the rice-beer by the process of distillation. The vapour generated in the process of boiling, is carefully condensed in a bottle or in some other available receptacle.

The process of distillation among the Ron-Rangs of Manmao area is as follows:

The rice-beer is first boiled in a degchi, on which a water-proof basket is set up-side down. A small hole is then made on one side of the basket. One end of a bamboo-tube is next fixed into this hole and the other end is passed into a bottle or some receptacle kept outside. Now the vapour passes through the bamboo-tube into the bottle and this distilled liquid is called *laho*.

The Mosang process of distilling, *laho* is slightly different. The rice-beer is boiled in a degchi, on which a cylindrical bamboo basket is placed. The basket has a perforated base in the middle, on which a receptacle is kept, leaving passage for the vapour from the degchi to escape. Then a pan containing cold water is set on the upper end of the basket. When the vapour passes throuh the perforations in the basket, and touches the cold base of the pan and condenses and settles in the pot undere it. The difficulty in this process is, that the pot for collection of *laho* has to be examined and watched during the process lest it overflows. *Laho* is also produced from the juice of the tapioca root.

Pt. The *pi* which is mixed with the boiled rice for fermentation is made of powdered rice. Some quantity of rice is ground into powder and mixed with water. Small cakes are then made with this rice powder. The cakes are preserved for a definite period when they themselves become fermented and bits of these cakes may then be used for fermenting the rice-beer.

Language

The different sub-tribes of the Tangsas speak different dialects, but the differences are so slight that they may be taken to form one language. Random samples taken by me of the five sub-tribes whcih came within the scope of my study lead me to believe that, making allowances for individual sonic tendencies, all the five dialects are identical. The following table of cardinal numerals will demonstrate the close relationship that exists between these five.

English	*Yogli*	*Ṙon-Rang*	*Khemsingh*	*Mosang*	*Lungri*
One	Asi	Washi	Ashi	Ashi	Asi
Two	Anai	Wani	Anai	Annai	Ani
Three	Atim	Waram	Atam	Atom	Adim
Four	Ballai	Bali	Ballai	Bali	Balli
Five	Banga	Banga	Bangi	Banga	Bangi
Six	Tarrak	Arak	Tarrak	Tarrak	Tarrak
Seven	Mishi	Misi	Mishi	Misi	Misi
Eight	Tichat	Ashat	Tichat	Tichat	Tichat
Nine	Takkao	Akhu	Takkao	Takkao	Takkao
Ten	Toksi	Rasi	Rosi	Rosi	Roasi

This shows that only the Ron-Rang dialect differs from the others in having an initial 'w' in the words for one, two and three and in the ommission of 'TA' or 'TI' in the words for six, eight and nine. This may be due to addition in the former case and dropping in the latter, of prefixes. Such additions and omissions of prefixes in different dialects of the same language are not uncommon linguistic phenomena. Excepting for these, all the words in all these five dialects are for all practical purposes the same throughout. Conclusions, however, based on resemblance as in the present case may not be very sound. There are reasons to believe that dialectal variations are far greater than what the samples given above would indicate. The most obvious ground for suspicion is that beyond a certain stage, the sub-tribes find it difficult to understand one another and are compelled to have reocurse to Singhpo as a medium of inter-tribe communication. So, nothing definite can be said about the degree of affinity between the different Tangsa dialects unless a detailed research is carried out on not only the fundamental vocabularies but also the structural traits of these dialects.

4

AMONG THE HILL MIRIS

Ethnic and Cultural Grouping

Writing in 1947, Haimendorf has objected to the distinction, made both in official and popular usage, between Daflas and Miris as separate tribal groups. In his considered opinion, they are one and the same. As this raises a difficult and rather controversial question, we may quote Haimendorf here at some length:

> 'The population of the upper Kamla Valley, reckoned in the reports of the Miri Mission among the 'Hill Miris', is, as we have seen, part of the Dol group, which embraces also many of the Dafla clans located today in the Panior, Kiyi, and Khru Valleys. To describe this population as a separate tribe would be unjustified and any line drawn in that area between 'Daflas' and 'Miris' would have to be entirely arbitrary. Personally I am of opinion that the sooner the distinctive terms 'Daflas' and 'Miris' are dropped, the better.'

In his notes on tribal groups in the Subansiri region, he has written: 'There can be no doubt that in the minds of the tribesmen and according to all traditional genealogies (genealogy largely legendary but yet reflecting actual tribal divisions) they form part of the Dol group.'

According to him, the Dol group is one of the three groups of the Daflas – *Dopum, Dodum and Dol.*

As L. N. Chakravarty has pointed out in his paper on the Hill Miris, they have been recognized as a separate tribal group by Dalton, E. Gait, Dr. Grierson and several administrative officers who served in the Hill Miri country. Alexander Mackenzie also regarded them as a separate tribal group.

As we have already seen, Haimendorf has acknowledged that at least there is a group of people (whom he has called *Gungu*) who regard themselves as a separate group. He has written of the Dodum Dalfus' claim that the Gungu have also sprung from their mythical ancestor Dodum and that they are indeed only another Dodum phratry just like Leli or Kemdir. But this theory is refuted by the Gungu themselves who have the tradition that their original ancestor was a brother, and not a descendant, of At Nia, the forefather of the Dol and Dodum clans.

It is clear that the Gungus regard themselves as a separate group, even though they acknowledge that their forefather was a brother of At Nia. Since they live very close to the Daflas, it is but natural that their mythical traditions, in the course of years of proximity, would get tangled with each other and influence each other. The Apa Tanis, who are also the neighbours of the Daflas, relate a mythical story in which *Taniba* the Apa Tani and *Baraba* the Dafla are brothers. Taniba was more intelligent and crafty and easily cheated Baraba who was a simple, wild fellow. Obviously, the Apa Tanis were extolling their own cleverness over the simple Daflas.[1]

On the question of racial characteristics of the Gungu, Haimendorf generally noted that 'the racial types that occur in the Dodum and Dol groups (Daflas) are also found among the Gungu.[2] Nevertheless, from his own descriptions, notable and distinctive racial traits of the Gungus also emerge clearly.

To quote from Haimendorf:

> 'Judging from purely visual observation (a most inadequate method of assessing the physical characteristics of a large population), I would say that the type with very large prominent features and high stature is comparatively rare, and that here and there is evidence of a strain of small, pointed faced, wavy haired element which recalls vaguely veddid type met with in certain Konyak Nagas, whereas on the upper Kamla, Selu and Sipi you find types which suggest mongoloid influences different from the Palaeo-Mongoloid sub-stratum of the area. *The Gungu do not show particularly pronounced mongoloid traits. Their skin colour is on the whole a reddish-brown and the eyes are often light*, but some individuals among the south Kamla Gungu have skins of a deep wheat colour.'

As compared to the above type, we may take notice of the prominent racial characteristics which mark out the Daflas. Haimendorf points to two distinctive strains which run through the Dafla group. The majority have features closely associated with what he described as Paleo-Mongoloid type. The more prevalent type is distinguished by a round, flat face with a broad snub-nose, prominent cheek-bones, eyes lying in flat sockets, and small weak chin. This type is also associated with a small stocky stature and a sallow yellow brownish skin colour. The other type, noted by Haimendorf, is distinguished by an ablong face, a prominent, often hooked, nose with a narrow bridge, deep-set eyes, a well pronounced chin, ruddy complexion, comparatively tall stature and athletic build.

Incidentally, we may remark that the latter strain also rather frequently distinguishes the Apa-Tanis who are close neighbours of Daflas. In spite of this occasional convergence physical traits, the Apa Tanis are rightly regarded as a separate racial and cultural group.

We have tried to show above that, though there might be similarities of physical and cultural traits between the Dafla and the Hill Miri, whom Haimendorf has called Gungu, nontheless notable differences are also present.

The *Report on the Miri Country* (1912) makes this important observation:

> 'Though it has been shown that the name Miri is unsatisfactory and inclined to be misleading, yet it has been so generally used that in the absence of any other general name for the Subansiri tribes who seem to be more nearly allied to the Kamla Miri than to the Abor neighbours to the east, both the people of the Kamla and Subansiri valleys must be included under that name.'

The report also observed that the classification of these hill people into tribes and clans was rendered difficult by the lack of tribal and clan organization; by the fact that they described themselves merely as men of such and such village, giving the name of the chief village in the isolated group they came from; and by the use of the word Abor to denote not only the neighbouring tribes but villages a few marches away with whom they had little communication.

The following remark of the Miri Mission on the relation of the Miris with the Daflas is also significant inasmuch as it shows that the

Miris have very slight connection with the Daflas and feel themselves as a separate group altogether.

'The Miris are separated from the Daflas by clearly marked mountain ridges. They have a small trade connection chiefly between the Khru river and Runga Nadi.'

Then after referring to a raid which one Miri village had led against a Dafla village west of Ranga Nadi, the report observed:

'Such incidents are rare, and Miris and *Daflas seldom come into contact, peacefully or otherwise' (mine).*

Language

On the question of the language of the Hill Miri groups, we may generally say that linguistic investigations into their language have not been carried out yet by experts and, pending such investigations, it is naturally difficult to come to definite conslusions or assign its place in the complex of languages spoken in the Subansiri area. We have, therefore, to be content with quoting very general observations, made on their language by explorers who themselves are no experts on linguistics. Haimendorf has this to say on the Language of the Hill Miris:

> 'The language of the Gungu group differs from the so-called Leli dialect of the foothills and the dialects spoken by the tribesmen of the Duri group on the upper Kamla. But the differences are not sufficiently great to bar understanding and men, say, of the Chimr phratry, are able to converse with Daflas of the Leli or Kemdir group as well as with people from the Selu or Sipi Valley.'
>
> Further on, he has remarked, 'Linguistic investigations are still outstanding, but observing men of different froups and areas brought together and attempting to converse with each other, one comes to the conclusion that the Gungu dialect must lie somewhere midway between the language of Panior and the upper Kamla area. For while men of these two regions find it difficult to make themselves understood, Gungu men seem to be able to converse freely with both.[3]

As against the above observation of Haimendorf, the following remarks of the Miri Mission might also be taken notice of:

> 'The Miris of the villages south of the Kamla stated that they had difficulty in understanding the inhabitants of the upper Khru and Kamla valley; but this was chiefly due to their fear of these people, and, when brought together, they were able to converse freely. They also had no difficulty in talking to Subansiri tribes, and the only variation in the language is slight change of dialect. *The difference between the language used by Miris and that of Apa Tanangs and Daflas is more clearly marked, but they have a majority of words in common and appear to have no difficulty in conversation with each other.'*

Comparing the two observations quoted above one might, perhaps, get the impression that though the variations in languages spoken in the Subansiri region are not fundamental but dialectal, yet the Miris do speak a language which is distinctive in spite of its affinities with, say, the Apa-Tani and the Dafla language.

We would, therfore, favour the view that so long as the Hill Miris consider themselves a separate and distintive group, and pending more thorough investigations on a scientific basis into the physical and cultural traits of the Miris, it would be safer and correct to treat them as a separate cultural group.

Appearance and Dress

E. T. Dalton, writing in 1872, described some of the groups or clans composing the Hill Miri as they looked at that remote time. He remarked:

> 'The Ghy-ghasis are a poor, meanly clad, badly fed, ill looking clan and stunted growth compared with the Abors; their villages extend as far as the eastern branch of the Subansiri.'

The Panibotia Miris received a closer attention from him and he described them more elaborately. The men of this clan possessed fine muscular figures; many of them were tall, standing over five feet eight inches. He also noticed that, in general features, they bore a resemblance to the Abors. This resemblance was, however, to some extent natural as between two basically mongoloid races. But they presented a marked contrast in dress as well as in the manner of their hair-style. Dalton noted that they gathered the hair to the front, where it protruded out from the forehead in a large knob secured by a bodkin. Round the head a band of small brass or copper knobs linked together was tightly bound. Chiefs wore ornaments in their ears of silver, shaped like a wineglass, and quite as large. A cap of cane or bamboo work with a peak behind was worn, when travelling, and over this cap a piece cut out of a tiger or leopard-skin, the tail of which was suspended down the back. Their nether garment was a scarf between their legs fastened to a girdle of cane work and their upper robe, and cloth wrapped round the body and pinned so as to resemble the Abor's sleeveless coat. As a cloak or covering of their knapsack, they sported over the shoulders a half cape, made of the black hairy fibres of a palm-tree, which at a distance looked like a bear skin. Their arms were the bow and arrow and long straight-sword, and the arrows were generally poisoned. They also made shafts from a bamboo which was said to be poisonous without any addition to render it so.

Side by side with Dalton's description of the Hill Miri, it would be interesting to read how another early explorer described them. We quote from the *Preliminary Notes on Miris* (1897) already mentioned:

> 'The Ghy-ghasis are small square-built, muscular men, with deep-set eyes, square jaws, flat noses and very large mouths.
>
> The Saraks resemble the Ghy-ghasis, but are inferior in muscular development.
>
> The Panibotias and Tarbotia are much superior to the Ghy-ghasis and Saraks, many of them being fine tall men of great muscular power. Their eyes are more obliquely set, and features are not so rough as the clans to the east, and they have a much more civilized appearance.'

It will be noticed that the contrast between the Ghy-ghasis and the Panibotias with respect to their physical stature and appearance had been set down by both the writers. Similarly, on the matter of dress, their descriptions are almost identical. The *Preliminary Notes* describes the dress of the several clans of the Hill Miri rather elaborately.

The Ghy-ghasis and Ghasis were very meanly clad, their whole costume consisting of a loin cloth and a sleeveless flannel Coat.

The Ghasis of the Sew river were perfectly naked as to the loins, but wore a sort of woollen mantle. Both these tribes had their hair cut square. The Panibotias and Tarbotias dressed much the same as Daflas; they gathered their hair to the front of the forehead, and, having made a bushy knot of it, passed a bodkin through it. Round the head they wore a fillet of leather studded with copper knobs. A girdle of cane sustained the loin-cloth. On their shoulders they wore a knapsack of a square form made of cane, and covered by a kind of shortcavalry cloak made from palm-tree fibre. They also sported a cane helmet resembling the Dafla helmet, but they added a piece of tiger or bear skin as a cover, with the tail still attached. Their arms were long straight daos, bows and arrows, and among the tribes north of Kamla, long spears.

It had also been observed that the Ankas (Apa Tanis) differed little in costume from the Panibotias. In the manner of dress, the neighbouring tribes often resemble or imitate each other, and such cultural exchange, touching on dress or hairstyle, is rather a matter of course than an exception. The Apa Tanis, for instance, tie up their hair in knots over their foreheads, secured with bodkins, much in the same manner as the Daflas, the difference being only in the manner of tying knots. The Apa Tanis make a more delicate and fine work of them.

Like the manfolk, the women of the different groups of the Hill MIri are also found to dress differently. The Ghy-ghasi women, as had been recorded by Dalton long ago, wear a small petti-coat made of filaments of cane woven together. It is about a foot in breadth and fits so tightly round the loins that it compels them to move in short steps. The women wear their hair long.

The female costume of the Panibotia Miris is rather elaborate, and, in many respects, peculiarly contrasted with that of neighbouring tribes. It consists of a short petticoat extending from the loins to knees......secured to a broad belt of leather, which is ornamented with brass nosses. Outside this they wear the singular crinoline of cane-work. The upper garment consists of a band of plaited cane work girding the body close under the arms, and from this in front a fragment of cloth suspends and covers the breasts.' This description of the dress remains largely true even to this day. Their usual working dress is, however, more simple. It often consists of a large piece of cloth, which might have been obtained from their neighnours or imported from the plains below and is worn over the shoulders, secured in front with a pin like a shawl.

With regard to the rest of their dress, we may follow Dalton's description which, with the exception of a few progressives, remains valid even today. They have bracelets of silver or copper and anklets of finely plaited cane or bamboo. Their hair is adjusted with neatness, parted in the centre and handing down their backs in two carefully plaited tails. In their ears they wear most fantastic ornaments of silver, which it would be difficult to describe. A simple spiral screw of this metal, winding snake-like round the extended lobe of the ear, is not uncommon amongst unmarried girls, but this is only an adjunct of the complicated ear ornaments worn by married ladies. They wear round their necks an enormous quantity of large turquoise-like beads made apparently of fine porcelain, and beads of agate, cornelian and onyx as well as ordinary glass beads of all colours. We may add here that love of multi-coloured beads, worn as necklaces and sometimes ear-ornaments, distinguishes almost all the tribes of the North-East Frontier.

Village and Houses

With very few exceptions, the Hill Miri villages are located at altitudes between 3,000 and 4,000 feet. Narrow and rough tracks, meandering up-hill and down-dale, connect the villages with each other. The Hill Miri villages are usually very small consisting sometimes of no more than one or two house-holds, but never perhaps exceeding 20 houses. The average size of a village may safely be placed at between 8 or 9 houses. The houses are usually long-houses, accommodating several elementary families under one roof. A house may be 60 to 70 feet long, standing on stilts and thatched with leaves. The houses lie very close to each other whenever a village is of any size.

The Hill Miris usually select the slopes of hills for siting their villages as a measure of natural protection. Otherwise, the villages are without any extra protective or defensive device such as some other hill tribes deliberately raise around their villages. It is the chief of a village who has to take upon himself the responsibility of looking after its safety as best he can. The Hill Miri village does not have a morung or bachelors' dormitory such as Naga or Adi village has. Among the Nagas the protection or defence of a village is the primary responsibility of the youths of the village who are members of a common village Morung. The Miris are however very careful not to display their property for fear of being pillaged by neighbours. They used at one time to bury their valuables at a place thought safe from prying eyes.

Their stores of grain are kept in granaries located a little distance away from the village.

It would be interesting, in this context, to cite extracts from the writings of early explorers who had left accurate descriptions of the village and house-plans of the Hill Miris. The Miris continue to construct their houses very much in the same manner as they did in the olden time when their country was visited by these explorers. Writing in 1845, Dalton noted that the houses were long, and raised considerably on posts of cleft timber, indiscriminately constructed on the top or side of the hill. 'But the level of the flooring is tolerably well preserved by varying the heights of the supporting posts.' He further noticed that each house held an entire family, including brothers and their wives, and married sons and their children.

In his *Descriptive Ethnology of Bengal* published in 1872, Dalton described the interior of a model Miri house in these words:

> 'It is 70 feet long; the flooring is of split bamboos on a very substantial framework, of timbers raised several feet from the ground; the roof has gable ends, and is thatched with leaves; under the gable a cross sloping roof covers an open balcony, one at each end. The interior consists of one long apartment 60 feet by 16, from which a passage at one side extending the entire length, is partitioned off in the large apartment down the centre; four fires burn on hearths of earth.'

Dalton also noticed that, along the long passage, a row of conical baskets with plantain leaves were lying against the wall. These baskets contained grain in a process of fermentation and the liquor, thus extracted, percolated into earthen vessels placed underneath the baskets.

The *Preliminary Notes on Miris,* printed in 1897, recorded an identical description of a Miri village and the house-pattern, almost exact in details. We may quote from it below as it makes interesting reading in the context of Dalton's description above.

> 'The villages of all the clans are very small, 18 or 20 houses being a large number; the average generally being 8 or 9; but sometimes as many as 40 people live in one house. The houses are 60 to 70 feet long, built on *changs*, and thatched with leaves. There is a framed-off passage down the centre of the house where fermentation of plantain leaves is carried on. The house is divided into

recognised partitions by the triangular tray slund from the roof over the earthen fire place after the manner of the Mishmi.'

The report also mentioned the fact that the villages were on the slopes of hills, never on the submit and were absolutely without defence, as very seldom there was feud between the clans or villages.

Though it will be found on a comparison that the two descriptions tally almost in every detail, the Report went completely wrong with regard to its reference to 'fermentation of plantain leaves'. As Dalton observed correctly, the plantain leaves were wrapped round inside the bamboo and cane frame only in order to contain rice or millet grain, but the alcoholic beverage, formed due to the fermenting process, actually percolated into earthen pots kept below. This process of distillation. It may be mentioned incidentally, is common with many of the neighbouring tribal groups in this region.

Economy and Trade

It should be noted that, under the impact of various development measures initiated by the Government the pattern of the tribal economy in the vast regions of the North East Frontier is undergoing rapid change. The tribal froups, for instance, are reacting vigorously to new ideas in cultivation and other fields of economy and trade. For our purpose in this paper, we shall be concerned chiefly with the traditional and historical culture and economy of the Hill Miris of the Subansiri. Our aim to present their ancient culture which they had inherited and practised from time immemorial. The changes that are coming upon their society in response to the change of winds and circumstances should form the subject-matter of a separate book rather than be attempted here.

The Miri cultivation may be described as what has been called *jhum* cultivation in this part of the country. It perhaps actually conforms to the shifting method of cultivation known over the world, with some local variations in techniques.

The Hill Miris confine their cultivation to whatever stretches of cultivable land are available around their villages. The availability of land is naturally limited, more so because of their practice of leaving considerable part of their land to lie fallow for a long period of time.

As had been noted by Dalton ling ago, they actually cultivated a patch of land for two successive years and then allow it to lie fallow for the next four or five years. They usually take up for cultivation a piece of land which has lain fallow the longest.

Dalton made a reference to an interesting custom to which the Miris adhered scrupulously. They had, like the Abors, a superstition which deterred them from breaking up fresh ground so long as their available fallow was sufficient; a dread of offending the spirits of woods by unnecessarily cutting down trees.

The crops, raised by the Hill Miri, are rice, millets, Indian corn, yams, sweet potatoes, a small quantity of tobacco, and red pepper. As the availability of land on the slopes of hill is extremely restricted, the amount of rice and other crops raised by them is hardly sufficient to carry them through the whole year. For lean times, they stock dried meat and fish. They are fairly good at trapping small animals and fish.

The *Preliminary Notes on Miris* (1897) took rather a gloomy view of Miri cultivation which might have been partly, though not fully, correct. It stated that among the Miris of the northern hills, with the exception of the Ankas (Apa Tanis), there was little or no cultivation, and even the Miri of the hills (nearer plains) were dependent on the plains for food, for their crops of Indian consumption. The northern Miris (north of Kamla) exchanged cotton clothes and mangit for food, while the southern did a small trade in tobacco. Their staple article of food was dried meat, but their supply of mithun and goats was very limited; so they had to trade with the plains for cattle which they obtained in exchange of mangit.

The Miri Mission, which had made an extentsive survey in the Miri Country in 1911-12, also described the Miri method of cultivation. It recorded that cultivation was of the most primitive description. There was no permanent cultivation but entirely *jhum* cultivation. Patches of jungle were burnt and cleared, trunks of trees laid along the hill-side to prevent the soil from slipping, no terracing was practised. The surface was merely scratched by hand with sharpened bamboos. These clearings were worked for an average of two years and then allowed to to back to jungle and fresh ground was taken up. Isolated patches were worked up to 3 or 4 miles from villages. The main crops were unirrigated hill rice, millet and Indian corn.

The report also noted that the harvesting time was October-November. The heads of grain are simply cut off and the stubbles left in the field to rot. The Miris construct temporary store houses for grain on fields which are at a considerable distance from the villages.

The grain is later removed to the village and stored in small granaries which are light structures made of wood and bamboo. Like the Miri houses, the granaries are raised on stilts and thatched with jungle leaves. The granaries are usually grouped together to one side of the village, a little further away. The grain is stored unhusked, and only a small quantity is taken out at a time for husking for immediate use. The appliances used for husking are simple wooden mortars.

'The Report on the Miri country recorded the following description of the food habits of the Miris:

> 'The chief food of the inhabitants is a kind of very solid bread made out of millet, pig's flesh and rice. They also eat fish, eggs, goats and fowls occasionally. They spend much time trapping birds and barking deer, which is the only large game existing in any quantity.'

A controversy has raged for a long time over the efficacy of shifting cultivation and it has been regarded as a sign of inherent backwardness. Some critics have laid it at the doors of primitive inertia and lethargy. As has been pointed out by a writer, this is actually a very wrong appreciation of what is called a primitive method of cultivation. A tribesman sometimes has to walk several miles, climbing hills and wading through streams, to work in his field. The process of clearing a patch of land for cultivation covered with trees and undergrowth, to say the least, is a very arduous task. D.S. Nag, in his book, *Tribal Economy*, has rightly pointed out that a system of agriculture is often the result and not the cuase of social progress. Several factors determine, at the outset, a particular method of cultivation adopted by a socalled primitive tribe. Geographical conditions, stage of economic development, technological advancement are some of the conditions which influence a method of cultivation. For instance, the Apa Tanis, who inhabit a flat land to the south-west of the Miri country, are the only people in this large tract who practise basically different method of cultivation and they hae certainly been favoured in this regard by the geographical situation of their low-lying and level land. We have also to remember that many tribes of the world have no form of cultivation at all and live by hunting and gathering food, though otherwise thay may posses a complex society.

The country inhabited by the Hill Miri is not so bountiful as that of the Apa Tanis and, besides, the hilly terrain of their land does not provide them with enough cultivable open plots. The following observation of Haimendorf is significant:

'There is indeed the strong probability that these Miris in the Hills between the Kamla and the plains were practically semi- nomadic and followed a routine of annual migration. They cultivated in the hills during the spring, rains and autumn and spent the coolest months in their bunting and fishing grounds in the plains.'

They came down every year and hunted in the tracts forest, along the foot-hills, and fished in streams and fords abounding in the area. Dalton had also noted this migratory habit of the Miris who spent a part of the year in foot-hills areas in quest of food. He remarked in his *Descriptive Ethnology* that no less than two-thirds of the population spent several months of the year in the plains, and their occupation there was to procure meat and fish, dry it, and carry it back to their hills.

There is not much to say about the cattle wealth of the Miris who are rather poor in this respect. Mention should, however, be made about mithuns (bos frontalis) first, which for the Hill Miris, as for most other tribes of this region, symbolize wealth and prosperity. They are still looked upon as a standard of wealth and, at one time, could be exchanged for wives and slaves. Mithuns served as a medium of exchange and even now, when money economy is finding favour with these hill-people with rapid improvement of their economic conditions, exchange value is still sometimes reckoned on terms of mithuns. These animals are only killed on occasions of special feasts and sacrifices. At other times, they are allowed to roam about in a state of semi-wilderness in nearby forests. In Miri villages, only the headmen can afford to possess a few mithuns, never perhaps exceeding thirty in the largest of villages. The Miri Mission had recorded, 'It is difficult to determine the number, as few are seen, and the people in some cases won't acknowledge they have any, afraid of their being seized, and in other cases exaggerate the number to increase their importance.' It however, goes without saying that the situation has totally changed since the Miri Mission conducted a survey in this area, and a feeling of security now generally prevails among all the hill tribes.

Sheep are almost absent, though there are a few goats which graze in the jungle around the villages.

Next to mithuns, pigs are regarded as a most valuable possession both by the rich and poor. Every family has a number of pigs which usually live immediately below the stilt-houses. They are the village scavengers *par excellence.* Pig-flesh, both fresh and dried, forms their principal meat ration. Besides pigs, every house also owns a few fowls. Eggs are regarded a delicacy and much used for religious ceremonies such as vaticinations.

We have already noticed that the Miris have considerable skill in catching fish. They do it, using their indigenous basket traps. The Kamla, the Subansiri and their many tributaries abound in *masheer* and other varieties of fish. Fishing is usually done between April and June, when the level of water is most suitable for fishing and trapping. Drying of fish is largely practised and dried fish is stored as food reserve for lean times, as already mentioned.

Haimendorf, during his visit to the Miri country, noticed the close contact which the Hill Miris had with the Assamese villagers of the plains through several months of the year. It was natural that such contact would lead to an exchange of goods and services. The Miris were expert in felling jungle, harvesting rice, weeding gardens, building fences and in many other odd jobs. They were paid daily wages in exchange of their labour. Haimendorf mentioned that, of all the tribal groups in Subansiri, the dependence of the Miris on the plains was the greatest. We have already noted that, besides being engaged in odd jobs, they spent much time during the winter months trapping game and fish at the foot-hills. But their main role was that of middle-men for almost the entire trade between the North Kamla Miris and the plains of Assam. The report of the Miri Mission (1912) also took notice of this fact. It would be interesting to quote here the remarks of the Miri Mission on the trade of the Miris, as it had found it during its visit to the country in 1911-12:

> The villages of the lower Kamla have become dependent on the plains for many necessary articles. They do not grow cotton, make cloth, or do any metal work and have lost knowledge of the few simple arts practised in the villages further removed from the plains. Much of their food comes from the plains, such as dried fish, and meat obtained at the foot of the hills within the Inner Line during the winter. Salt, cloth, knife blades and ornaments are exchanged for rubber, various dyes found in their jungles, and skins, procure their simple requirements. The villages further north are more self-supporting. They grow cotton in just sufficient

quantities to weave cloth for themselves. They do a little primitive metal work.'

The products which the Hill Miris carried down to the plains for sale consisted mainly of chillis, bamboo shoots and some other jungle products. Occasionally, they might have sold an indigenous sword or animal skin, but from a commercial point of view, such transactions were of little importance.

The things which the Miris carried up from the plains to their home in the hills were many. At one time, salt was the most important item for which the Miris had to depend almost entirely on the plains of Assam. The South Kamla Miris found trade in salt very profitable as they were the intermediaries on whom the North Kamla Miris had to rely for import of salt. The art of weaving was virtually absent in the villages of lower Kamla Valley and consequently cloth had to be imported from down the plains. The South Kamla Miris bought cloth in the bazars of the plains not only for their own use, but also did a little trade in it with the villages on the other side of the Kamla. The rich among the Miris had some preference for hand-woven Assamese silk cloth. The South Kamla Miris also received a limited supply of cloth from the Apa Tansi and villages on the Khru and Upper Kamla.

Next in importance to salt and cloth was iron. The Lower Kamla Miris obtained such iron implements as daos, knives and hoes from the plains, and sometimes traded these equipments with tribes situated farther north. The Apa Tanis fashioned their own daos, knives and swords. But even they were dependent on the plains for their supply of iron. They were not, therefore, in a position to produce implements for in excess of their own need. At one time, iron hoes were almost unknown on the north side of Kamla and agriculture was carried on with implements fashioned out of the shoulder blades of mithuns. Apart from important items of import mentioned above. Haimendorf points out, the South Kamla Miris also bought in the plains bell-metal cups, brass pins, tin mugs, silver ear-ornaments, bangles and varieties of glass beads. They often bartered these with tribes far up the north of Kamla. The tribesmen from the north seldom trekked down to the plains in quest of trade or otherwise, but the rich people, sometimes sent down their slaves for earning wages with the purpose of carrying back cloth, salt and iron implements for their masters. But all this was very long ago. The South Kamla Miris had been accustomed with the use of money as a medium of exchange from a long time past, owing to their closer trade relations with the plains. But the tribes farther to the north had a preference for payment in kinds. Till recently, and perhaps even today, by adherence to long established customs, values of articles are expressed in terms of commodities. Thus, values are reckoned on terms of the exchange rate of a mithun, a pig or a dao. There is usually a recognized scale of values between items of exchange, and this provides the starting point for bargaining. The scale also may slightly vary from one place to another. We may cite one example, as recorded by Haimendorf, of the scale of exchange values, in order to gain some idea as to how it operates among the Miris. A full grown mithun is equal to 50-60 carrying baskets of paddy and one pig. But when the Miris are obliged to buy paddy from the Apa Tanis in times of scarcity, they might be left with no choice but to accept only 30 carrying baskets of paddy in exhange of a full grown mithun cow. The Miris produce barley enough for their own subsistence and they are often at the mercy of the Apa Tanis who are extremely commercial-minded.

Haimendorf points out that, among the various tribes of Subansiri and Kameng, the Apa Tanis are the most trade minded. It goes without saying that this is largely due to the very sound and stable economic base of their society. The Apa Tanis are not only self-sufficient in food, but they are also in a position to do small trade in it with the neighbouring tribes. Besides, they are good at weaving and can also produce iron-implements. The Apa Tanis extracted a salty substance from a kind of herbacious plant and the Miris sometimes were obliged to buy it from them when they could not procure enough salt from the bazars of the plains. The Miri country was regularly visited by the Apa Tanis, in exchange of items of trade, bought from the Miris pigs, fowls and sometimes dogs. Pigs, however, ranked first among the goods which were in great demand from the Apa Tanis who were themselves not experts in animal husbandry as these people. The Miris also sold to the Apa Tanis coloured beads, small prayer bells(known as *deo-ghanti*), fibre rain-cloaks, fibre rain-hats, plaited cane and grass belts. They gave, in exchange of a simple Apa Tani cloth, a piglet or a rain-cloak; a middle sized pig for a broad- bordered Apa Tani cloth; a small pig for an Apa Tani dao and a rain-hat for a short dao or, perhaps, a fowl. The prayer-bells were regarded as of great value by the Miris who had a reverential attitude to them and sometimes ceremonially worshipped them. Miri families often treated them as heirlooms.·Highly valued articles were equated against the supposed exchange values of these prayer bells. The Miris, however, sold only small bells to the Apa Tanis for three or four pieces of cloth as well as beads. Big prayer bells were regarded as worth several mithuns.

According to Haimendorf, the exchange of goods between the Miris and the Daflas did not strictly come within the purview of commercial transactions. He consideed such transactions as more in the nature of ceremonial exchange of gifts which did not flow along regular channels of trade. The exchange or barter of goods took place as between friends or visitors in a casual way or more of ten in the course of organized and ceremonial payments.' The volume of goods, comprising beads, bronze plates, cloths, daos, prayer bells, which thus passed from village to village, was not inconsiderable, even though the movement was slow. It was obviously the contention of Haimendorf that Miris were bound to the Daflas by a bond of kinship, and cultural and ethnic affinity.

Social Institutions

We have already referred to the division of the Hill Miris into many phratries, each comprising several clans. The descent is counted on the patrilineal line, and the Hill Miris are reputed to have a fairly accurate memory of their genealogies. Like many other tribes, they love to trace their genealogies as far back as their mythical ancestor *Abo Teni*.

B.K. Shukla, who was till recently the District Research Officer in Subansiri, mentions in his unpublished report on the Hill Miris that they usually count back their genealogies in an ascending order up to thirty generations. They are, however, conscious that many more must have occurred between the limit of their memory an their mythical first man, *Abo Teni*. Shukla notes that names of prominent ancestors are often reprated four or five times in the process of reckoning of genealogies. The Hill Miris explain this, saying that the names of an ancestors are more important than a correct account of generations that went before.

It is very probable that clan exogamy was the rule among the Hill Miris at one time though, as noticed very early by the Miri Mission, there was a tendency to seek a bride near one's own village. This general rule of clan exclusion in contracting marriage alliances has suffered great changes in recent times. This could have been due to various factors. The unstability of the region often led to movements of population from one place to another both in the past and also in comparatively recent times. The localization of a clan in one fixed area was not, therefore, always possible. As lately as the 1950 earthquake, many villages were broken up, and families were obliged to migrate and even settle among people far away from their own group of clans. Movement of population from one place to another is probably one of the important factors which contributes to the break-up of social barriers, leading to liberalization of rules. Shrinkage of population is another great factor which may compel a group of people to introduce far-reaching changes in their social structure. Social separation of different lineages of the same clan, due for instance to migration to new places of residence, may also facilitare intermarriage within the same clan. While strict clan-exogamy has undergone some changes, bringing about new dynamism in interpersonal relationship, it would not be true to say that rules regulating marriage have completely broken down. Even now, certain lineages will acknowledge fraternal relationship with certain other specific lineages and, as rule, refrain from taking a girl as wife from these lineages. The fact that the Hill Miris generally lay great emphasis on genealogies point to the conservative core of their society.

Marriage

It appears from the account of Shukla that various forms of marriage are recognized among the Hill Miris. First in sanctity and importance comes the *nyida* marriage with the full-scale paraphernalia of a regular marriage.

Nyida is primarily an arranged marriage in which the boy's father makes the initial move. If he has a girl in view, he starts with cutting open the liver of a chicken and taking omens on it. Provided the reading is favourable, he starts on a ceremonial visit with his kinsmen to the girl's father, taking suitable presents with him. The present usually consists of a big bump of pork. The proposal is not mooted immediately or directly. The conversation carried on in symbolic language. In reply to the query of the girl's father as to the purpose of the visit, he ma;y say that he has come in search of *tattum bilam* or *sikam beedum,* both being some kinds of nuts and, symbolizing woman's virtues. If the father of the girl should wish to signify his unwillingness to the proposed match, he will answer saying that his louse is bereft of such things. He may nevertheless show courtesy by expressing his willingness for a lasting friendship and offering presents in return. In case however he is agreeable, he will now proceed to take omens before the match is finally decided upon.

The next step in the negotiation is called *nim-surr* which obliges the father of the boy to make another payment of two mithuns. Shukla mentions that the real bride-price is one cow mithun, but actually social prestige and customs demand exchange of more gifts on both sides. Before the final exchange of gifts takes place, kinsmen from both sides gather in the house of the bride where they are entertained with food and indigenous beer. This is also an occasion when songs, mostly of a religious nature, are sung. The father of the girl may take the opportunity to voice his disappointment with the bride-price paid as well as his demands through songs.

If everything goes well, the final stage is reached when the girl's parents and kinsmen should make arrangement t escort the bride to the groom's house. An auspicious day is decided by omen. The girl is then dressed appropriately for the special occasion. The mother gives her head-necklaces, on the head she wears a kind of decoration called *dumlup*. She is also supposed to carry a sword. As the bride's party approaches the groom's house, the village youth stages the *hoi-pekdan* which is a mock opposition to the bride's entry to the house. There is much dancing accompanied by shouts and swinging of daos. The dancing party expresses annoyance at the supposedly late arrival of the bride. This mock drama is not, however, allowed to continue for long. After the boys have had their fun, elderly men of the village inervene and shout at the boys to clear the way for the bride.

The bride then, along with the party accompanying her, makes a ceremonial entry through a specially constructed gate to which is tied a fowl or a goat. The bride's father has to sacrifice it with his sword, and, after he has done this, he is suppposed to have made his peace with the local spirit. If the spirits are not propitiated in this way, the bride's party is likely to call upon themselves ill luck in the form of diseases such as dysentery, fever etc. Shukla also mentions that, it is the custom with some families having the means to sacrifice a mithun before the arrival of the bride's party. The bride is then required to cross over the carcass before she climbs the notched ladder to the balcony of the house through a decorated arch made of leaves and bamboo shavings.

The dancing party is now allowed to enter the house and to continue dancing as best they can within the limited space;, until it is time for the feast. The dancers beat metal plates as musical accompinaments. The guests huddle around blazing fires in hearths. They feast on cooked meat and rice, and are served with lavish quantities of home-made liquor in bamboo tubes. Groups of people eat from the same plate. This is also the occasion when the priests relate stories of the creation of the earth and the sky, the sun and the moon, through the medium of songs. The genealogies since the time sof the mythical *Abo Teni*, the exploits of hosts of spirits identified with Nature, someway or other controlling the destinies of meb, form the themes of other songs. The memories of the priests are put to hard test on such occasions. The people gathered also find time to discuss about the exchange of gifts that has taken place. The occasion is rounded off with the final presentation of gifts made by the bride's father. This is called *kin-kimbo* which consists of valuables like manjis, beads and swords.

The finale to the whole procedure is however yet to come. The last ceremony is called *yulo* which is performed for obtaining the blessings of the spirits responsible for dispensation of good luck. Shukla has described the ceremony as follows. On the second or the third day, a shrine is constructed near the house. This shrine is an elaborate structure to which are tied one or two mithuns according to individual means. In the beginning of the sacrificial ceremony, the village girls come with rice flour and beer, and sprinkle them all around the shrine. The bride then mounts the scaffold of the shrine and pours bits of rice-flour and beer on the head of the mithun. The next part of the procedure belongs to the groom's mother who now comes forward with a quantity of rice flour, made into a dough with liquor, and ceremonially feeds the mithun. After these preliminaries have been completed, the bride-groom, following the instructions of the priest, steps in with a bow and arrow, and lets go an arrow at the mithun. No sooner is the arrow released than a cousin of the groom, waiting in readiness, gives a mighty blow on th head of the mithun which now collapses. Other kinsmen then attack the animal with long daos and pierce it through the heart, thus finally killing it. The next day, the guests depart, taking with them shares of the sacrificial meat.

It is no wonder that the Hill Miris attach the greatest importance and sanctity to the marriages performed according to the *nyida* rites. If a *nyida* wide should run away with another man, the husband will consider it a great affront. He may refuse to be compensated with the return of bride-price alone and should he fail to recover her through negotiation, he will have the tacit sanction of his society to make'war' on his rival. The Hill Miris believe that selling away a *nyida* wife will incur the wrath of gods who may send misfortunes.

It should be apparent that the *nyida* form of marriage is the privilege only of the rich people who can afford it. So there are other forms of marriage recognized by the Hill Miris. The marriage, which comes next to *nyida* is termed *tado hale*. It requires payment of one or two mithuns as bride price, but there is no question of dowry or return payment of gifts from the side of the bride's father. If the wife of a marriage contracted according to *tado hale* should prove unfaithful and goes to live with another man, the husband may let her go without arousing the displeasure of the gods. In this case, he will be usually satisfied with the return of the bride- price paid by him.

There is yet another way in which, a man may get a wife for himself. He may persuade a girl to elope with him without the knowledge of her parents. They may later live as husband and wife with the implicit approval of society. This form of marriage, called *nim-moli*, becomes a cause of much confusion and bickerings between parents on either side owing to the question of unsettled bride-price. The situation is made worse as, in such a case, the girl is usually a willing partner in the whole drama. Mediators are then employed, and, after protected negotiation, they may bring about a settlement of the question of bride-price, and counter gifts from the girl's father. A planned elopement may not necessarily take place always. A girl may simply go to live with a man of her choice. The society usually gives its approval to such an arrangement later. This is called *nimo kedna*. The formalities of payments have naturally to be gone through at a later date.

The patterns of marriage among the Hill Miris, as already indicated above, is patrilocal. But exceptions are not unknown. Under special circumstances, the boy may be willing to go to live under the roof of his father-in-law's house. If the father-in-law, for instance, is old and infirm, having no son to look after him, the son-in-law may continue to live with him and ultimately inherit his land and other material possessions. Under normal circumstances, however, it is considered derogatory for a boy to live with his father-in-law.

Position of Women in Hill Miri Society

Dalton mentioned long ago that polygamy was socially valid among the Hill Miris. As a matter of fact, however, it was of necessity confined to the wealthy class; the chiefs, for instance, who had the means to buy many wives. There was no acknowledged limit to the number of wives a man could have, except for the limit his means of buying additional wives. Dalton added that value was placed more on the girl's social position than on her beauty. But chiefs' daughters were generally the belles of the clans and there was great competition among suitors for girls having beauty to match with their social positions. Dalton also mentioned an instance where the price put on such a beauty amounted to two or three mithuns, twenty or thirty pigs, and an equally large number of fowls.

In his *Descriptive Ethnology*. Dalton referred to occasional polyandry among the Miris. We may as well quote him here, 'with poorer classes man has to work hard to earn the means of buying a wife; and from this results in a few instances the practice of polyandry.' Two brothers might pool together the proceeds of their joint labour to acquire a wife between themselves. This, however, is a bit of information which cannot be confirmed with any accuracy without proper investigation. Shukla, in his most recent report on the Hill Miris, has not mentioned this as a direct or oblique institution.

It has been noted generally that the position of women in Hill Miri society a similar to that of Dafla women. Dalton wrote in 1872, that the Miri women made faithful and obedient wives. They were trained never to complain or give an angry answer, and they cheerfully reconciled themselves to their lot. They appeared to bear the hard burden imposed on them, which included nearly the whole of the field labour, an an almost equal share of the carrying work on their journeys to plains. The above remarks of Dalton will naturally give the impression that the Hill Miri women were a hardy and active lot and their importance was no less to their menfolk either at home or field. The situation has not changed to any very great extent since Dalton made his observation.

According to traditional code, women are completely subservient to men. The husband has the right, theoretically at least, to take the life of his wife, if he feels justified in doing so. This, however, is a privilege which no husband, perhaps, ever exercised. Fidelity after marriage is expected on either side. If a wife is known to be involved in sexual intrigue with another man, the husband will chastise her, try to correct her ways, and may do whatever lies in his power to bring the offending rival to book. He may force him to pay compensation for the damage done to his prestige. In case, however, the wife actually deserts and goes to live with another man, practical wisdom may prevail upon the wronged husband to be contended with the return of bride-price paid by him. Alternatively, an aggrieved wife may answere her unfaithful husband by running away with another man of her choice. There are of course other factors which in practical life contribute to a sene of independence in girls.

While living with parents before marriage, the girls do their share of work at home and in the field. They are even allowed, with the knowledge and active encouragement of their parents, to acquire valuables such as beads, swords and many other things of their fancy. The parents may give their daughter from their piggery a pigglet or two, and encourage them to rear these as their own. In course of time, these piglings multiply and augment their personal possession. Rich people's daughters are known to display more initiative; they may even own lands and work them separately. In olden time, chief's daughters and other wealthy persons daughters could even own slaves for whom they had paid from their own earnings. The property thus acquired, the girls take with them to their new homes after marriage. Such girls, who grow rich by their own pluck and initiative, naturally have greater independence, and may actually feel free to choose their own partners in life, dispensing with all question of bride-price.

In the management of house-hold affairs, the wives have very decisive influence. As pointed out by Shukla, the position is as though the wives are the real owners, and they decide how best to utilize the house-hold property such as field produce, pigs and fowls. The granaries are at their disposal. In a polygamious family, the wives may have separate property, and they can augment it with their own initiative and intelligence. The difference between the wife and unmarried daughter is that the wife cannot take her so-called property with her, if she should decide to leave her husband for another man. In other words, so long as she continues to manage the home, she has a very real say in everything. The husband usually does not interfere, and, even when he does, he would take counsel with his wife first for the sake of family peace and understanding.

In one sphere at least, women may appear to labour under a stigma or social disapproval. Women, for instance, cannot officiate as priests, their role being confined to arranging feasts and sprinkling rice flour and beer on the heads of sacrificial animals. The place of honour as priests in conducting ceremonies belongs exclusively to men. This should, however, give no cause for the supposition that women are mere drudge of slaves to the menfolk. They obviously do not suffer from any disadvantage or from a sense of inferiority, as the separate roles are culturally determined from time immemorial. On the other hand, they are fully conscious of their own importance in the Hill Miri society as it is constituted.

Political Institutions

Dalton's observation, made as early as 1872 with regard to the political institutions of the Hill Miris, is worth quoting at some length. Dalton wrote:

> 'They live in small communities under hereditary chiefs and, in some instances, one family has obtained sufficient influence to be acknowledged as chiefs over cluster of communities. They have no Morang, or town hall, in which the elders meet and consult during the day, nor do the youths, armed for the protection of the village, keep watch by night. The villages consist of ten or a dozen houses of as many families, built pretty closely together in some position rather difficult of access, and it is left to the chiefs to look after its safety as best as they can.'

Dalton's above description remains correct so far as it goes even to this day. But he seems to have gone completely wrong with regard to the institution of hereditary chieftainship. As pointed out by Shukla, Dalton confused what in fact was a kind of natural leadership as a hereditary institution. Even today, there are a few persons who wield very real influence over their respective villages. One might get the impression that they have the last word in everything. The acquisition of such leadership could be attributed to various factors. Wealth is certainly one of those factors, and at one time, it depended largely on leadership during war. Many of these natural leaders were responsible in the past for bloody raids on other people. The raids were conducted either as reprisal, born out of some grievance or traditional enmity or sometimes simply for the sake of spoils of war and slaves. It so happened that often such leadership passed on from the father to the son, and thus traditionally for some generations. This fact might have led Dalton in to believing that this leadership was hereditary, and he felt justified in institutionalizing it as actual chieftainship.

As a matter fact, Hill Miri society does not have constituted central authority. They are too individualistic, and are just not made up for unquestioning submission to any central authority. Yet Hill Miri society is not an amorphous mass of people, all pulling in opposite directions. In the fiest place, the tribal code of conduct is clearly determined, and accepted as binding. Any breach will be frowned upon, and will call indirect retribution upon the offender. Besides, clan allegiance, although in recent years it has undergone some changes, is quite strong even now.

Hill Miri society also lacks a formal council of elders, which is found among other tribes. But the heads of families in a village do meet, whenever circumstances demand, and take agreed decisions on matters of common interest. In such informal meetings, as well as in matters affecting the welfare of the village, a person who is looked upon as a leader by virtue of his wealth, wisdom and abilites, naturally dominates the proceedings, and almost seems to hold the final decision. Naturally, it all depends on the personality of the leader and the extent of influence he wields over the members of the village or clan. The real source of cohesion with in the village or clan-group should, however, be looked for elsewhere. This actually is to be found in a system of reciprocal rights and obligations, fixed by the unwritten tribal code, binding the members together, besides their common heritage, clan affiliations, legends and mythological belief in a common origin.

Nevertheless, as in any other society, personal animosity and quarrels do occasionally arise, calling for the intervention of the neighbours. But such cause of occasional dispute is soon resolved within the frame work of the tribal code. The usual procedure, resorted to in case of serious breach of peace, is appointment of intermediaries, called *gingdung*, who do their best to bring about rapprochememt between parties in accordance with the tribal sense of justice and propriety. The parties to the dispute naturally find themselves obliged to submit to collective social pressure.

In the past, the method of settling a personal grievance was left primarily to the aggrieved party, as amongst the Apa Tanis and Daflas, until it posed a threat to the public peace. He would capture a mithun or sometimes the wrong-doer himself, if he could and keep him prisoner with his foot encased in a heavy piece of log. He would then announce a ransom for the release of the prisoner. It was then considered a social obligation on the part of the kinsmen of the prisoner to produce the ransom for his release. If instead of the wrong-doer, the aggrieved person had succeeded in apprehending any other member of the wrong-doer's clan, it would have been looked upon as equally justifiable according to the tribal principle of collective responsibility. On the other hand, the opposite party to the dispute was also free to retaliate, repeating the same procedure, and thus the drama went on for some time until a formal peace, called *dapo*, was concluded between the partties. The Administration, however, has now put an end to this practice of taking prisoner and keeping him in stock. The people are now encouraged to settle their private disputes through the mediation of the *gams*, or village leaders, who are usually given the red coats, an insignia of their standing with the Government.

B.K. Shukla reports that there has recently been a move among the Hill Miris to establish a *bango* or a council of elders on the moder of a similar institution among the Padams and Minyongs of the Siang district to the east. The *bango* is proposed to be constituted with 11 members, mostly of the red-coated Gams. It, however, remains to be seen whether the *bango*, when it begins to function, proves an improvement upon their own traditional method of settling disputes. They seem to have, however, their own misgivings as to how far the *bango* can actually prove effective unless it is vested with some authority to impose its decisions on the disputing parties.

REFERENCES

1. Dr V. Elwin, *Myths of the North-East Frontier of India* (Shillong, 1958) page 142.
2. Haimendorf, op.cit.
3. C. Von Furer-Haimendorf-*Ethnographic Notes on the Tribes of the Subansiri Region*

the bamboo or jungle-wood roof is covered with grass or straw. There is just one room which is divided to form the kitchen and the sleeping apartment. They dislike anyone entering their houses in leather foot-wear. Even such of them who use footwear leave it outside before entering. Most families have pig-styes and poultry-runs either attached to or near their home-steads. There has been a march of culture into their society, and a great majority use wooden furniture, and brass and alminium ware. They keep the yard surrounding their houses clean, and maintain an attractive kitchen garden. Their homes are on hill tops, and to minimise the food problem they live scattered.

These tribes have a taste for agriculture, and cultivate land whenever, it is available. Some have large holdings in the forests and villages. Rearing pigs, poultry and cattle is a common occupation. Prior to the enforcement of prohibition toddy tapping provided employment for many. Even now illicit tapping to derive an income is practised by most of them, especially those who live within forest tracts. Large numbers are seen employed as plantation labourers.

Kudiyas have an elected priest and Yejaman (headman) who is also known as Gurikara or Malamudiya. The great esteem and attention which the headman enjoyed in their early society have considerably disappeared. However, even now he is permitted to inquire into their affairs, and among some groups he has the right to punish an offender. Disputes are referred to a council of four or five elders, and the senior present presides over the meeting. The headman is an important personality at marriages, and funeral ceremonies. Some headmen act as priests specially for performing ceremonies to stop the influence of bhoodams (evil spirits) and as oracles. The office of the headman is hereditary and a competent son succeeds the father and, failing, him, a senior nephew.

Marriages are after attaining puberty. The more primitive sections make an attempt to have the marriage on the eleventh day after puberty. Cross-cousin marriages are coventional. The Urmale section of these tribes avoid conjugal relation with the paternal and divisions are not significant. More important are the phratries and clans.

Phratries and Clans. The three major divisions of the tribe subdivided into a number of exogamous phratries, which in turn, comprise a number of patrilineal clans. Owing to the lack of data from the widely separated and hitherto unknown areas, it is not possible to give an exhaustive list of all the phratries and clans. What is presented below is only a partial list based on the existing group in the Panior, Palin and parts of the Khru valleys, and in the area around the Nyapin Administrative Centre.[1]

Major	*Divisions*	*Phratry Clans*
Dol	Durum-Dui	Tasu, Likha, Chuhu, Pil, Hijang, Harku, Takyang, Chonyu, Yowa, Tade, Tajing, Byabang, Byajang (Nengbia), Byari, Ganku, Gami, Dohu, Dolang and Dobam.
	Dukum-Duri	Tari, Tai, Hora, Huryang, Ryangpa, Ryangra, Ryankyo, Ryangme, Takyo, Tame, Tadang, Tali, Lindum, Linko, Gida, Gichik, Biri, Dadung, Damang, Khyoda and Joram.
Dodum	Kemdir	Pei, Pochu, Nara, Ralo, Toku, Tab, Telih, Taha.
	Dumchi-Chili	Yumri, Yumdo, Khasang, Rengu, Nabom, Hidu, Hibu, Gyamar.
	Pekhi	Devya, Sodu, Sobum, Niri, Kholi, Tao, Techi, Tana.

Whereas it is possible to give at least an outline of the sub-divisions of the Dol and Dodum groups, little is yet known of the subgroups of the Dopum Daflas. There are a few scattered clans of this group particularly the Gnuri, Gnurang, Hilang, Heba, Deying, Hodu and Hopu. Nothing is known about the phratries of this major group. Some of the clans of this group, such as Tede and Deke are extinct.

In the villages around the Nyapin Administrative Centre exist a number of clans who claim to have descended from Atu Nyah through

Riku. Thus, they constitute a separate major division. We do not yet know the phratries of this group, but the important clans are the Tedar, Tayer, Tayi Take and the descendant of Riku, do not intermarry. Other scattered clans are the Charu, Pate, Lido, Linya, Liyo and the Lidung. The Gollo clan, which Dr. C. von Furer-Haimendorf includes in the Dol group,[2] actually belongs to this Riku group. The well-known priest of this clan, Gollo Tegin, lives in the village of Tapo Gollo near the village of Mengo. He traces his descent from Riku, through Pale, Gnuri, Mabu, Tayang, Dago, Kagnu, Kojum, Tago, Kanu, and Tamang in a direct line.

Without going into the details of the phratries and clans, two features of the Dafla clans should be noted. In the first place, the clans are not totemistic. Each clan is named after an ancestor, who is considered to have been real. The clan consists of a few lineages or groups of men and women who trace descent from that ancestor in the patrilineal line. Secondly, all the members of the clan regard themselves as brothers and sisters. Thus clan exogamy is the rule for marriage. This criterion is further extended to the phratries which are also exogamous. The inter-relationship of clans within a phratry is very loose, but for the purposes of marriage, the members consider themselves as consanguineous.

Beyond this, a clan does not function as a close social unit. Not all its members occupy a common territory. The whole clan is not a political unit for war and peace, nor is it a unit for economic and religious purposes. In fact, only those members of a clan who are also bound together by the bonds of individual kinship and neighbourhood, form a unit for the above purposes. This leads us to a consideration of the structure of the Daflas family and the extended family or kin.

The Family

The Dafla family consists of the man, his wife or wives, and unmarried children who live under the same roof. Its structure, as of any other family, keeps on changing with the change of members composing it. The man may bring another wife, a daughter goes to live with her husband, or again the death of a member brings about a change. Nevertheless, the above description gives the usual pattern. In the polygynous house-holds the husband lives with the eldest wide, though he sleeps with each wife in turn. Variations in this practice, however, may occur in special circumstances. Thus in the case of Toko Chada, his first wife, who is barren, willingly agreed that he should live with the second wife. Byabang Ekha of Radeng too lives with another wife. His first wife is old though still hard-working and she did not object to the new arrangement. It is difficult to lay down any definite criterion for the deviations from normal practice. Old age and barrenness are, however, the usual factors that often make a man live with the second wife.

The above picture is by no means complete for within a single homestead also live a man's brothers and patrilineal kinsmen, their wives and children. This group of families may roughly be described as a joint family. Its members normally recognise and obey the authority of the senior man of the lineage or head of the house. But when quarrels become frequent between the families, one of them may move to live in the house of another lineal relative, or establish a separate home in the vicinity. Each family within the homestead is to a great extent, independent of the other. The clearings are separate and the produce is not jointly storked. The economic and blood ties, however, are not lessened by the domestic independence. All the members of this unit work together in each other's clearings turn by turn. The men join in hunting and fishing and participate in feastings and socio-religious activities.

A part of these members, there are other lineal kinsfolk who, though not living within the same house, live at least in the same locality. In a lesser degree they too form an economic unit in the enterprises of daily life.

A particular behaviour emerges pattern among the members of the home- stead. All elderly male members of the ascending generation are respected. A child not only obeys his father, but also his uncle and grandfather. Obedience to elders is part of training of Dafla children. However, when son is adolescent, the father as a rule takes his opinion on domestic matters. A different pattern exists for the women who come as wives. The attitude of a grown-up boy towards them appear to be one of avoidance. Avoidance is practised to preclude the stealing of sexual favours form a women during the lifetime of her legal husband. As we shall see, all such women can rightfully be inherited by a man after the death of his brother or father.

Among the Daflas descent is reckoned through males only. Thus, it is agnatic or patrilineal. For the sake of convenience in remembering their genealogies, people follow a simple rule. While giving the name to a son, they add the last syllable of the father's name to his name in the beginning. Thus, Herin's son is named Ringdo for the reckoning of descent, though ordinarily he may have a popular name like Tado. Descent is important from the point of view of inheritance of widows, since only close agnatic descendants inherit. The Daflas democrate this group from the rest by partaking of the blood of a sacrificed pig together. None who is not a member of this group can have the privilege of sharing it. Adoption is very rare. A slave, though not formally adopted, takes the clan name of his master.

Position of wives. Dafla customary law is silent over the rights of women. In the minds of the people, for all practical purposes, a wife is obtained for a specific payment. Consequently, the husband claims all rights over her person and the labour of which she is capable. In fact, if a person punishes, or even kills her for a misdeed such as adultery, her kinsmen may be offended, but they are not entitled to legal redress. She cannot leave her husband legally, unless someone compensates him for the loss. This is one reason which makes divorce difficult. Theoretically at least, unless a person is prepared to pay with mithuns, neither husband nor wife can divorce each other.

In the field of religion, women have hardly any privileges. A woman does not take part in the religious ceremonies, except in the preparation of beer for ceremonial use. She may watch but may not participate. The same is true of political activities. A woman has no say in public affairs. Except for the sake of evidence, her presence is not required in the assemblies which decide cases.

These considerations, and the factor of polygyny should not however lead us to think that Dafla wives are merely chattels, only a little better than slaves. There is no such thing as a high or low position of women, but it is only relatively high or low with in particular domains. Dafla women have more privileges and freedom in the household than in the political and religious spheres. They also own a certain amount of property.

Each wife has a separate hearth by which she lives. She has a plot of her own which she cultivates. Indeed, she has to work hard in the clearings, but the husband cuts the crop and helps in the cultivation. She has poultry of her own and may have pigs and goats. The economic partnership requires that she should do the household work, bring firewood, and provide her children with food, edible roots, mushrooms and vegetables. She is not required to offer food to her husband every day. It is a matter which entirely depends upon the mutual understanding of the wives themselves. The obligations which she is supposed to fulfil are in fact those which she willingly performs to keep her husband pleased. Whatever, the mutual arrangement, a loving wife provides her husband with beer almost every day.

On the other hand, if she is displeased with him, she can easily disturb the peace of the house. Bickerings may result in quarrels and she may go to the back balcony of the house to cry and weep. She may abuse the husband and attract the attention of the people in the village. This naturally brings shame on the husband. If the quarrel goes too far, she may run away to any other man who gives her shelter. Occasionally, such cases do occur and they lead to a lot of complications.

With our ideas of monogamy, it is perhaps difficult to realize how a man can live peacefully with a number of wives. It should be remembered that here fidelity extends to several wives instead of one. He should try to divide his favours as equitably as possible. A father takes active interest in the training of all his children. Paternal duty requires that he should try to get all of his sons married by paying the bride-price. He should also see that his daughters are married and fetch good wealth. Once he fulfils these duties, the sons and daughters pursue a normal career. A Dafla is greatly relieved of his burden when his sons are married.

Traditionally, the eldest wife has a greater say in household affairs, and has in her charge the *majis* and *talus* which she secretly buries in the ground. Many wives virtually control their husbands in such matters as the sale of a mithun or their children's marriages. This is due to their personality rather than to any right granted to them under customary law.

The Life-Cycle

A Dafla child is a gift of the Wiyus. A 'woman may sleep with her husband every night and yet not conceive,' says Toko Dum, wife of Likha Teji of Likha village, 'It is only when Duini and Polo are pleased that she may have a child.' As a prerequisite, a fundamental physiological necessity, the fact that a girl will not conceive till after her first menstruation, is recognized. Conception is linked with the acto of love, though it is not one but a series of sexual efforts that establishes physiological paternity. However, once a woman conceives, her husband's work is over, since it is for the Chengtom Bot Wiyu to shape the baby in the womb. Normally, a young woman conceives within one to three years of her married life, failing which appropriate sacrifices are made to the Wiyus. Barrenness is considered a misfortune and a barren woman is miserable all her life.

Dreams play a great part in foretelling the sex of the unborn during this period the woman does not eat any meat procured form the jungle, nor any meat that has been brought by a priest after a sacrifice.

Complications in delivery may occur at times, an these are always attributed to mischief caused by the Wiyus who are immediately given offerings by the priest. An abnormal delivery may result in the death of the mother. According to Dafla tradition, if a woman dies in delivery and the omens in the egg confirm that the baby is unlucky, the dead mother and the living baby are buried together.

Early childhood and training. The Dafla baby is born and brough up in Nature. In its first months it is never away from the mother's breasts of someone's arms. Wrapped in a blanket or cloth that the mother or sister puts on, it enjoys the warm security of their bodies. It sleeps in comfort with the mother's nipple in the mouth. By the time it is six to eight months old, it has learnt to remain on the back well supported in a sling. Now the mother can safely leave it for hours in the care of another, a daughter or a son. If the baby cries, the finger is inserted in its mouth as a substitute for the nipple and rocked or sung to. Inside the house, lying on a mat, it watches the glowing fire whole the mother busily prepares the evening meal. Both father and mother may teach it the first terms of address, *ane* and *abu*, mother and father. The imparting of early education continues, most interestingly, by the repetitive method.

When a child begins to walk, it is not a source of trouble. Clothes are hung well above its reach. Beads, clay pots and gourds are kept on the racks, and there is always someone who watches. Children at this age are taught to keep away from the fire. The lessons in hardship are almost a matter of environmental conditioning. Naked, they are bitten by *damdims* and other flies. Inside the house, smoke and darkness beome a normal part of life, and they come to enjoy it as a cosy and comfortable environment. Dafla children are not given lessons in cleanliness and they dislike water. Otherwise, theirs are happy and warm lives, loved by everybody with affectionate display.

By the time a boy is three or four, has learnt many things: how to use the rickety ladder, run errands such as calling some one from a neighbour's house, and play games by himself or with friends, although there are only a few organized games. He knows too that he must obey his mother. When he troubles her at night, she says,'Look yonder, '*orum*,' and the child goes to sleep immediately. Should his mother spit on his face, he sobs with shame and understands the rebuke intended. If he is sulky enough to snatch her clothes, he is beaten thoroughly. Thus, he gradually learns the difference between socially acceptable and unacceptable behaviour. At this age, he is taught to carry and look after babies, and perform such simple tasks as bringing water.

Children above six help their parents in several ways. At this age a boy may carry a small or big dao, and develops a child. A dream of purchasing a smoking pipe indicates a son, and a *rini*, the bell for decorating the woman's neck, indicates a girl. A dream of banana plants laden with fruits, or bamboo shoots sprouting up from the ground indicates the coming of children.

Pregnancy is recognized in the second month, and after five months, when there are foetal movements, the side on which the movements regularly occur is taken to signify the sex of the baby. If it is on the left, the probability is a son, for a man holds the stave of his bow in the left hand. Movements on the right side indicate a girl. During pregnancy, certain food craveings are observed and the women commonly eat baked earth from the hearth and ashes of millet chaff. The period of gestations lasts for nine to ten months and a baby born earlier than the ninth months may not survive.

Pregnancy intrudes but little upon a woman's regular work. She continues her cultivation, grinds corn, cooks, and brings firewood and water for the household. The change is gradual and inconspicuous. The feminine ideal, at least during the first pregnancy, requires not only a show of modesty but also a pretence of innocence. Pregnancy is not a subject for proud exhibition and a girl will never talk about it in the presence of her elders. Modesty and shyness lessen, however, as she gets accustomes to it with the advance of age. Custom does not demand any period of abstinence.

Morning sickness and vomitting are infrequent, though, in the advanced stages, there may be pain in the back, which is considered normal. But where there is acute pain, the priest may be called to make sacrifices to Wiyus. The woman is supposed to observe certain taboos during this period. For instance, she does not eat from a bamboo tube or a metal plate for fear that she will bleed excessively during delivery.[3] Nor does she go to a house where death has occurred for fear that the child will dies. Likewise, the husband does not fell big trees, not eat in a house where death has occurred. Among may tribes in India there is the belief that the sight of an eclipse harms the baby in the womb. No such belief is held by the Daflas and the pregnant woman may view an eclipse without any fear of evil.

Childbirth. Childbirth is a simple affair. Normally the woman continues her daily work until the labour pains start. The place of delivery is the enclosure where the fowls are kept, though it may occasionally take place in the house. There are no professional midwives. Only one or two old women may attend. The delivering woman rests on her knees and the attending woman holds her shoulders from the back. If the baby is not delivering woman rests on her knees on the delivering woman's back and ask her to exert pressure. This process usually results in a safe delivery. Nobody touches the baby until it is fully delivered. The mother then ties a thread at two points on the umbilical cord, approximately two inches apart. It is cut between the two points with a sharp-edged piece of bamboo kept ready specifically for that purpose. The placenta is thrown under the house, and is not subjected to any special care as to its disposal. Often it is eaten by the pigs. The baby is immediately washed with lukewarm water and the mother comes with her child to her hearth and sits near the fire.

The priest is called the next day. He takes omens from a chicken's liver and gives the baby a suitable name, in keeping with the patrilineal line of his ancestors. The baby girl may be named after the month, for example, Pra, or be given one of the traditional names such as Yamang, Yarang, Yasap or Yanyang. The next day, following the naming ceremony, the child is washed again and the visitors are offered drinks of beer and, if possible, food. The mother washes her clothes the next day, and then again on the sixth day, after which the baby can be taken out of the house and the mother can attend to her normal duties. The stump falls away from the baby within five or six days. Post-natal abstinence lasts for a month. A man breaking the taboo invokes the wrath of the Wiyus who may kill him.[4]

Sense of duty. Failure in guarding the field may earn a beating from the father. When the child is eight to ten years old, he goes to the jungle with grown-up boys and may bring firewood, a little game, or fish. The boys fulfilling these responsibilities, however small they may be, naturally come to possess a sense of maturity and even of superiority. The girls are usually busy in tasks that the mother assigns to them, such as fetching water, carrying the babies, bringing firewood, helping in the cultivation, cooking, and other houshold chores, in short, all the tasks that they will have to perform when they go to live with their husbands. The entire training is meant to prepare a boy or a girl for their future career as husband or mother.

The socially approved habits of smoking and spitting are learnt at an early age, and practically every child carries his pipe and tobacco in a pouch. No other habit is more pronounced than spitting. This becomes necessary because of incessant smoking and chewing of raw tobacco or tobacco-ash. People spit near the hearth and while talking, in and outside the house, in fact, anywhere they go. Spitting on the palms is essential for a firm grip on a dao or a stick. Spittle is applied to the palms before releasing an arrow, and is essential on the head before a shave. It is applied to all kinds of cuts, burns, bruises and ulcers. It appears to be an unfailing cure for *damdim* stings, and for pain following an awkwardly released arrow. On certain occasions, however, it has more meaning. As indicated above, a vexed mother may spit on a son who demands the major share, and this will send him sobbing. In such cases, it serves as an effective check on the child's unapproved behaviour. Spitting may, at times, be taken as a joke, as when someone tells a lie and another spilts; but if a man is offended by another's lies and spits in front of him, it is an expression of contempt.

Puberty. Puberty among girls is marked by the first menstruation at the early age of twelve or so. However, there are no formal ceremonies to mark her entry into the age in which she becomes ripe for procreation and motherhood. A girl is not embarrassed at her first menses, for she has already secretly learnt what it means. A menstruating woman is not surrounded by many taboos; consequently, though she may feel a little awkward, she has very few practical inconveniences. She should, however, not touch the ceremonial horns of mithuns and skulls of pigs hung on the main wall of the house, nor any of the ceremonial structures representing the Wiyus in and outside the house. She must not have sexual congress with her husband for five nights and should not eat wild boar. But these apart, she has nothing to avoid. She can cook and do other household work, brew beer and go to the jhums. There is no taboo on touching people, nor on eating with others. 'It is our organ that is dirty,' said a Dafla woman,'and not our hands'.

The pubic cloth is unknown, so the skirt that a woman puts on below the main garment, serves as the sanitary towel. She may bleed on the way and wipe herself with green leaves, and even if she is careless in throwing the leaves away, no harm will come to her from the Wiyus. Nor is a man embarrassed at finding a trail of blood on the track, or at accidentally touching the blood of a woman working in the jhums. Dread of the menstrual blood which is so prominent among some tribes of central India is absent here. The sixth day after her period commences, she washes her hair, hands and thighs, in a secluded corner slightly away from the house, or sometimes in a small stream. She does not wash herself or her skirt in big rivers for fear of offending the water Wiyus. As she grows older, menstruation is taken as a routine that occurs every month and which ends only when a woman has become old.

Puberty among boys is marked by the wearing of a hair knot, and a mature boy is described as one who wears a *podum*. The age for wearing a *podum* is about sixteen or seventeen years. Variations, however, may occur when it is worn even earlier. The podum indicates that the boy has reached the age when he can and should take up his duties as grown-up member of the society. There are no ceremonies, no day fixed, and no omens looked for in the egg. The priest's services are not required and tying the hair knot may be done by the boy himself or by any other person. The Dafla *podum* is attractive and at this age, adds to the handsomeness of the wearer who is proud of it. Age brings with it a little freedom from parental control, though love-making and romance may start even earlier.

Premarital love. Marriage is not normally preceded by love, yet wooing often results in a happy union rather than frustration. Obviously, a girl whose bride-price is already being paid in instalments should act with prudence and is usually guarded against the overtures of other young men. Yet there are times when the heart wins over the conflicting clains of the mind, ignoring the consequences. The passionate romantic urge a young couple is beautifully put in the following *abyu* (love) songs from Yuba:

> Both of us are in the prime of our youth
> Let us be friends
> Let us cling to each other
> As two young leaves of a banana
> If we are to climb a hill
> We will climb together
> If we are to cross a river
> We will cross together.

and again:

> Let us cultivate the fields together
> And grow old
> Our hair will grow grey
> And our teeth will fall
> But we shall live.

It will be erroneouss to presume that love among these simple people is merely an outburst of passion. The carnal aspect is not minimized, but love rests on deeper foundations. In every case, the young lover's ambition is to get married and establish a happy home. The exchange of gifts is a recognized way of showing attachment. The lover, for example, may give his beloved some fine beads and she, in turn, may offer him the finest beer. Seclusion is the essence of romance but, whereas many a lover may confess that he has fondled his girl, rarely will he admit that he has gone beyond that. The love situation gradually becomes known to the parents. If the bride-price is paid to the parents, she can get married and live with her lover in the new status of wife[5].

Maturity. With the coming of age, a Dafla aspires to get the best out of his resourcefulness. He tries to marry as many girls as he can afford, and more than ever, the rearing of mithuns assumes great importance. He tries to accumulate valuables such as beads and *majis*, and settle his cases or take revenge. 'When I was of your age,' said Nilom Serra, a rich old Dafla of Nilom village, I had married three wives. I took part in several raids. I killed a man who had brought disease to my village.

But now I am old and ailing. Those days we different. Then I was strong and everyone feared me.' Likha Teji of Likha village remarked, 'I have eight wives and I am happy in my house. My father died when I was very young. I have married them all with my own resources. But I have no mind to marry any more. I have sons who are growing up. I have to look to their marriages also. My eldest son is already married, but I am paying mithuns for the others.'

Marriage, begetting of children, and bringing them up are the tasks to be completed during this stage. For some Daflas, privileged with eight or ten wives, it is easy to live a comfortable life. A rich Dafla can often be seen living an idle life, drinking beer and gossiping or settling cases. It is the woman whose lot is hard. She has to manage the household, cook, bring water and firewood, care for the children and bring them up. Her major burden is cultivation. She is fully occupied in her clearings throughout the year, as she is responsible for all the produce for the year's consumption. These duties are arduous and only efficient and hard-working wives are able to run the house- hold smoothly.

Old age. Old age among the Daflas is not necessarily respected unless a man is distinguished priest or craftsman. With the decline of age, the authority of a person also wanes. Sons have respect for an old father, and his advice may still be taken on important matters. But they do not always obey him. Old men and women, unless too old or disabled, have to work and help in the cultivation. It is only when one ceases to be a useful member of the society that life becomes miserable. There are quarrels and everyone shirks the responsibility of support. People with several wives to look after them are considered lucky insofar as they do not have to face this difficulty. However, all of them at this age crave for death as a release form their miserable condition.

Marriage

Reasons for polygyny. The Daflas a number of reasons for their limited polygyny. The commonest is that women are indispensable for agriculture. As a Dafla remarked, 'What good it there in having a number of mithuns which may die of sickness? Get more wives for mithuns and they will produce a lot of crops.' Another reason given is sexual variety. Thus, Likha Teji was curious to know how people with one wife manage to sleep when she is in her courses. A Dafla woman from Kugi said, 'Our men dislike old women and are always after young girls.' Yet another reason is progeny. In many cases, where a woman is barren, she actually demands that her husband marry another girl. This was the case with Toku Chada of Poru. Though married for a number of years, his eldest wife did not have any child. She was able to force her husband to take her younger sister as his wife, but she too failed to bear any child. Being persuaded by both the wives, Chada has already begun paying the bride-price for a third wife. Lastly, polygyny is supposed to be a token of a man's status. A Dafla with many wives not only has the privilege of having additional hands for raising his economic status, but may also become a lavish entertainer, serving guests with beer and food. A few of them can, as stated before, even afford to remain idle.

It may appear, that since many of the Daflas are polygynous, a section of the people may find it very hard to get any wives at all. This danger, however, is mitigated by two factors. Firstly, the amount of bride-price paid for each wife limits the number of women a man may marry. In practice it is the privilege of a few rich, who can afford as many as eight wives. Secondly, it is often possible for the unmarried to inherit the widows.

Considerations for marriage. (Love, as already mentioned, is not a pre-requisite for marriage, nor is age a bar). The customary acceptance of the disparity in age often makes it possible for a rich old Dafla to marry a girl of fourteen, or again, a nubile girl may be married to a young boy. The best age for marriage for their children, so the Daflas think, is adolescence. In many cases, this is conditioned by economic factors. Thus a rich man is not only able to marry a number of wives himself, but to bring as many brides as possible for his sons as well. Consequently, sons of rich men get married earlier. Different is the lot of poor people. A man with few mithuns always finds it hard to get a girl for his son or an additional wife for himself. The difficulty is solved if he has one or more daughters, for then he can accept the bride-price for them and pay it for a wife or a daughter-in-law. As a result, daughters of poor people often get married earlier than their sisters who are rich.

Finding a suitable girl is not difficult, since girls all over the area are usually known to the parents who arrange the marriage. In many cases, a boy himself may take the lead in selecting hsi bride. He may visit the house of hs maternal uncle frequently, each time giving him little presents of meat, beads or daos. The maternal uncle is obliged to make presents in return, but he gestures from the boy by way of presents are well understood. He may ultimately suceed in winning the maternal uncle's daughter. Wealth and family status are important considerations to be taken into account. Generally the boys and girls have little say in such matters and tend to approve the decisions of their parents in settling their marriages.

Betrothal and payment of the bride-price. Initially, the boy's father talks about the proposed mariage to certain people, who indirectly try to know the views of the girl's father. If he favours the proposal, it is known in advance. Then one day the groom's father goes to the house of the girl's father with certain presents such as meat, cloth and a dao. These things are customarily accepted. In the discourse which follows he tells the purpose of his visit. It is now that the bargaining begins. The girl's father generally says, 'Take beads, *kojis, majis or talus*, whichever you like. But where and how should I find a firl for your son?' The talks continue for hours to settle the bride-price, after which the boy's father returns home.

After a few days he takes omens from the livers of chickens. If they are good, he goes to the girl's parents, this time with one mithun, pig's meat, one piece of *endi* or other cloth, one dao, five bundles of salt and many baskets containing fermented millet for beer. The mithuns and the articles are carried by kinsmen who compose the party along with the prospective groom.

When the party reaches the girl's home, her father too takes omens. He smears the mithun's horns with a paste of rice flour and beer. The articles of bride-price are accepted. He kills a pig and numerous gourds of beer is prepared for a feast in honour of the guest. The party stays for three days. Every night during their stay the priests on both sides sing *id* songs. The singing often takes the form of a contest in which the priests of each side try to outwit those of the other party.

The payment of the bride-price is made in annual or half yearly instalments, or at such intervals as may be convenient to the boy's father. Each time the girl's father gets a part of the payment, he gives cloth, beads and daos in return. The return gifts may be only a fraction of the bride-price or form a substantial dowry—depending upon the status of the families.

Marriage. After the stipulated bride-price has been paid, the girl comes, according to the rule of patrilocal residence, to live with the husband. There are no formal ceremonies which mark the consummation of marriage. Only the husband and the wife are both clad in new clothes and wear a number of ornaments. The marriage party with the bride and groom returns home carrying presents given by the girl's father. On the way they sing song, drinking beer frequently. At the approach to the village the path is closed with a number of bamboo arches. Offerings of eggs or chicken are made to the Wiyus of the jungle and they are prayed to return to their abodes if they have been coming along with the party.

When the bride comes to the husband's house she is received at the *tumko*, where she sacrifices a fowl. Immediately afterwards she enters the house. The only ceremony a few days later is the Yulo in which a mithun is sacrificed. Kinsmen and relatives join in the feasting and make merry.

Other ways of finding a mate. Marriage by the payment of the bride-price is considered ideal. But there are two other ways which are also significant. A frequent practice is to elope with the girl who then goes to her lover's house. This is normally possible only for a couple of paramours, whether married or unmarried. The girl's parents make a search and try to bring her back, if necessary, forcibly. If someone has already paid for her, this results in complications. However, if the lover insists on keeping her and pays the bride-price to her father, the latter is then obliged to restore the original bride-price to the first husband. In certain other cases, a man forces a girl to live with him, this inevitably leading to serious brawls continuing for months and years. Elopement is, however, one of the established ways of getting a wife, though in such cases, elopement and compensation do not exclude each other.

Another method practised is marriage by service, where the prospective son-in-law spends a couple of years with the girl's family, doing all the necessary work. Among the Daflas the incidence of marriage by service, though it exists, is rare as it is considered undignified. Sometimes a girl's father may take a fancy for a boy whom he thinks suitable for his daughter. If the boy's father agrees, the former comes to live with his would be father-in-law. He goes through the usual routine work of agriculture, hunting and fishing and is supposed to keep the latter happy. He eventually gets his wife and may return to his house. In the instances recorded, however, it was found that they had settled in the houses of their father-in-law and did not intend to return to their parents.

Implications of bride-price. In all kinds of unions where the girl goes to live with her husband, the Daflas insist on the bride-price. The contract actually binds the girl's parents in more definite terms than one would imagine. Thus, if the girl dies within a few years without any children, the husband may, by custom, claim back whatever he has paid for her. His prerogative clearly extends not only to sexual privileges and the life-long services of his wife, but also to the bearing of children. Barrenness alone, however, is not sufficient reason for claiming back the bride-price. To the Dafla mind, even a barren woman is economically useful and she, in turn, does all she can persuade her husband to marry one of her own sisters.

The bride's father has yet other responsibilities. If the girl runs away with some other man, he must help in restoring her to the husband; and if she returns home on account of the maltreatment by her husband, he should compel her to go back to him. the obligations imposed by the bride-price very often force the parents to coax her away from obstinacy. Sometimes she may be beaten, or even be put into a stockade to make her submissive to the husband's wishes.

The case of Yasap, a girl from Ganku village, will illustrate this. Yasap was married to a man of Tok village. Since her father was dead, the payment was made to her brother Epa. When she went to live with her husband she had no liking for him. She would not sleep with him willingly nor talk to him. The husband ill-treated her, beating and abusing her. There were many quarrels for which she felt hurt and disgraced. She tried to escape, but was caught. Her husband cut off her hair and threatened to kill her by witchcraft if she ventured to run away. Only with difficulty did she reach her brother's home.

Her husband tried to take her back, and even her brother was reluctant to keep her in his house. But Yasap refused to go. In a few months her husband, unable to recover his mithuns, caught Epa's mithuns one by one to make good his losses. Epa was annoyed and threw the whole blame on Yasap. If she would not go to her husband, he said, she could no longer stay in his house. Yasap, though adamant, was helpless. She was unwelcome in her own paternal home, and her brother abused her in the filthiest language she was compelled to leave and live in a neighbouring house.

This did not quieten Epa, who now asked her to go anywhere she liked. He was only interested in getting back his mithuns. Ultimately, she agreed to marry a young man of Lungba village, who promised her brother that he would pay for her. Yasap has gone to live with her new husband, though the bride-price still remains to be paid.

Inheritance of widows. The implications of the bride-price appear to be far-reaching when we note that Dafla customary law specifically prescribes the allotment of widows to the dead man's heirs. Thus, after the father's death, the sones inherit his wives with the exception of their own mothers. On the other hand, in theory at least, it is always possible for a father to keep his deceased son's wife for himself. But in practice this rarely occurs. Daflas also permit the levirate which provides that, if a man dies, his widow may become the wife of one of his brothers. As we have seen earlier, disparity in age is no bar to marriage. It is not rare, therefore, to find a young boy inheriting a widow of his father or brother who may be more than thirty years of age.

For the inheritance of widows, commonsense adjustments are made. Unmarried sons or brothers are taken into account; the wishes of the widow too are considered. The outcome is appropriation with agreement. It is only when a widow intends to leave the house that quarrels occur. Then, as a rule, the person who takes her is required to pay at least part of the bride-price. Normally, no Dafla expects quarrels over the inheritence of widows. In many cases, when a widow is too old, she may continue to live in the house without being inherited. This is more likely if, owing to her old age, no one is willing to keep her as a wife. Again, even when a widow is young, a man may waive his claim in favour of a close consanguineous kinsman.

REFERENCES

1. *For a fuller account of the Dafla phratries and clans see C.von. Furer Haimendorf, Ethnographic Notes on the Tribes of the Subansiri Region* (Shillong, 1947), pp.1 ff.
2. *Ibid*., p. 2.
3. This belief is limited only to the Panior valley. Women during pregnancy eat food served on leaves.
4. This belief is again limited to the villages of the Panior valley. In other areas, the abstinence periods varies from 10 to 15 days.
5. This presupposes that the girl's parent are under no contract to offer their daughter to someone else. In case another person has already paid a heavy price, the love may end in frustration, for the girl is quickly sent away to live with him.

6

LIFE AND TIMES OF MINYONG

Land, People and Environment

Boundary. The Siang Frontier Division is the home of different sections of Adis, Dr. Verrier Elwin has described the Siang Division as 'one of the most fascinating and exciting parts of NEFA: the scenery, when it is not hidden by cloud and rain, is superb: the people are charming, hospitable and filled with a zest for life: tribal institutions still retain their vitality. It is a country of song and dance, of hard eager work, of fine spinning and weaving, where the 'rich and varied tapestry' of NEFA is displayed."

The southern boundary of this Division starts from the southernmost point of the eastern boundary – the old Sissirimukh, and runs straight in a south-westernly direction upto the fourth milestone on the Kobo-Pasighat Road. It then turns north-east to the junction of a nameless stream with the Remi river at Oyang. Then again it takes a south-western course upto the point, where the river Jiya Dhol cuts across the Rajgar Ali. From there it follows the right bank of Jiya Dhol towards north to a point due east of a spur along which it continues westward till it turns again southward to Siplimukh – the point where the Sipli meets the Subansiri.

From the point where the Sipli meets the Subansiri the western boundary of Siang Frontier Divisions runs along the left bank of the Subansiri to the point where it meets the boundary between Tibet and India in the north.

The northern boundary line starts from this point and runs along the Indo-Tibetan boundary to a point on it about a mile south- west of Khangri Khangro La Pass.

The boundary in the east starts from this point, and runs in a southernly direction along the range dividing the Siang and Dibang valleys to Dirap and continuing south-eastwards to a nameless stream with its source below the Egadi river. The boundary then runs down the midstream of this river to the Sissiri river and then to the junction of the Sissri and Siang. It continues by the left bank of the Siang and acroos the mouth of the Lohit to the bank of the Brahmaputra as far as Rongdoi Ghat.

The land of the Padam-Minyong and allied groups covers over 8,000 sq. miles, and their habitations are concentrated on both banks of the Siang and the Yamne rivers, extending in the north upto the border of India and Tibet, and extends as far as Pasighat and few miles below in the south. To the west the boundary is demarcated by the Gallong settlements, and by the Siyom river. The eastern boundary as marked by high mountains and on the south-east, the last Adi habitations are the Dambuk, Meka and Rayeng group. In the north-west corner their habitation extends as far as Tadadege and Mechuka.

Topography. The country to the right of the Siang is less hilly, whereas the area lying between the Siang and the Dibang has great snowy ranges ranging from 10,000 ft. to 15,000 ft. in height. On the north there are high mountains and the whole area consists of a series of spurs of these mountains thrown out at right angles. On the east of the Siang there are subsidiary ranges running east and west throwing spurs in a southernly direction. The 'outer ranges' south of the Division gradually merge into ranges running from north-east to south-west and thus form a wall shutting off the valley of Assam from view. The valley of the Siang above the village of Kebang is clearly visible for many miles, but the valley below Kebang consists of low ranges of hills, densely covered with forest. The southern portion of the counry, unlike the right bank of the river Siang, between the Domjur and the Siang rivers is comparatively flat and densely wooded except for places where there are settlements. The left bank of the river Siang is full of steep inaccessible mountains and consequently fewer habitations are found on this side. The area between the left bank of the Siang and the right bank of the Yamne river to Dambuk, the last Adi village on the south-eastern side, containing the villages Ayeng, Mebo, Silluk, Dapui, Memesepo, is for most part flat and favourable for habitation. The area below Renging on the righ bank of the Siang upto Ledum is also more or less flat.

Rivers. The Tsang-po flows through Tibet and takes a turn southwards, approximately at the latitude 29.35N and longitude 95.20'E. At this bend the river encircles some high mountains the Namcha Barua (24.445'). Beyond this turn, there are rapids for about 30 miles below, the river enters Indian territory, where it is known as the Dihang or among the Adis, the Siang. Once the river breaks through the mountain ranges, it does not run north to south, but first flows south-south-west and south-south-east and lastly straight south to Kebang. On the whole, the course of the river is at right angles to the lie of the hills. All through the Division, the river is fed by a bumber of tributaries. Some of these are like moderate-sized rivers of the plains. The river enters the plains at Pasighat. A few miles downstream from Pasighat the river divides into two. The width and current of the river form the point where it enters the Indian Dominion to Bordak village are not great. It is not navigable because of strong current and innumerable rapids throughout its course. A few miles below Pasighat the river becomes navigable in all seasons. In the mountainous section above Pasighat, there are a few places where the river can be crossed with the help of dugouts in winter or in early rains. The two banks present completely different pictures, one sloping down to the river, while the other is sheer cliff.

The Yamne rises somewhere in the high snow-clad mountains in the north-east beyond Modi village. From its source, the river flows south-west until it meets another big tributary bearing the same name, which flows down from due north near the Milang village. It then turns south and, fed by many tributaries, flows down forming a curve towards the south-west near Dukku. It then runs south-east to meet the Siang below Jero village.

Another important triburary of the Siang is the Yang Sang Chu which originates form the mountains in the south-eastern side and flows north-west to meet the Siang near Jeru on the right bank of this side of the Indian border.

The fourth important river is the Siyom which rises in the Pari Mountains in the north-west corner and flows due east through the Bori country and then takes a turn south. A few miles down, the river again turns towards the east near Along village, an important stage in the Gallong area, and finally meets the Siang near Panging.

Flora. Almost the whole of the Adi Hills is covered by dense forest. There is a great variation of flora in this area due to the difference in altitude and climate, starting from grass, reeds, swamps to large trees. In the south of the Adi hills, the forest is full of evergreen sub-tropical vegetation with thick undergrowth and creepers. In the north the vegetation gradually changes. Here large trees are replaced by rhododendron and cypresses, while the central parts are clothed in bamboo and cane. The common vegetation in the south are Simul (*Salmalia malabarica*, Schoot), Hollock (*Terminalia myriocarp*, Heurck & Mvecull), Pichola (*Meliosma simplicifclia*, Halp), Borpat (*Ailanthus grandis*, Prain), Walnut (*Juglans regia*, Linn) and the Oak, (*quereus* sp) Chestnut (*Castanopsis*), Screw (*Pandanus*) pine and Orchids of different varieties in the north. The southern areas are rich in fruit-trees like Mango (*Mangifera indica*, Linn), Jack- fruit (*Artocarpus integrifolia*, Linn), Lichee (*Nephelium Chierensis*, Sononer), Yellow Raspberry (*Rubus* sp), Orange (*Citrus Aurantium*, Linn) and Pine apple (*Ananas Camosus*, Linn Merr).

Fauna. Of the commoner mammals different varieties of monkeys, langurs, civets, Himalayan black bear, flying fox (fruit-bat), shrews, giant squirrels, rats and mice may be noted. Big game includes tiger, leopard, wild boar, porcupine and various kinds of deer of which the sambar, hog deer and barking deer are common. The curious Takin (*Budorcas taxicolor*, Hodgson) is found only in the higher ranges of the Adi hills.

The birds are representative of the whole Indo-Himalayan-Burmese Region. Green magpie, Tree-pies, Grey and Sultan tits, Parrot-bills, various Laughing thrushes, Babblers, Sibia, Siva, Rose-finches and Pheasants live in higher altitudes from 3000' upwards. Other commoner birds distributed over most extensive areas except on the bleakest high hill-tops, are different kinds of Bulbuls, Cuckoo-shrike, Minivets, Thrushes, Forktails, Redstarts, Flycatchers, Warblers, Munias, Finches, Martins and Swallows, Wagtails and Pipits, Flowerpeckers, Sunbirds, Pitta, Broadbill, Woodpeckers, Barbets, Bee-eaters, Hornbills, Parakeets, Trogon, Owls, Hawks and Eagles, Pigeons and Doves, Jungle fowl and Partridges, Snipes and Sand-pipers and Ducks.

Of the reptiles, the Gavial, Turtle and several kinds of Lizards are the most familiar, and Blind-snakes (*Typhlops*), Tree-racers (*Elaphe*),

Rat-snakes (*Ptyas*), Racers (*Coluber*),Bronze-backs (*Ahaetulla*), *Wolf-snakes* (*Lysodon*), Keel-backs (*Natrix*), Cat-snakes (*Boiga*), Whip-snakes (*Dryophis*), Cobra (*Naja*) and Pit-vipers (*Trimeresurus*) are also frequently seen.

Among the amphibians, various species of Frogs and Toads are met with.

Mountain carps of various species, Loach, Mahaseers, Cat-fishes of various kinds. Eels and Murrels are the common representative of the fishes of this area.

Of the Arthropoda, the most interesting representative is Peripatus belonging to the primitive group Onychophora. Several species of freshwater Shrimps and Crabs represent Crustacea, and Moths, Butterflies, Bees, Wasps, Ants, Flies, Sand-flies, Cockroaches, Crickets, Dragonflies, Beetles etc., are the common insects.

Climate. So far as the solar climate is concerned, the Siang Frontier Division may be considered a monsoon region falling within the hot belt according to Supan's [1] classification of climatic zones, But the solar climate is modified by great variations of the topography brought about by an intricate mountain system which cuts the country into numerous deep gorges and narrow valleys. A cross-section from the north to south will reveal a gradation in altitudes ranging from the ranges of eternal snow in the extreme north to the low hills bordering the valley of the Brahmaputra in the south through a succession of hilly tracts in a descending order of heights. The physical climate is, therefore, entirely different from that of a rather uniform land occupying the same geographical position. Due to this great variation in the physical features of the different parts, the division presents a varigated climatic picture.

To speak in a general way, the temperature is high with little variation in the year in the lower parts. The seasons depend more on rainfall than on the temperature, and the Adis divide the year into two main seasons (i) the rains, and (ii) the winter. But as gradually rising hills cut off the upper parts from the inflow of the moisture-laden winds of monsoon, the precipitation decreases in intensity as well as continuity as one proceeds northward. On the whole, however, the distribution of rain and rain-shadow area is very complicated on account of the tortuous paths taken by the winds through the gaps and passes in the labyrinthic folds. In the lower regions, the rainy season lasts from the last week of March to September when the sky is overcast almost all the time, and the rainfall is very heavy. The valley of the Siang, cutting a passage through the hills for the monsoon clouds, is specially noted for comparatively heavy rainfall. A steep descent of the streams, draining the entire accumulation of rain-water in the upper regions in their rapid downward courses, causes sudden swellings in the lower reaches occasionally flooding the adjacent lands which are completely cut off from the plains. It is the most unhealthy part of the year with enervating warm humidity and quick wild growth of underwood jungle so well known in these areas. From October starts the dry season which continues till the end of January. The temperature gradually falls, and so do the rivers. Heavy mist lies over the land which clears only in the morning. This season is noted for strong gorge winds. Between January and March, a brief spell, which migh be termed spring, intervenes. This season is not particularly distinguished by the people themselves. To them it is merely a transition from winter to summer, as in the first part, it continues the cold of the former and ushers in the rains by intermittent showers of the latter.

This is true of the lower parts of the Division and in the valleys, on the windward side of the ranges. The leeward sides are naturally less wet and more open to the cold northern winds. The usual change of climate is noticed as one proceeds to higher latitudes and altitudes. The high lands are characterized by a cooler climate, the intensity of cold depending on the lie and height. The peaks of the outer Himalayas stand high above the snow line and represent an arctic climate in this torrid zone area.

Different Groups – Origin – Migration and Present Distribution

The Adis are divided into different groups, such as Padam, Minyong, Pangi, Shimong, Ashing, Pasi, Karko, Bokar, Bori, Ramo, Pailibo, Milan, Tangam and Tagin. Of all these, the Padam and Minyong are the largest groups.[2]

The origin, migration and present distribution of these different groups are described from north to north-east and then southwards.

From the legends available, it appears that the ancestors of the Ramos and the Bokars were brothers. The Ramos descended in a direct line from Dungram, the elder brother of Dumgumi, the ancestor of the Bokars.

The Ramos appears to have originally settled in the valley of Tang San Po in Tibet. Their ancestors left their original settlement, moved from place to place in Tibet and finally crossed over to the Tadadege area and settled within the Indian territory. Their last migration from Tadadege to Rapum, which they still inhabit took place long ago.

At present, the Ramo area consists of Rego, Rapum, Hiri, Puryi, Kiposhi, Paduche and Harme villages. Rego is the last Ramo village on the way to Mechuka. There is one village, called Dorjeeling, where bvoth Membas and Ramos live together.

The Bokars claim descent from the first man, Abo Tani. Abo Tani had several sons. One of them was Nikar, whose eldest son, Karbo, was the father of Bodung, who in turn had two sons. From the younger son, Dungumi, urns the direct line of descent of the present day Bokars.

The ancestors of the Bokars used to live in place known as Mate in Tibet. Due to pressure of Population, they started migrating and settled near about Tadadege, in a place which is at present known as Pui. Another version claims that their ancestors came down from Tibet and settled near the Shimang river, presumably near the source of the Sike river, a tributary of the Siyom. According to yet another belief, the Bokars came originally from Samelo, near Lhasa, from where they were driven out by the Tibetans Thereafter, they migrated and settled down on both sides of Tungula Pass in Yumi and Nayu valleys. The Bokars are very alike to Ramos and Pailibos and bear no resemblance to the membas or Tibetans. There are altogether twenty-two small villages in the Bokar area. The biggest is Gesing. The less important villages are Pangri, Yangrang, Taihiyong, Rote, Pidi, Ruying, Kate, Luto, Ramni, Hemi or Mote, Pote, Karle, Manigong, Ingo, Pulom, Simegong, Papigro, Tadadege, Lapugora, Yorkongdo and Namasiba.

The Bori villages are situated on the tops of the hills on the both the banks of the Siyom or Yomgong and the Sike. The area is surrounded by high ranges of hills on three sides – in the east by the Luyor range, in the west by the Piri hills and in the north by the wall formed by these ranges closing together. The important villages of the Boris are Yiyo,

Dupu, Payun, Pame, Gasheng, Gatte, Gameng, Paying, Bogu and Mega.

It is believed that the Pailibos are descendants of Bomong. As far as we know, they used to inhabit an area originally near about Dosing. They started migrating southwards, but due to natural calamities, they had to turn back by the right bank of the Siyom and finally settle in the area near about Yapuik. They at present inhabit a small area of rough terrain on the right bank of the Siyom. Their neighbours on the south-east are the Gallongs from whom they are separated by the Bayor hills; to the east are situated the highly populated Bori villages; to the north-east are the Bokars and on the north-west the Ramos. They are a small tribe, and their important villages are Yapuik, Irgo, Yapu, Tadogitu, Tagur, Lipo, Pauru, Boge, Silli and Tato, which is the last Pailibo village on way to Mechuka.

The Tagins are believed to have migrated form Penji, a village in Tibet, to Tadadege region. From Tadadege, they seem to have migrated to their present settlements.

The Ashing area starts from Tuting in the north and extends as far as Ramsing village in the south. The northern-most village is Tuting on the right bank of the Siang, to the south of which is Ninging. Pango, a moderately big Ashing village, lies south of Ninging. In between Pango and Bomdo, the largest settlements of the Ashings, are the two comparatively small settlements, Minging and Mosing.

The Tangams originally inhabited that part of the Adi country which extends from the gorge, which the Siang breaks through, to as far as the 29th parallel of latitude. More than a century ago, they were pushed down and were evicted from their best lands and forced to migrate towards Kuging.

They are now found distributed in Nyereng and Kuging on the right bank of the Yang Sang Chu, east of Jedo. Mayum is situated on the left bank of the Tsangpo, north of Jedo.

The Shimongs seem to have migrated very late. From their original home somewhere on the other side of the great snow ranges of the Himalayas, they came down to the Nigong valley. They could not move further south beyond the present Shimong village, as the Minyongs, the Padams and the Pangis were already in occupation of that area.

Thus in course of time, they had to turn back northwards as far as Jedo.

They occupy the norternmost region on the left bank of the Siang. Jedo being the northenmost village situated between the Yang Sang Chu and the Siang. The area occupied by the shimongs extends as far as Gobuk in the south. The principal Shimong village is Shimong. The next large village is Gete which lies on the bank of the Siang, north of Shimong. Less important villages form north to south are Anging, Singing, Paling, Rikor, Puging. Gobuk is the southernmost village on the bank of the Yamne.

The Karkos believe that one of their ancestors, Dunkor, migrated from the upper Siang valley unobstructed upon Gosang village. Fom Gosang, they migrated to Didung and finally to Karko village. They followed the Padams in their migration. The Karkos occupy today the region on the right bank of the Siang, the area lying between the villages of Ramsing and Pankang.

Milan, Dalbin and Modi, the three villages that form a triangle between the upper reaches of Yamne in the north and the Sidip in the south, belong to another section of the Adis known as the Milans.

The ancestors of the Milans are believed to have migrated from Pango to Karko and then to Riga. From Riga, they were forced by the Minyongs to cross the Siang and settled for some time in Riu. They were further compelled to migrate and settled in a place between the present Damroh and Milan. From there they spread to their present habitat.

It is said that the Padams come from the north and were originally the inhabitants of Bomi, a place near Ramsing. They started migrating, and passed through Sira Pateng, Dempui, Nugong, Ringong, Kilive, Pegu, Silluluak, Tayek Puigo. From Tayek Puigo, all the clans of the Padams other than the Legos. migrated to a place called Ngling. The Lego clan went to Milan and finally to Damroh. The Irang clan of the Padams also left the main body and went to Jokan and finally to Damroh. The main body of the Padams went to a place called Anatko in the Komkars' land and from there to Kesing and then joined with the Irangs and Legos at Damroh. The Padam area now starts from the Sidip on the left bank of the Yamne, covers the whole of the region on this side and extends as far as the Siku river in the south and the Dambuk village in the south-east. The northernmost Padam village by the side of the Yambe is Damroh, the next two villages towards the south being Padu and Silli. Bordak is the last Padam village in the higher region of the Adi hills. In the lower region there are five Padam villages, all on the left bank of the Siang. The first of this series is Ayeng situated at the foot of the hill by the side of the Siku. The next village east of Ayeng is called Mebo. Further east, there is a group of three villages named Silluk. The villages of the Padams on the eastern side are Dambuk, Meka and Rayeng on the bank of the river Sissiri, and are under the jurisdiction of the Lohit Frontier Division.

The Panggis are believed to have inhabited a part of the Siyom valley. They were too pushed southwards across the Siang by a more powerful section of people and finally settled in the Yamne valley. The Panggis occupy the main Yamne valley and are confined to the right bank of the river. The important villages are Jeru, Sibum and Gekku.

The ancestors of the Minyongs used to live on some snow-ranges near about Telilidung. In their southward migration, they did not follow the course of the siang. Instead, they came down the Angony valley to Mani-Pere and crossed the Takek-Adi near Dibok and finally settled at Riga past Pangkang. Later they managed to cross the Siang near Tayek-Puigo near about Riu and spread over the area from Kebang. Yemsing and Pangin as far as Ledum. The Minyongs nowadays occupy an area on the right bank of the Siang and a part of the valley lying between the Siang and the Yamne. The northernmost Minyong settlement is Pankang and Renging the southernmost. The Principal Minyong villages are Riga, Komsing, Riu, Panging, Kebang, Rotung and Reging. There are, however, a few small settlements of the same group, such as Pangkang, Dosing, Jorsing and Yambung.

The Pasis took a different route in their migration. They were driven from Singong (Sira Pateng) by other powerful groups of the Adis and migrated south, halting at Nugong, Ringong, Koliyive, Pegu, Silluluak and finally crossed the Siang at Tayek Puigo. They then proceeded to Ngling and settled in a place halfway between Damroh and Adi Pasi. From there they followed the right bank of the Yamne south-wards to Kuying Yive and then to Sire Kumu, north of their present village. They settled at Adi Pasi for some time, and then due to the increase in population, they came down near about Pasighat and settled in Ramkang and Monku. At present, Adi Pasi is the only Pasi settlement – a solitary village in the upper regions, lying between

Damroh and Padu. Their other settlements are in the lower region, a few miles from Pasighat. These villages are known as the Balek group, composed of Romkang, Tigra, Balek, Roing, Rasam, Monku, Kellek, and Gine.

A Study of the lengends relating to their original home, would suggest that the Adis came into India from the north across the Himalayan barrier. The real cause of their immigration cannot be ascertained at present. It may have been occasioned by some great natural upheaval in their home-land or by large scale racial movements set in motion by political happenings in these regions. Nor can it be said whether they came in a single mass or gradually in small batches in successive waves through centuries. In the former case, it is just possible, they might have come in a sweeping mass down to the plains of Assam and been driven back afterwards into highlands, they occupy now, by a superior power. Anything definite cannot be said upto this point: but it is comparatively easy to picture their later dispersion. Once they had settled in the moutainous regions below the Himalayas, growing communities would be forced to send out colonists in search of new lands. These colonists would establish settlements which, in their turn, would find others. In this way, expansion would continue in a sort of chain work. It may be taken for granted that, in the initial stages, the expansion was from east to west, particularly, in the Siang area. The southward expansion occurred later, when this area was fully occupied and could not accommodate any further settlement.

Characterization of a people is a very difficult task. We are often given a subjective picture that depends more on the temperament, attitude and approach of the observer than on the real character of the people. The occassion and the purpose of the observer's visit also in its turn determine to a great extent the nature of observation. This explains why the Adis have been painted in different colours, often contradictory, by different observers in the past. For the purposes of our present study, the reports on the character of the Adis by previous observers are considered under two heads. The first were by those who accompanied military expeditions. They naturally were prejudiced and unfriendly in their outlook. It is from this class that we get unfavourable pictures of the Adis who are said to be 'a blunt, independent and warlike race[3] who are 'large, uncouth, athletic, fierce-looking dirty fellows'[4] 'a much taller race than the Mishmis, but clumsy-looking and sluggish[5] and so on. The state of belligerency that existed between the Adis and the governments in the plains has led some writers to attribute bellicosity to them just as in any war either party reproaches the other with aggression. It is in this light that Hamilton's remarks on this people have to be taken. 'For a long time past the Abors have been cocks of the Assam border. Very independent, quarrelsome, they had come to regard themselves as the rulers of this far-distant corner of India.'[6]

There is another class of observers who go to a people with an open mind or in a spirit of loving curiosity. From them, a better picture and one nearer the truth generally, is obtained. N.M. Krick belongs to this class and this is how he writes about the Adis:

'The Padam is very active, jolly, a lover of freedom and independence, generous, noble-hearted, plain-spoken, more honest than the average Oriental, not over-moderate in eating and drinking, at least as far as quality is concerned. I have not lived long enough among them to be able to speak of their morality. I confess I have never been able to discover what they understand by modesty; they seem to possess much of the child's simplicity.[7]

Dunbar tries to give a more balanced picture.

'The more debased amongst the hillmen would, it is admitted, justify Portia's judgement on her German suitor, but the better type of Abor and he is by no means uncommon outside the Minyong and Panggi clans, does not fall so low. He certainly does his share of the work by clearing the "jhums", helping at harvest and building the houses and bridges. If he is full of curiosity and avariciously inclined to set an inordinate value on his services to strangers visiting his country, he possesses a certain dignity, is hospitable, cheery and honest, and may be relied upon to carry a load to the place he says he will take it. This I have found by experience he will do without supervision. He is not, according to his own standard, treacherous, for unlike the Mishmi he will not deliberately invite any one into his village and then murder him. But in his character cunning takes the place of bravery, and he does not, most emphatically, court war like a mistress.[8]

W.B. Hore tries to explain why the first impressions made by the Adis on an outsider are likely to be unfavourable:

'The Abor is suspicious and sulky with strangers, but this is soon changed to a friendliness which sometimes becomes embarrassing.'

'All the tribes are agricultural rather than warlike: indeed, fighting for its own sake is not an Abor custom. They are, however, quite ready to fight for their independence or in revenge for real or fancied wrongs.

'Treachery of the worst type has always been attributed to the Abor, but as a matter of fact he compares favourably with other savages in this respect.

Treachery is after all only a relative term, and the Abors consider our method of outflanking a stockade to be treacherous. The Abor code seems to be roughly as follows, with uninvited strangers. A warning is almost invariably given to a stranger visiting the country uninvited, that, if he will pursues a certain line of action, or forces his way to a certain locality, be killed. If this warning is disregarded, the Abor considers it perfectly fair to lull his victim into a state of false security by rendering him every assistance, in order that later on he may be killed with the least possible chance of relatication. Measured by European standards, the Abor of course is treacherous, and most of the regrettable incidents that have occurred in the past have been caused by our forgetting that we were dealing with savages, and by our attributing to them, with no possible justification, our own standard of honour.

'The Abors are a kind-hearted people and children and animals are invariably treated well.

'Their method of slaughtering doemestic animals is, however, not very humane.

'The Abor will tell the truth or will lie, with equal cheerfulness according to the whim of the moment. This makes the collection of accurate information a matter of some difficulty.

'He can, however, always be depended on to give an entirely untrue account of a path when first called on to describe it, and to greatly exaggerate its difficulties.

'This partly arises from the fact that he takes a pride in being supposed to have traversed a dangerous road and partly from his desire to dissuade strangers from exploring the country. This aversion to the intrusion of strangers is ever present and is due to the fear of disease: also to the fact that should disturbance occur, the village which permitted strangers to pass through would be held responsible by the rest of the community. This is especially the case when the boundary between the tribes has to be crossed: under such circumstances much passive opposition may be expected.[9]

A study of these reports on Adi character suggests that the people impress a visitor unfavourably at first, but improve on later and closer association. The factors that react unfavourably on the mind are the general appearance both physical and environmental. Some fundamental differences they have in their notions of morality and right conduct have also caused some misunderstanding of their real nature. In order, therfore, to eliminate subjective distortions as much as possible, it is proposed to depict their character on the basis of scientific observations of traits by presenting them as they are without any reproach or approbation.

The Adis belong to the Mongoloid stock and as such their character may be presumed to conform in a general way to that of the Mongoloid people as a whole. Now—'A great optimism and a cheerfulness of temper, combined with a bonhomie and a camaraderie that are the result of a sense of happy go-lucky freedom, appear to be the most salient qualities of the character of the Mongoloid peoples. Self-reliance and courage, as well as resourcefulness, are other good points in the Mongoloid character. On the debit side, however, they appear to be rather credulous, and at times they can be very cruel to both man and beast; and, besides, they lack depth of thought and possibly also a depth of feeling or emotion. A habit of indolence, after their immediate needs are satisfied, seems to be an occasional characteristic; but when roused to action, they are capable of concerted and sustained work. They are factual and not philosophical, pragmatic and practical rather than argumentative. They have also an innate sense of decoration and colour and of rhythm.[10]

On the credit side the Adis have many of these excellent characteristics. Once the fear of attack and enmity disguised under the mask of friendship which constantly haunted the Adi mind in the past, disappeared from their lands, with the spread of the *pax indica*, the sullennesss and suspicion, noticed by early observers vanished like the morning mist, disclosing the native frankness enlivened with a warm congeniality of heat and bright joviality of spirit which have charmed every visitor to their lands. One cannot read the reports of friendly jouneys undertaken in their lands including the remotest parts, without coming across high tributes paid to them for their spirit of hospitality and winning manners. Every one has been struck by the high spirit they maintain inspite of great hardships and privations, natural calamities and diseases which would have rendered any other people depressed and miserable. At Ninging, to give an example, 'there was an old woman with one arm. Sometime ago it has been bitten by a snake and had, as they put it, 'rotted away"... the arm broke off at the joint and she recovered."

At Miging also by way of another example, 'a man had his leg bitten by a bear and suffered in the same way. The wound seems to have become gangrenous, the leg swelled monstrously and at last it too broke off at the point.'

'Think of the incredible suffering', Dr. Elwin exclaims, 'that these two people must have endured; consider too the invincible will-to-live and the physical strength which, enable them to survive such ordeals.' Of the Miging man, he says, 'every time we met there was a beaming smile, never a complaint and never a hint of begging for anything. Here was the true Adi spirit – proud, independent, courageous, filled with a zest for life.'

On the debit side the want of a depth of feeling or emotion seems to be confirmed by the callous manner in which they sacrifice mithuns. Judged by our standards and looked from our angle, the strangulation practised by them seems to be extremely inhumane. But we must remember that religious saction and long practice acclimatize a people to acts which would appear to them in different light if the context of the situation was changed. Nobody would accuse the Buddhists of inhumanity, but it is in their literature that we come across 33 traditional methods of tortures described with an equanamity as diabolical as that of Dean Swift in his famous'Modest Proposal'. Except for this, the Adis are noted for their love and affectionate treatment not only for their fellow beings but also of the dumb animals which they do not domesticate in the true scientific sense, but which live with them almost on an equal footing. This is an anomaly, but such anomalies are to be found in all the peoples of this world. So, the Adis cannot be described as cruel and insensible to the sanctity of human and animal life in an offhand manner.

These are, however, more or less superficial traits which depend on extraneous circumstances. One of the basic features of Adi character taken as a whole is their co-operative spirit which distinguishes them form the Idus and the Gallongs, their immediate neighbours in the east and the west. This quality has enabled them to build up a society where the individual blends imperceptibly into the society and to combat the unkind nature which surrounds them with a unfailing brave heart, similing faces and to enliven it with their colourful dresses, merry songs and sprightly dances.

The tribes taken separately display individual traits some of which may be noted.

The Boris and Ashings have a certain self-abandonment about them. They have indomitable spirit. They are free, casual and independent. The Pailibo young people look bright with similing faces and are self-respecting.

The Ramos seem to be better off than the Pailibos and seem to be more independent and clever.

The Bokras are by the most disciplined and self-contained of all these groups. They give the impression of being men of the world.

The Shimongs, the Pasis and the Padams on the left bank are energetic, and the Minyongs have a great village solidarity.

Adi character treated in this objective manner 'does not stir into life and show us the hill-man standing out, a living creature.[11] Specially it fails to do justice to the fairer section of the people – the Adi women. It is they who bear the heavier part of the burden of life, and it is they who smile brighter in the face of hardship and distress. And yet their unsophisticated innocence has been misrepresented by those who have been taught only to admire artificial modesty in women. A life history of a simple Adi woman will show how false these aspersions are. She like all Adi girls had an *angong* (seeetheart) in the first prime of her youth. But she was not like him, all flesh and no soul. She did not take this relationship just as a passing amour to be forgotten as soon as over. It was a serious business of life – and sacred – a whole existence to her. But her *angong* was a mere gallang–all passion and no love – and without the least compunition – unhesitatingly took the choice of his parents as his wife. In deep agony at the news with a weeping heart she went to him, to seek confirmation and explanation. Before she said anything the unfeeling lover jeered at her and declared to his friends that his bride was a beauty far fairer than his *rasheng* love. With a bleeding heart she came back without a reproach escaping her lips, no, not even in gesture. A lonely life she led thereafter for she did not marry and had no second *angong*. She lived in the memory of the dream she had in her *rasheng* days. The gods however were not so forgiving and cursed the marriage of the false lover. He was unhappy with his wife, and came back to her to seek solace in a *rasheng* union. But how could she agree? To him she belonged – but so sacred was the spiritual bond that no light-hearted pleasure could be suffered to sully it with its gross sensuality. 'I can love no more – no, not even you', she said. Blinded by passion he sought pleasure in forbidden company – was found out and disgraced. And none wept for him in his days of disgrace, but she whom he had betrayed so shamelessly.

And when I met her – years after, she was still leading the life of unfailing constancy – faithful to a memory – without a lover – without a husband.

Such self-effacing sacrifice, uncomplaining forbearance and unswerving constancy can be met only in imaginary heroines of idealistic romances, and this girl gives the lie to all who talk of looseness in moral and lack of ethical principles in Adi society only because their standards differ from ours.

Language and Literature

The Adi language, including Miri and Gallong, belongs along with Dafla and Apatani to what may be termed the Central Group which dominates the linguistic topography of the North-East Frontier Agency. This group is fortunate in having received the attention of more linguists and anthropologists than any other Agency speech form. But literature on the Adi language proper is still very scanty. The Linguistic Survey of India treats the Central Group as a whole, fixing its emphasis maily on Dafla and Miri because it was only for these two that sufficient material was available at that time. The Research Department of the North-East Frontier Agency has deferred academic research on the Agency languages and has given priority to practical objectives such as – preparation of text-books, anthologies of folk-literature and dictionaries. The Anthropoligical Department of the Government of India undertook extensive tours in Adi areas from 1948 and collected data for a systematic and scientific study of the Adi language. But the results of its researches are yet to be published. Besides Lorrain's dictionary, a few text books, a grammer and some stray references and observations in books on wider subjects nothing special is yet available. This is not the place to try a systematic analysis of the language and I shall notice here only a few features that appeared to me to be characteristic of the language during the course of my study of the cultural aspects of the people.

Classification of the Agency languages has long been a subject of controversy and a final decision is yet to be reached. The linguistic Survey of India includes the Adi language in the North Assam group of the Tibeto-Burman branch of the Sino-Tibetan family, only on the basis of its geographical position. In spite of obvious objections to this classification we have to be contented with it at present, till this language is more thoroughly studied. The language itself consists of a number of dialects and it is , perhaps, the richest in the Agency in dialectical varieties. Padam, Minyong, Pasi, Panggi, and Gallong are the most important of these dialects while Gomru spoken in three villages of Milang, Dalbin and Modi is conspicuous by the apparent magnitude of its divergence from the other dialects.

It is agglutinative in type. The vocabulary consists of bases and a number of empty words which are used as particles, suffixed to the bases, to indicate their mutual relations when used in sentences. Though it perhaps does not reach the classic perfection of the Turkish language, yet the system of use of these particles is very simple and regular. They are added to the bases with the least phonetic change in them. It abounds in vowels of which, central'i' and 'e' strike as peculiar to ears used to the Indo-Aryan sounds only.

Among the consonants, retroflexes are absent and alveolars are used instead of dentals. Phonetic changes are noticed in nasalization of final plosives before following nasals and changes of surds into sonants and sonants into surds, according to the nature of the sounds that follow.

Monosyllabism has been claimed to be one of the characteristic features of Tibet-Burman languages. But in Adi, words with two or more syllables are far more common than words with single syllables. It may be that monosyllabic base words have been combined with prefixes or suffixes or other base wods to give us the forms now in use. It is thought for instance, that 'A', 'E', 'I' and 'U' occurring at the beginning of words in this language and in Dafla and Miri, are different forms of an otiose prefix which is added to bases to give them force of adjective or noun. This theory seems to be supported by a number of words. *Ager* means work, and *ager-ger* is a verb, meaning to work. It will be noticed *ger* is the main base; the original sense of action is modified by the prefix 'a' and the main base is repeated to bring back that sense. But it is not easy to trace back the original monosyllable base in every word. The function of the otiose 'a' in Adi has been compared with its use in other Tibeto-Burman languages and its origin, therefore, may be ascertained only after a study of all these languages. A most interesting feature is the process followed in forming compound words. If the two component base consist of two syllables each, both drop the first and join the second into a single word. Damro is the name of the parent village of the Padams. It is said to be a compound of two words, Padam and Aro where Padam drops its *pa* and *aro* its *a*. This dropping of the first syllable is very regular when it is unaccented. This system is followed not only in coining new expressions for new ideas and objects but also in forming masculine and feminine forms. For instance, *perok-one* gives *rokne* or *rongne*, and *perok abo – rokbo or rokpo*. It is very effective, no doubt, in enriching the voabulary of the language, but is rather difficult sometimes to race the component parts in their original forms. To take one example, it is not clear whether *paglak* was formed from *kapak alek or tapak alek*.

The Tibeto-Burman languages are said to evince a difficulty in forming words for abstract ideas. But Adi has got a definite system of forming abstract nouns from verbs and adjectives. This is done by adding *nam* to the verb and adjective bases. This is a remarkable trait and here is a point, perhaps, for further research to find out whether it is feature of native growth or an innovation due to contact with the plains.

Adi verbs do not distinguish persons and numbers, nor is any distinction of the time of happening made beyond the three broad tenses present, past and future. But Adi conjugation takes into consideration the condition of the action taking place, and the attitude of the speaker of the agent. *Tuwai*, a past tense paricle is added to the base in order to denote discontinuation of an action rather than the actual time of its occurrence. *Dung* and *e* are two copulative verbs comparable in use with English *'be'* and Tibetan duk and re. Ai added to dung implies that the reporter saw the agent to do the action while *tung* implies just the opposite. *Ardungai* or *tidungai* conveys the inorganic of the speaker about the condition of the agent or the action at the time of reporting. By adding *yai* or *yape*, the speaker suggests the probable completion of action provided there were no obstruction while performing it. From these, it will be clear that Adi conjugational system is based more on moods than on terms. Conjuctions are not used but it seems *delokke*, (literally meaning thereafter) is gradually being treated as an equivalent of 'and'. All sentences are simple in the sense that clauses are unknown. The function of relative clauses is performed by participles. Negatives are formed by adding *mang* to the bases and sometimes when conjugational particles follows, the final *ng* is dropped.

The Adi language till recently was without any script. But it is rich in oral literature, both religious and secular. The religious literature is represented mainly by rhapsodies known as *abangs* relating myths of creation, origins of social institutions and the original history of the people. The exact number of *abangs* is not yet known and the collection may be said to have merely started. One of them deals with the origin of the *moshup*. It is divided into three sections. The first narrates the creation of this world and titanic struggles between the originator of the human race and his adversaries. In the second part, it deals with the progress and race and the development of agriculture and war. In the third, it recounts how the *moshup* came into being and stresses its importance in the social structure of the Adis.

Similarly, there are *abangs* on the origin of the mithun, the most acceptable sacrifice for the gods. Fragments of *abangs* relating the origin of hunting and the use of poison have been already given in original with English translation. The *buri* is a special kind of *abang* which is sung by men only to celebrate the building of a new house in a village. It narrates how man first came to build houses and live in them. It is sung solo, followed by a chorus after each stanza.

The *abangs* may be compared with the *Puranas* of the Sanskrit literature and the sagas of the Teutons. They are written in an archaic esoteric language which is unintelligible to the uninitiated layman. They exist in the memory of a special class of Miris and even among them, only the most experienced and learned remember them correctly, and understand and can explain their exact significance. This class, however, is gradually dying out and if the *abangs* are not recorded early, soon a time might come when they will be lost to the world. Dr. B.S. guha has collected a few and is engaged on a special study on them.

More sublime in tone are the funeral hymns known as *penge*. These are traditional compositions written in rhythmic prose and the endowed with the simple grandeur of Biblical psalms. In them, the soul of the decreased is directed along the path of the land of the departed and in this, they resemble the Vedic funeral hymns, especially the famous *Setu sema* and the Tibetan Book of the Dead. They are imbued with a pathetic appeal that moves the audience to tears as they are reminded of their sad bereavements.

Ponungs are lengthly ballads that draw their themes from the *abangs* and sing of the origin of things and of the Adi race. They assume familarity on the part of the audience with all the details of Adi mythology and the treatment is rather by allusion and mere hints than by full narration and detailed description. Their language too, as that of the *abang* literature, is archaic and they, moreover, use obsolete poetical names of tribes, places and persons. For these reasons, they are extremely difficult to understand for those who are not acquainted with the Adi mythology. Even the local people, excepting professional Miris, though they may know some of the *ponungs* by heart, have no deeper understanding of these ballads than a vague general idea of the topics treated. The *ponungs* are, however, very popular and are regularly sung to the accompaniment of dances for days together on religious occasions, each *ponung* being known after the religious festival in which it is sung.

This name has been extended to secular compositions which celebrate some non-religious special occasions, such as the arrival of an honoured guest. They are short lyrical extempore pieces depicting the sentiment of the composer at the time of the occasions celebrate. They too, however, have traditional forms beginning with well-known traditional lines which are used as refrains. But the successive lines which form the body of the songs are usually changed to suit the occasions and the predilection and power of composition of the singers. So, they are mostly fluied in form, changing from locality to locality and singer to singer. Every song, in this way has got numerous versions formed round the same nucleus.

Abes may be taken to represent the political literature of the people. They are the introductory speeches delivered by *kebang abus* in *kebangs*. Naturally, they are prose, fixed in form and phraseology with attempts at innovations and alterations interpolated here and there. They are recited in a cadence peculiar to them which lifts them from the plane of ordinary conversational prose of daily intercourse.

All this literature is more or less public in character in so far as they are meant to be recited in or to entertain public gatherings. There are two other classes of compositions which are of a more personal nature. There are a number of love-songs which nobody sings in public. They are meant to be whispered into the willing ear of a lover or a lady-love in seclusion and privacy. Lullabies are crooned by girls while rocking babies on the back.

Nowadays, new fields in literature are being attempted, specially by young writers who have had the benefit of the school or college education. There has grown up an appreciable amount of writing, especially poetical compositions, in praise of the development work initiated by the Administration, exhorting the people to co-operate with the Administration in its schemes for the progress of the land, deprecating addictions such as opium and delineating the duties of the younger generation to their land and people. These are, however, still limited within the educated class that is forming, and it is yet to be seen how they are accepted by the people. These compositions in some cases, have departed from the traditional Adi norms and have borrowed themes and forms from the more developed neighbouring languages. The old religious literature, on the other hand, is showing signs of losing its hold on the people, especially the young generation that is going in for modern education. Conversance with it is decreasing day by day and though Adi men and women do not yet find it difficult to recognize a particualr piece when it is recited, yet there are few that can claim a full knowledge of the themes. Familiarity with the refrains and rhythms of the secular *ponung* is still wide spread, and as soon as a Miri starts a song, the dancers immediately react with the relevant movements with apropriate rhythms and instantaneous reptition of the refrain.

Traditional Adi literature has been orally transmitted by generations of Miris who form a class of professional rhapsodists. It is not possible in the present state of our knowledge to ascertain how far they have been able to hand it down faithfully in its original form. The system of transmission no doubt cannot claim the perfection and rigorous exactitute insisted on by the transmitters of the Vedas, yet the great difference between its languae and the speech of the common man today speaks for its ancient character. This process, however, is coming to an end – even sons of Miris renowned for their knowledge of the ancient lore are showing a marked preference for the modern methods of book and pen, and a great reluctance for memorizing a dying literature that fails to appeal to them any longer.

The Village

Location. The country of the Adis is a land of villages in a truer sense than the rest of India. Not a single township, except for Pasighat and Along recent creations of the Administration, is to be found in the whole land, and their language also has no word for 'town'. The distribution of the villages along the course of the three main rivers, the Siang, the Yamne, and the Siyom and their tributaries, is an indication of the immigration of the tribe. It seems from this distribution, that they kept close to the river courses in their expansion. But they always avoided the low lands lying by the river beds. They preferred rather the nearest tops of the hills with declivities towards the rivers and steep unnegotiable falls on the opposite side. This is invariably the case until we come down to the southernmost part of the Division adjoining the plains, where we find villages such as Ayeng, Mebo and others, situated in level lands by the side of the rivers. This may have been due to the example of the plains villages.

A study of village locations suggests the principles that guided the Adis in selecting them. The first need was to be near a river, ensuring constant and dependable supply of drinking water, facilities for washing and fishing.

The second need was security. In the early period of expansion, there was a widespread sense of insecurity among the tribes. Every village lived in constant danger of being taken by surprise by new waves of adventures in search of fresh grounds for settlement. A vicious pattern of intertribal feuds, attacks and counter-attacks, over possession of land contributed to a sense of uncertainty and mutual suspicion. Under such conditions, the primary consideration for selection of a village-site was to ensure natural protection and a good defensive position against surreptitious attacks. In a hilly country covered with dense forests, these two precautions were possible only on hill-tops which overlooked the neighbouring landscape. The features which were considered most suitable in such hill-tops were a gentle slope leading to the river which would solve the problem of water supply to the village, and difficult approach on other sides. Isolated hills with sloping descents to the water points, perpendicular and precipitous on the other sides were, therefore, considered the best. In cases where such isolated hills were not available, exteemities of spurs were selected as village sites. Access to the villages was carefully guarded and artificial barriers and impedients were erected to strengthen the natural difficulties already existing. Steep and difficult climbs and man-made obstacles usually, therefore, confront one while going to any Adi village. When all other factors were favourable, difficulties of water supply were solved by constructing bamboo pipe-lines for carrying water from streams of springs, in which remarkable skill is displayed. Sometimes, water is carried by this means from considerable distances.

The third important factor, which had to be considered, was the availability of suitable land. The main source of sustenance of the people is agriculture. It is shortage of food caused by overpopulation that forces them to find new colonies. They are ever conscious of the difficulties that shortage of food might cause. Therefore, sites otherwise suitable were not favoured, if agricultural land was not available in sufficient quantity. Agricultural land, in ideal circumstances, should be as close to the village as possible, with scope for future expansion to meet future demands as the village grows in population.

It is very difficult to say if scenic grandeur was consciously taken into consideration. But the fact remains that Adi villages are noted for the beauty of their location. The grand panorama, which every village commands all around, with rivers meandering far below through wooded hills, their gurgling flow gleaming in silver streaks through screens of the dark foliage, is such as could not be surpassed by the most fastidious of modern plannings. This feature is so uniform a characteristic of Adi villages, that it is hard to believe it to be purely accidental. The question of beauty may not form an item of deliberate planning, but that an innate aesthetic sense which distinguishes this people, plays a great part in the location of their villages, cannot be denied.

Plan. That villages were founded not in a hapazard manner, but always followed careful planning in accordance with a well-defined set of principles, evolved by them after long experience and, perhaps, based on ancient traditions, will be apparent from the picture Dunbar[12] gives of the founding of a new colony. At first, a selected number of men goes out for prospecting. The time selected for this is about early in December after the harvest is out. This is the time when the springs are at their lowest and the question of water on the prospective site can be best settled . This is also the time when the sun is in the lowest in the horizon and the amount of insolation can best be studied at that time. They do not come back immediately after this. They settle down there on the site that they consider the most suitable for the location of the village, start clearing the forest and erect the first huts. Only when they are satisfied with the place after their experiences and observations during the short stay, they move their belongings and families to settle there down permanently. Others join them at later periods, if the reports are found favourable. And in this way, the new settlement grows.[13]

Social Life

Birth in Adi society creates less stir than death. The family life goes on as usual, without much disturbance and there are no religious rites to encumber the normal process. The mother continues with her daily work almost to the very moment of delivery. During pregnancy, she has to observe a few simple rules of diet. She should not drink water from the leaves fo the wild potato, 'otherwise the child will be born with defective eyesight'.[14] The Doric pheasant should also be abstained from, for it might give spots and marking on the body of the infant. She should not kill snakes or frogs, 'lest, the child be born with a darting, snake-like tongue, or crooked limbs.[15] In some places doves and jungle fowls and *pitta nepalensis* are also taboo. In no case should she eat the head of any creature. Double fruits should be shunned by both the parents to avoid the unwelcome birth of twins.

The first child may be born in the house of its maternal grandfather. Uptil then the father is perhaps a *magbo* and has not started house-keeping of his own. In that case, the child brings with it the problem of a new household. Now the father has to take the mother with the new born child to a new house and that entails feasting and elaborate preparations and ceremonies.

When, the pains start, any woman, who is known for her skill at child-bed, is called in for assistance. The mother is taken into the corner of the ordinary living room. Children and the male members keep out of the house and only the authorized women attendants remain in the room. The mother clings to a horizontal pole and delivers in a kneeling position. If there is any difficulty, she stands up and is assisted by the women attending her. If the labour is difficult, pigs and fowls and sometimes mithuns are sacrificed to Nipong. A string is tied round the umbilical cord in two places and the cord is cut with a split bamboo sharpened into a knife. The placenta and the cord are then taken away into the jungle and are either thrown away or buried in a pit dug to receive it. The period of defilement lasts for three to six days. During that period the mother neither touches the fire-places nor cooks. On the expiry of the period, she goes to the water-point and cleans herself and her clothes there. The water-point itself is not used, but a stone is brought and placed at a little distance from it, on which a ceremony and the ablutions are performed. Her father's father, father's mother, mother's brother and mother's brother's wife form int a circle round her, to protect her from evil spirits. After washing, she returns to the house and takes her seat near the fire-place. The name-giving is not an important event. As a rule, the father or any old man names the child at the time when the umbilical cord is cut. The name is usually of two syllables, the last syllable of the father's name forming the first of the son's. The day of the birth may be celebrated with a feast to the children of the village, if the parents can afford it. The mother starts going to the *arik* along with the child after the purification period, but refrains from any hard work. Field work in real earnest starts a little later. After about a month, she performs the ceremony of Erang Abo to which all her relatives, her mother's brother in particular, are invited and entertained in a feast.

For the first six months, the baby lives entirely on mother's milk. Afterwards, the mother starts giving rice, merum, and sweet-potato to the child, three times a day. She, however, chews it into a paste before giving it to the child. As soon as the child cuts its teeth, it starts taking all kinds of food without any restriction, but first chewed into a paste by its mother, Breast-milk continues until conception of the next child; this period may be taken as two years on the average. *Apong* may be given as early as the age of one. In case breast-milk fails after birth, the child is fed with *apong* mixed with the juice of sugar-cane, or mother's brother's wife or sister, provided they have children of the same age, may suckle the baby. In order to ensure a copious supply of breast-milk, the suckling mother takes *apong* mixed with juice of a number of leafy vegetables. The child's hair is first cut in the local fashion after ten days of the birth.

Up to six months, the child continues to be the whole time responsibility of its mother and is carried by her wherever she goes. Afterwards, when it starts crawling. It is placed under the care of its elder sisters or brothers. The elder girl carries it on the back tied up in a *gale* and most of the day it passes there in sleep or rocked into silence, if awake. The father does not think it unworthy of him to take care of it and whenever he has leisure, and the mother is away in the field, he looks after it and fondles it. Only in the evening, the mother comes back and takes over the baby and suckles it, sitting by the fire-side. From this tender age, in this way the Adi man and woman start a life of independence from parental guardianship and care. This goes on from the age of crawling to that when the baby turns into a toddler. Only the watchful eye of the aged and the senior boys and girls (which is not however as watchful and fond as a mother's) continues to be the only restraint on the child's free movements.

By this time it learns to observe the behaviour of the elders and imbibe the ways of life. It knows and accepts the routine of duties of the grown-ups, their times of coming and going, the division of responsibility towards it among the father, mother, brothers and sisters and other members of the family. In absence of the constant company of a fond and indulgent mother, it rarely develops way-wardness obstinacy and grows a sense of restraint regarding its own wishes and fancies. An Adi baby at his age is usually a quiet type of being rather grave, smiles and prattles little, and cries but rarely. It recognizes the indifference of the world around to its baby complaints and sufferings and takes lessons in roughing and self-help.

In this way, the child grows up mostly uncared for in its own way more in the lap of the nature than that of its mother. It imbibes rather than is taught any knowledge. The father may occasionally tell it something about the spirits and deities and ancient heroes, customs and festivals. With the village society it gradually adjusts itself as it grows. Games and sports are not many. 'Knot tricks are known and children play knuckle bones with pebbles. In addition to bamboo spears and swords and toy bows and arrows the children make pop-guns with a pithed stick as the tube and a half berry as the pellet.[16] Sometimes, 'they make little bamboo *merang* and idols in imitation of those made by their parents'.[17] A few other games have already been noted, but altogether an Adi child's life up to ten years of age is a blank with no engrossing diversion and so, hallooing groups of boys and girls intent on abosrbing games and excited over 'wins' and 'lost's are rarely met with in Adi country. Within this period, however, the difference between the life of a girl and t eboy begins to manifest itself. A giel, as soon as she learns to take care of herself and that she does very early, is expected to do odd jobs to help her mother and elder sisters. She is asked to look after her younger brothers or sisters, to fetch water from the water-point in small bamboo tubes, to carry fuel and other articles from the jungle and *ariks* in small baskets. She has still less games or sports to play than a boy. A boy idles his tiem away in play or otherwise with no particular duty. But she has odd errands always allotted to her. Thus, they grow up in different ways, one already a small helping hand in the family, the other just a blank adjunct to it till they attain the age that qualifies them to enter the community life through two different organizations, the *moshup* for the boys and the *rasheng* for the girls.

Moshup. The *moshup* or bachelor's dormitory for boys is a very important institution in Adi society. 'There are two underlying principles on which the institution is built, namely, the creating of the habit of discipline among children at their formative stage of life and in the developing of a spirit of co- operation and collaboration so that the tribe can act as a unit, and fissiparous tendencies within the body politic of the tribe may have very little room for growth. In addition, it develops among the young a spirit of responsiblity, alertness and habit of taking risks in the face fo danger which are essential for the existence of the tribe. Although emphasis is laid on the training for the groups to work together and face a common danger, there is also a provision for showing respect and consideration to the elders of the tribe, specially those who are old and infirm and dependent on the younger members for their living.[18]

The institution is called by different sections of Adis by different names. The Minyongs call it *dere*, Padams term it *moshup* among the

Milan and other allied groups, the institution is known as *ngaptek* and Boris and Ashings call it *bange*.

The *moshups* are usually constructed in the centre of the village from where different approaches to it can be watched and guarded. The construction is carried out by the people of the village, and is similar to that of the dwelling houses with the difference that it is a longer construction without any compartment as a rule. The back side of the *moshup* is covered with wooden planks as protection against cold wind and other three sides are left open. In some villages *moshups* are covered on all sides with provision for numerous exits. The entrances are on the low side and on the high side there are rows of pigsties. The walls, the floors and the partitions, if any, are usrally made of rough when plansks and not well fitted. Logs of netched woods are used as staircases and are many in number. There are a bumber of fireplaces fo *merums* in a *moshup*. These *merums* have occasionally parition walls in between. The number of *merums* in a *moshup* corresponds to the number of sections in the village which also are known as *merums*. Each *merum* has a separate entrance to the *moshup*, and has a platform or a shelf for keeping the belongings of its members. There are suspended trays over each fireplace on which are kept the trophies of animals killed during community hunting.

Pedong Nane was the daughter of Liming Litung born of Sedi Melo. Pedong Nane married Idum Bote, a son of Sedi Melo. They had numerous children of whom were Robo and Doni. In a great *Kebang* held to bring about peace and order in the world, presided over by Tusing Imite and Lero Rodange Migong, an equitable distribution of the and the wealth of this world was made among the children of Sedi Melo. In this distribution, Doni and Robo got the largest and best shares, but later on, rivalry grew between these two in which, Doni prospered and incurred the jealousy of Robo who was supported by all others. Jealousy at last broke out into an open hostility in which Robo with all the evil spirits and wicked beings as his supporters proved too much for Doni, the man of peace. His parents-Idum Bote and Pedong Nane, therefore, decided to save him from the machinations of Robo. For this purpose, a shelter was built where Doni could learn the art of war and where he could live under the protection of the good spirits and be thus saved from the harm attempted on him by Robo. This is the origin of *moshup*.

For the construction of *moshup* such trees, bamboo, canes and leaves are used, as are not good as fuel. For instance, the posts for the *moshup* are made of Tapit and Takinag trees, and the Tale, Tagiang. Tagmo and such other trees are used for other purposes of construction. These trees are used as they are either favourite of the good spirits or repugnant to the evil spirits. After the first *moshup* was completed, the spirit of Nui, the great hunter an the gods of the under world, good friends of Nui, were called to live there. *Apong* and yeast were brought to the *moshup* for the hunters. Ginger was kept in it becaue of its good smell and a large number of poisoned arrows was also kept ready. To feed the hungry spirits, a large quantity of food was also stored. This is how the first *moshup* was built and the same custom and procedure are observed even today.

The *moshup* is used as a sleeping house by all young men from the age of ten till they take wives to their homes. Any man of the village or stranger can sleep in the *moshup.* Boys belonging to different *merums* on completion of their day's work for their househod and after their night meal come to the *moshup* to sleep round their own *merums*. Younger members are expected to light the fire in the fireplace, from wood collected by all the members of the *merum*. Each *merum* is in charge of a senior boy and he is responsible for the maintenance of the discipline of his *merum* and is empowered to punish any defaulter. 'Side by side with the *merums* there is another health called *romsom* where the old and the infirm male members of the families belonging to the *merums* sit together, gossip during the day and may even sleep at night. Each *merum* has a *romsom* attached to it, both of which must act as a single unit and supplement each other'.[19]

The *moshups* are used for holding different types of *kebangs*, more specially *kebangs* relating to war and communal hunting. They are also used for different types of feasts and festivals. During some festivals, girls are allowed to dance inside the *moshup*. Hunting expeditions are organized by each *merum* under the guidance of a senior and experienced member for the training of the younger members.

'The personality structure of the Abors grows through the *moshup* in a manner most suitable for the welfare of the tribe where struggle for existence is very great and where there is very little scope for the weak and inefficient persons of fissiparous nature.[20]

Rasheng. The *rasheng* or the dormitory for girls is erected in each village on the same principle as the *moshup*. The *rasheng*, a small hut having only one square room with a fireplace in the centre is constructed by experienced old men who in return are supplied with rice and *apong*. The *rasheng* members help in collecting the raw materials. The adolescent and unmarried girls of the village sleep in their respective clan *rashengs*. It remains unoccupied during the day. The inmates come after their night meals and carry on their spinning and weaving until they retire to bed. They return to their respective houses early in the morning. Like the *moshup* each *rasheng* is under supervision of a senior and experienced girl. It is the training institution for the girls in discipline, comradeship, responsibility and leadership. Here they are friendly and free, and learn to obey the seniors, and are taught that disobedience is punished. After adolescence, a girl really starts her romantic life and in the *rasheng* she starts her courtship which leads her to choose her mate in future life. Young boys from different *moshups* come and join the girls in the *rasheng* in the night. A girl is free to entertain anyboy of her choice and there is no reflection on the character of the girls or the boys for doing so. The *rasheng* is not only a training institution for all serious teachings of life but also gives opportunity to its inmates to develop finer aspects of life. Older experienced girls teach the younger, different types of dances, their traditional songs, and heroic myths. The younger members get some training in spinning and weaving from their mothers but more from their senior *rasheng* friends. 'It also helps ..... the growth of a spirit and comradeship among men and women and a life of healthy relaxation which provides the outlet for the release of tensions and repressed forces which otherwise would have developed into fractionism and marred the development of a healthy tribal life.'

The *moshup* and *rasheng* are central institutions where boys and girls get practical training in the traditional mode of life. Here the boys and girls are allowed to find their way into the mysteries of life; in addition to the social and communal life, to the mysteries of sex. In this, the dormitories may be considered as schools of preparation for matrimony. The training period falls into two: one what may be termed probationary period and the other, the advanced and qualifying period. In the first period, the novices are placed under senior members who act as their tutors and guides. They have to obey these instructors and carry out their instructions. After taking meals in their homes in the evening, they go to the dormitories and do odd jobs such as fetching fuel for the *merums* and water for *apong*. Usually, in the beginning, they fall asleep early round the fire-place and know not what goes on in the night. But gradually as they grow up, they start noticing the conduct of the older members and learnings things by simple observation as they have been doing at home. From what they see and what they hear, they discover the meaning behind the meetings that go on between the *moshup* boys and *rasheng* girls and as inhibition is one of the least drawbacks of an Adi character, their growing curiosity does not remain unsatisfied for long. In this way before they reach adolesence, they become well informed about sex and soon start love adventures of their own. The girls are allowed to join *ponu* parties and come into more intimate contact of the same age group of the opposite sex, and liasions start which are free from any embarrassing apprehension of irremediable catasrophe if the first uninformed and uninstructed selections do not come out successful. Partners are changed if they do not come up to expectations. Want of partners is not allowed to stand in the way of such experimental contacts, if it can be helped and refusal by free girls on the groudn of dislike alone is not countenanced by the social code. In this way, experimentation goes on till an adjustment is reached. If both the partners are satisfied with each other, they think naturally of establishing their relationship on a permanent footing. Though the will of the intending partners is supreme and they may unite in matrimony inspite of opposition from their elders, yet the custom is that the actual negotiation should be done through the parents. The boy makes his desire known to his parents either himself or if he feels shy, through his friends. If his parents agree, the mother of the boy prepares one chunga of *apong*, two or more smoked squirrels and ginger paste. With these, as presents, she repairs to the girl's house and makes a formal proposal on behalf of her son to the girl herself as well as to her mother. If the presents are accepted, the proposal is considered to have been agreed to, and from that day on, the boy and the girl become formally engaged. The girl from that day starts wearing a cane appendage on her neck. This engagement gives the boy right to visit the girl's house and spend the night with her there. In the beginning of this friendship, the boy spends the evening only in the girl's house and spends the rest of the night in the *moshup*. He starts staying the whole night with her in her house at a later stage if the girl agrees. The boy shows his attachment to his girl by presenting *apong* and meat to his woudl be parents-in-law from time to time. With the Ettor festival following the engagement, starts a formal exhange of presents, which is known as *lungkang*. During that festival, the girl prepares a large quantity of *apong*, meat and food and sends them to the boy's home, and the boy responds by killing a pig and sending it to the bride's. This formality is observed every year as long as the girl continues at her father's.

This is among the Padams. Among the Minyongs, the parents of the boy consult all the elders of their clan as soon as the son proposes to marry. If the elders agree, an elderly woman is selected as *arebina*, go-between. She goes to the house of the girl with presents of *apong*, squirrels and meat, which is known as *apong kadung*, and places the marriage proposal before the parents of the girl in a traditional formula which means—I have come to you for vegetable (*oying-kadung*). If the parents agree, the *apong-kadung* continues for one mouth; if during this period nothing unfavourable turns up, a day is fixed for *reying- apong* (final decision). On that day, the mother of the boy takes a plentiful supply of mithun meat, pig, fish, squirrels and *apong* to the house of girl. There, all the matrons of the clan to which the girl belongs, are invited and entertained in a feast. The mother of the boy distributes the food which is flavoured with salt and ginger paste only but never with chilly. Each woman is given one squirrel to carry back home. The meaning of *reying-apong* is the *apong* that cools the heart. On the completion of this ceremony, the engaged pair is declared as a formally married couple.

The girl, after the marriage, may continue staying with her parents if the boy in the mean time has not been able to have a house of his own and still lives with his parents. It is expected, however, he should have his own house and take his wife there with the coming of the first child. The maximum period allowed for keeping a wife at her parents is generally up to the birth of the third child. But if the girl refuses to leave her parents and follow her husband to his house, there is no legal compulsion to make her do so and the matrimonial relation may continue with this dual residence in such cases. Cases have been known where the wife has joined the husband after as many as twenty years after marriage. During the period of the wife's residence at her father's the husnand is known as *magbo* and thenforward has to perform Yegling which is the first ceremony in his new status in the wife's family. It is an optional one and is performed only if the *magbo* can afford it. In it a pig is sacrificed and the portion between the neck and the lower ribs with one foreleg intact, is offered to the parents-in-law. The other foreleg goes to the sister of the bridegroom. The clansmen received the heart, the liver and the intestines. No game killed in chase may be offered because poisoned arrows are used in chase and so presentation of hunted game is considered discourteous to the parents of the bride. After Yegling whenever there is a sacrifice in the family of the bridegroom, or games killed in *ampi kiruk*, the chest portion goes to the parents- in-law.

Among the well-to-do with whom the economic aspect of matrimony is very important, the wishes of the girl or the boy are not always consulted. The father of a rich girl is naturally against a union with a poor family and so is the rich father of a boy. Where the families are equal in status and wealth, consent is not normally withheld, but where one family is rich and the other poor, parental consent is very difficult to obtain. On the other hand, the liking and dislikes of the children are ignored for marriages of convenience settled by the parents. If the proposal comes from the parents of the girl, there is no formal procedure, they simply communicate their desire to the parents of the boy, who are then expected to start the formal procedure, if they agree to it. If the girl is of age and agrees to the earrangements by her parents, she allows the groom selected to visit her at night. If she does not, the groom goes on trying to make her agree. If he succeeds in winning her over, he is received by her at night in her own residence, which amounts to her acceptance of him. As long, however, as the girl. If the marriage is settled by the parents in the childhood of the parents, the boy and the girl refuses to accept the groom selected by her parents, she demonstrates her unwillingness by continuing to pass her nights in the *rasheng* in the company of her own chosen mate. The groom in such cases cannot raise any objection. If the *rasheng* choice culminates in matrimony, then only the groom selected by the parents may demand from his successful rival compensation for what he has paid as the price for the girl are free to separate if both agree to do so and render the marriage null-and-void without any complications. No compensation can be claimed by the contracting parties in that case. If, however, it is the girl only who objects but the boy is aggreeable, her objection has no legal value and she can have her man only if he pays the traditional compensation to the boy. Boy's objection is legally valid inspite of the consent of the girl and the marriage is annulled without any compensation.

Every girl is considered an asset to the family to which she belongs. So, depriving a family of a girl by taking her away in marriage has to be compensated by payment, commensurate with the status of the family and personal belongings of the girl, such as *tadaks*. This payment of the bride-price is known as *are*. This is no fixed lumpsum payment settled at the time of proposal or marriage either in cash, household property or domestic animals. It takes the form of a continued supply of meat by the husband and his relatives to he parents of the wife. The husband gives his entire share of fish caught in organized fishing and half his catch by a trap or rod; of rats and squirrels caught, half the number goes to the girl. If the catch is poor, the wife's family claims the whole of it. The whole share in a community hunting goes to the girl and only a hind leg of the game bagged individually. One foreleg with five ribs of a wild boar or a bear killed by the brothers of the husband or his clansmen is treated as a share of the clansmen of the bride to whom it goes through her parents. The father-in-law gets the upper portion of a mithun sacrificed by the husband, but if sacrificed by his brothers or clansmen, the entire chest including the neck is presented to the girl's parents. Wife's father gets the hind leg of a pig so sacrified. Of the pigs sacrificed on the Sulung festival, the neck and the chest exclusing the ribs and the lower jaw are presented to the girl's parents. Both the boy and the girl exchange their shares of meat whenever that forms an item of menu at home.

There are two ceremonies which are performed when a man is lucky in marrying a girl from a rich family who comes with personal possessions rich in *tadaks*, specially when these beads amount in price to fifteen mithuns. The first of these ceremonies is known as Maruk. It may be performed any time after the marriage at the convenience of the husband. There is no fixed time, but it has to be performed at the time of the Uning festival. For it, a huge quantity of food consisting of ten loads of rice, at least two pigs, ten tubes of *apong*, four to five of cooked rice, two to three loads of dried meat, the same quantities of smoked rats and squirrels is prepared by the husband. A mithun has also to be presented on this occasion. All the youngmen of the clan rig themselves out in their war-dance costume and go out with the presents in a gay boisterous procession towards the home of the bride. The youngmen of the bride's clan also proceed towards the home of the groom in the same way but without any presents. Both parties meet half-way and there they stage a mock-fight, the bride's party blocking the way and the groom's party trying to force pasaage. Daos are taken out and flourished menacingly but harmlessly, the air reverberating with war cries and helmeted heads bobbing up and down as so many combed heads of fighting cocks. This goes on for about two hours. By this time both the parties feel tired, the tempo comes down and the bride's party yields pasage to the groom's party, which passes on in a joyous mood. A few yards from the house of the bride, they are received by the women of the bride's clan with *apong* and food which are offered only after the mithun and the food brought by the groom's party are handed over. All the clan-members of the bride assemble by this tiem and the bride's parents also kill some pigs or mithuns and both the parties join in a grand feast. The second ceremony is known as Minyam. In it, pigs are offered in place of the mithun.

This is the usual and normal marriage. But there are other forms which, if less common, are in practice and have the sanction of the society. One of them may be described as marriage by exchange. In this, a boy desirous of marrying a girl undertakes to fill the gap in her family by supplying a suitable girl for a marriageable boy in exchange. By this method, the difficulty sometimes felt in paying the *are* is solved. In case the marriage in exchange does not take place on account of unwillingness of the girl who may run away with someone else, the bride-price that would have been due had there been no exchange, has to be paid.

Elopements also are not uncommon. This may happens with non-Adi persons also. Such irregular marriages are tolerated by the society as usually those who elope, leave the country and live in distant lands outside the tribal jurisdiction. But all the same the customary compensation equivalent to the bride-price is always claimed in these. Cases are also known where marriages by abduction have taken place.

Till an Adi youth settles down with his wife in his own house, he continues a member of his father's family or that of his father- in-law, where as a *magbo* in its fullest sense, he has to stay and render services to him, in exchange of the hand of his daughter. He starts his independent life with his wife beside him and as usually the wife joins him with one or more children born at her parents, he begins his independent life as the head of a full-fledged family. He gives up sleeping in the *moshup or* in the father-in-law's house and starts looking after his own wife and children. But the property continues in the father's name as long as he is alove. His children grow up in their turn and gradually transfer their allegience to the dormitories and finally to their own families. In this way, an Adi family rarely develops into a joint family with two or three generations and lateral descendants living under the same roof and the supreme authority of a patriarch or matriarch. As soon as the elementary family reaches its fullest development, it splits itself into independent units. During the life-time of the father, however, the joint property holds the different units together in an economic bond. Seen from this angle, they may be said to constitute a family federation of autonomous bodies independent in their internal affairs. The only exception of this general practice of sons starting household of their own may be found in the case of the youngest son who may continue in his father's house with his family.

Monogamy is the general rule and rarely a second wife is taken before the first has died or has been divorced. But instances of a man with two wives are not rare. Co-wives, however, living under the same roof have never been known to cause domestic strife or inconvenience or trouble in any way. Strange though it may be, the proverbial dislike of step-mother for step-children is very rare and no case has been recorded and no report has been heard of quarrels between the co-wives leading to rupture in a family. Within the family, the supreme authority rests with the father. This continues unchallenged till the children have reached the dormitory-going age. After that, the responsibility of training with growing age is divided between the community and the father, the community being represented by the dormitories. As soon as the son gets engaged, the family loses a further claim on him because thenceforward his shares of games killed individually or as a member of organized hunts, go to his parents-in-law. All claims on him cease to exist when he starts his own household or becomes a *magbo* atached to the family of his father-in-law. As long as the father is alive, the family can only claim his labour in the field. In the case of a girl, after the dormitory-going age, the family surrenders its control over her nights but her whole day she devotes to household duties. In the early morning, she helps her mother in cooking food and feeding the swine and the fowls; then she accompanies her to the field and there sows, weeds, or reaps according to the season and comes back in the evening with loads of harvest, of fuel or of water. On reaching home, she pounds and winnows roce and puts rice to boil. The evening meal over, she is free to visit the *rasheng*. She is ow considered as one of the senior members of the house and is often consulted in household affairs. There she waits in her father's family till the time when her husband builds his house for their independent family life.

Residence is patriolocal in the beginning and nuolocal in the latter part of life for both man and women. The patriolocal residence normally ends with the birth of the first child which is a signal for a change over to a nuolocal residence. Exception to this rule occurs when a man due to various reasons fails to have his own house at that time, and serves a period of a *nagboship* at his father-in-law's.

Within the family, the world of man is clearly distinguished from that of the woman. There is no segregation, nor is any seclusion of women observed, but each has a special sphere of activities clearly demarcated. From the early childhood, a girl knows the type of work she has to do and the boy knows his. So, a boy always looks up to his elder brothers and father for guidance in regulating his behaviour. In the same way does a girl derive her instructions from and builds up her behaviour on the pattern of her mother and sisters. This devision of labour is scrupulously observed and both the man and the woman accept the traditional pattern without any question and grumbling. Of course, their idea about activities suitable for man and woman differs from ours. An Adi man for instance, does not mind looking after a child while his wife is away from home in the fields. He may even lend a hand in cooking. But in no case will he handle a loom, so will a woman refrain rigorously from felling trees and setting fire to debris in a jungle clearing. In social life, no woman will formally join a *kebang* though she does not hesitate in making her voice heard and her opinion felt.This distinction of man and woman maker itself manifest in the behaviour of the household members and unconsciously young boys and girls have their character and outlook moulded in the traditional form.

Descent is traced through the father. The children take the clan of the father. But in case of children of extra-marital relations, the boy belongs to the father's clan and the girl to the mother's.

An Adi family, as has been shown above, consists of a nucleus of father and mother with separable units in sons and daughters. The parents too, are not tied together with unbreakable bonds as divorce and desertion may occur with no great difficulty. So, economic stability of the family has to depend to certain extent on a sense of economic security of all the component elements. This adjustment has been achieved by dividing the property into two categories, personal and joint. The bulk of the joint possessions consists of land. When a village is founded, each family is allotted a piece of land. This land belongs to the family as a whole and as the family splits economically after the death of the father, the land is also divided equally among the sons. Another item of immovable property is the house. Though the house is used by the family as a whole, it belongs to the father and each son can claim a share in it after his death. But as usually the older sons start independent household during the life time of their father, the youngest son by the virtue of his being the last to remain with him, comes to an automatic possessio of it after his death. None have been yet known to dispute such possession by the yougest brother. But in case all the sons separate before the death of the father, the house is equally divided among them. The widowed mother should in normal cases, be the responsibility of the eldest son, but in practice she prefers to live with the youngest son as he generally continues longest in the parental house.

Besides these two types of immovable properties, every house has its movable property in the form of domestic utensils, implements, live-stock and ornaments. Ornaments are personal properties. Beads and silver ornaments brought by a girl from her father's house and those given to her by her husband are her personal belongings. These are generally inherited by her daughters and daughers-in-law. In the same way, the father may have beads inherited from his father, his trophies of war and chase, his bows and arrows, daos purchased by him and items of dress woven for him by him wife. Some of these go to decorate his grave. Beads of real worth are not wasted in that way but are substituted by imitation ones. The real *manis* are inherited by the sons and they pass down the family as family heirlooms. Rice pounder, *danki* and such other valuable possessions of which only single items are available in a family, are divided among the brothers by mutual understanding. The live-stock is equally divided. Where physical division is not possible, as for instance where only one mithun is possessed by a man, the division is made either on the basis of value or it is included in the miscellaneous list consisting of single item possessions such as *danki* and rice pounder and apportioned among the sons according to their need or desire. In such cases, arbitration mey be felt necessary and the village elders sit in *kebang* on it.

In the centre of this world of concentric circles of affinities, the Adi grows and leads his life of graded and well-determined responsibilities and attachements. Disturbances when married partners disagree, leading to divorce, occur and lead to fissions in the family nucleus. But these are governed by customary laws and cleavages are healed and new nucleii formed without any great difficulty and turmoil. A man and woman thus grow old in their houses amidst their children who separate to go to their own or to their husband's and the time comes when the parental couple is too old to go to the fields and to take part in the arduous duties there or at home. Then they start staying at home enjoying their well-earned rest, basking in the sun on the open platforms or enjoying the warmth of the hearth inside, and looking after the children and doing very light work such as basket making, only to keep their vacant hours occupied. They are treated with respect and consulted and obeyed in all important household affairs. Though not active as before, the village society never lets them fall into oblivion. Their voices reach the *kebangs* and in the annual community hunting, they are treated to a banquet with the best and largest shares of the games in the *moshup* where occasionally they pass their time just to be in touch with young life. In some places, they have separate institutions known as *rikiyap* all to themselves where old age dozes and dreamms and meditates and slowly slides down the corridor of time to the eventual goal of life in peace and tranquality. And when it comes at last, the family and the village stop all other work to bid farewell and pay the last homage to the departed soul. If death comes first to the father the widowed mother goes to live with the youngest son or may marry again her husbasd's elder or younger brother. If she has no son and remains a widow, she is taken care of by her husband's clansmen. The death sometimes, comes premature and if a baby is born dead, it receives aerial burial. The crops is packed in a covered gourd shell and hung high from a tree. Deaths by accident whether on child-bed or in the wilds or in water are looked upon with awe and longer *gennas* are observed.

So is the Adi born, and so he lives his span on this earth and so he passes out of it to enter a new life in another sphere where his own familiar world waits for him in a new form with the same facilities and status that he enjoyed here.

REFERENCES

1. A. Supan, *Grundzuge der Physischen Erdkunde* (Leipzig, 1896).
2. Another section of the Adis, the Gallongs, of the Siang Frontier Division has been described by Shri L.R.N. Srivastava in a separate booklet.
3. From a letter by Major H. Vetch, Political Agent, Upper Assam, dated 3rd January, 1848.
4. J. Butler, *A Sketch of Assam* (London, 1847), p. 110.
5. E.T. Dalton, *Descriptive Ethnology of Bengal* (1872), p. 22.
6. A. Hamilton, *In Abor Jungles* (London, 1912),
7. Rev. N. M. Krick, 'Account of an Expedition among the Abors in 1853' (translated by A. Gille), *JASB*, Vol. IX. (Feb. 1913).
8. G.D.S. Dunbar, op. cit., p. 66.
9. W.B. Hore, *Report on the Abor country* (Simla, 1913) pp. 21-32.
10. S.K. Chatterjee, *Kirata-Jana-Krti* (Calcutta, 1951) p. 32.
11. G.D.S. Dunbar, op. cit., p. 61.
12. G. Dunbar, op. cit., p. 32.
13. Nilima Roy, 'Habitations of the Adis of the Siang Frontier Division' *Vanyajati*, Vol. V, (July, 1957), p. 125.
14. G.D.S. Dunbar, op. cit., p. 57.
15. Ibid., p. 57.
16. G.D.S. Dunbar, op. cit., p. 58.
17. Ibid., p. 58.
18. B.S. Guha, 'The Abor Moshup as a Training Centre for the Youth, *Vanyajati,* Vol. I, No. 4, 1953, p. 83.
19. B.S. Guha, op.cit., p. 84.
20. Ibid., p. 85.

7

SOCIAL STRUCTURE OF WANCHO SOCIETY

The Wancho society is divided into two important social divisions : Wanghman, the Chief and Wangpen, the commoner. This division dates back to the days of the first creation of a Wancho village and there is no tradition or folklore to say the exact times of this division. As is customary and usual in a society with a Chief, a Wancho Chief is entitled to marry several girls from the commoner class. The marriage of a Wangham with a Wangpen girls has given birth to two intermediate classes : Wangsa and Waangsu. A Chief is sacred and so is his blood. So his son born out of a Wangpen wife has something superior in him given by his father and something inferior given by his mother. He can neither be a Wangham because there is Wangham blood in him, nor can he be a Wangpen because Wangham blood is also in him. Thus all the children of a Wangham from his Wangpen wife or wives are assigned to an intermediate class of Wangsa, just a rung lower than the Wangham. Below Wangsa there is another class. All the children of a Wangsa father irrespective of the class their mother belong to are relegated to a still inferior class known as Wangsu. Four social classes have thus come to be established. On the highest rung of this social hierarchy is the Wangham with all his glory and purity and scredness. Next to him is the Wangsa degarded because of the Wangpen blood. A Wangsu goes a step furhter down and does not give rise to any other inferior class. On the last and the lowest rung is the Wangpen with no royal blood in him. All these four social classes have various special responsibilites and obligations, rights and duties, and interpersonal relationships.

The Wangham is the head of the village as well as of the society. The head of the village has got to be a Wangham and, since the post of a Wangham is hereditary, a Wangham has to produce a Wangham son. For this he has to marry the daughter of Wangham born of a Wangham wife. Such a daughter is known as Wangcha. As polygamy is the rule without exception among the Wancho Chiefs, a Wangham may and often does marry than one Wangcha. The first son born out of any of these is entitled to the office of Wangham. If a Wangham does not have a son from any of the Wangcha wives, the office of the Chief, on his death, goes to the nearest kin, his brother's son being given the first preference. But, if it so happens that his brothers also do not have sons born out of their Wangcha wives, he asks the Chief of his parent village to send to his village one of his younger sons to succeed him. This arrangement is also followed when the Chief of the parent or the paramount village has no son, or other eligible heir. He then asks the Chief of the village which branched off from it to send his eldest son, who then shifts to the parent village and inherits the office of the paramount chief on his death. The next person in the line of succession then becomes the heir apparent of Chief of the dependent village. But in no case can a son of a Wangham born of a Wangpen wife, a Wangsa, becomes a Chief. Since office of the Chief is sacred, the holder has to be sacred and one can only be sacred if one is born of a Wangcha mother, as only a Wangcha is the symbol of purity and sacredness in Wancho society.

For the purpose of marriage these four classes broadly form two groups. The Wangham, Wangsa and Wangu or, so to say, the royal classes form one group and the Wangpen, the commoner, the other. The *jan*, comprising several villages, regulate marriage; the village, though, functions asthe basic unit for marriages. All the descendants belong to the royal classes living in all the villages of the *jan* are related to each other by blood ties and so marriage among them is forbidden. Similarly all the Wangpen of all the villages of the *jan* are related and cannot marry among themselves. Within the endogamous village these two groups functions as exogamous units. Members of the royal classes give their daughters to and take daughters from the Wangpen class and *vice versa,* except of course the Wangcha who can only be given to a Chief. But since a Chief has to marry a Wangcha for an heir, he has to marry in such a village which is outside his *jan*. As the village from which the Wangcha comes cannot be brother village, it has to be a hostile village. Belligerency and marriage relations go together between two villages. Because a village cannot be a belligerent to nor can it establish marriage relations with a brother village, a village has to be found which can fulfil these two requirements. Hostililty with some village is as necessary to establish as marriage relations. If there is no hostile village from where the heads will come for the head-hunting rituals sanctioned by the society? Thus, the Chief has his affinitive relations both in his own village through marriage with Wangpen girls and in one or more hostile villages through his wives.

Wangsa is a status only for one generations given to the Chief's children by a Wangpen wife, known as Wangu. So long such a child survives he remains a Wangsa. His children are degrades to a still, lower status of Wangsu. This helps in reducing the number of Wangsa in the village. If the Wangsa were made into a permanent class it could create problems for the society by becoming potentials rivals to the heirs of the Chief. All of them would then regard themselves superior to the Wangpen and ultimately the Wangsa could outnumber the Wangpen in the village and so the privileges demanded by the might become more than what the Wangpen could afford to bear. If Wangsa were allowed to increase their number, one day they would become very powerful on the village and could pose a threat to the Chief's authority. Numerical strength has always been considered as a main source of power in the Wancho villages, and villages with considerable population have always dominated smaller ones and subjected them to their authority by sheer threat of annihilation.

A Wangsu is the descendant of a Wangsa. This class is permanent and more stable. A Wangsu cannot be further degraded in the social scale and all his descendants in all the succeeding generations remain Wangsu. By virtue of having the Chief's blood in them they are considered a little superior to the Wangpen but are not entitled to much social prestige. For the purpose of marriage they come under the royal class and cannot marry anyone belonging to the same class in the same village or *jan*. They can marry among the Wangpen in the same village. Since they are not considered as potential claimants of chieftainship and there is not threat from them to the Wangham son of the Chief's office.

A Wangpen remain a Wangpen for all time. There is no change in his social status. His marriage relations with a higher class do not enable him to rise in social scale nor can he go down the scale as he is the lowest. Though he can marry a daughter of a Wanghan, other than a Wangcha, or that of a Wangsa or Wangsu he does not get any benefit out of it. The group of the three royal classes is the only marriage group in the village which can provide girls to him. Though, in theory, the men of the two marriage group can marry girls from their own class outside the village and the *jan* in practice, it is rarely done. When mates are available in one's village nobody bothers to find one from outside, especially from a hostile village which would have been impossible for the entire populations of the village. In one's own village one knows all the girls, who has played with them, made love to them and it is the fitness of things that one selects a mate from them.

As woman have to bear the burden of domestic chores, they have also to bear the social mark of their identity, given especially to Wangpen women, who crops her hair in order that they may be identifed. Women of the other three classes keep long hair and decorate it with the help of various beauty-aids at their disposal. But this long hair and cropped hair patterns go on changing alternately from one generation to another. A Wangpen girl has cropped hair because she is born a Wangpen even if she is married to a man of any of the three royal classes. But her daughter will be the daughter of man of a royal class and so she will have privilege of long hair. Again the daughter being a Wangsa or Wangsu has to be married to a Wangpen and her daughter will be the daughter of Wangpen and so revert to cropped hair. This system is very interesting and both patterns of hair can.be seen in all the families. Mother and daughter have to adopt different styles, while mother-in-law the same style. There is, however, no change in the hair style for men. Men of all the four classes keep long hair and let it hang down behind on the necks. They either tie the hair in a burn at the nape of the neck or encase it in a covering made of leaves. The hair then looks like a solid stick dangling on the back. There are two distinct styles for trimming the front hair. Some shave a little portion above the forehead, others make a parting line between the hair falling in front and that falling behind. This parting line is made by cutting and removing the hair in a straight line across the head from ear to ear. The front hair is not allowed to grow longer and is cut along the forehead so that the trimmed line touches the forehead. Women of the three royal classes also keep long hair and treat it as the men. They do the crop occassionally. Both sexes use hair brushes.

Premartial sexual relations are permitted in Wancho society. Since the two groups of the royal classes and the commoners class are exogamous in the village, boys and girls of one group mixed freely with those of the other. When a boy falls for a girl he starts paying her more and more attention. While on the way to the *haram* or coming back from it or working there or at any other meeting place, he starts offering her *chhali*. When he comes by some beads he quietly passes them to on her. If he is gallant and well-off he might present her with her mirror just to remind to her how beautiful she is. He might also give a small ear-ornament. This may not be of much material but of great sentimental value. All these attentions and presents endear him to his sweetheart. At night when the unmarried boys and girls assemble at the Chief's house, or in the house of some other village elder, the boy sings *lai lunga le* in which he praises her beauty and says that he is madly in love with her.

Since a Wangcha is considered pure and sacred by the people, one would conclude that her premartial life would be equally pure and sacred and that she would be going as a virgin to her husband. The fact is far from it. Since the Wangham and the Wangpen form exogamous marriage groups within the village, the Wangpen boys do get indulgence from a Wangcha. While the other girls in the village are allowed premarital liberty it would be unfair to force restrictions on the Wanchos.

The marriage of a Wangcha is more difficult to arrange than that of an ordinary girl. She has of neccessity to be married to a Wangham and the Wanghams are not as common as the commoners. Marriage wiht many a Wangham may be ruled out by unfavourable omens. These circumscribe the field of choice of a suitable match for the Wangcha. She may have to wait for several years before she gets a husband, and during all these years she cannot be asked nor expected to remain a virgin. She finds her lovers from among the Wangspens. It would be erroneous to suppose that she remains content with one lover. It is a matter of great pleasure and prestige for a Wangpen boy to have relations with a Wangcha for a sweetheart. And they are eager for liaisons with her; she, on her part, may quite often oblige them. But she has her own perfences according to which she picks and chooses. She has to be discreet and avoid embarrassing consequences. Though a premarital conception does not bring any serious complication in her social position or relation, or in getting a suitable mate, it is not considered decent for a Wangcha. Wangcha is sacred and she cannot be relegated to the status of a common Wangpen girl because of a lapse in her dealing with the youngmen of the village. Her lapse is not decent not because she has done anything degrading but because she has not been careful enough. A Wangpen can never think of marrying a Wangcha. He may have enjoyed her but when you ask him whether he would like to marry her, he shakes his head vigorously and says,'Oh, no, no, no. It will be a great sin to marry a Wangcha.'

While marrying off a girl, nearness of the groom's house from the village is given prime consideration. Though theorotically members of one social groups can get mates from the same social group from an unrelated village, in practice, they do so from the other group in the same village. Harvest time is the best for settling and performing marriages. There is enough then to feed people and to celebrate the ceremony in a benefiting manner. How can a father entertain people in a lean period? Not much wealth passes from one family to the other in form of bride-wealth. In conformity with the economic condition of the average families, bride-wealth is just nominal and there is rarely any higgling over it. The girls takes with her bead necklaces, armlets, wristlets and other petty ornaments. The greatest happiness to her is that, besides getting the pleasure of living with her husband, she will be living very close to her paternal home, and this affords her a sense security.

The Chief of Longkhau, as that of Maihua, is not a Wangham, the first in the social scale but a Wangsu, the third. The people say that when they migrated from Tsangnu their Chief was not a Wangham but a Wangsa, why so is not clear. Sometimes it so happens that a parent village sends a Wangsa Chief to a newly branched or conquered village so that the new or the smaller village may not boast of its social position and ever thinks in terms of equality with the parent or the dominant village. This was what happened in case of Bonya as the present Chief there is a Wangsu. But why a Wangsa was sent initially to Longkhkau when it was more or less an independent and newly founded village could not be explained by them. Later on, Longkhau came under the political control of Pumau and the latter also played the same diplomacy which Pongchau had played with Bonya. To secure its control over Longkhau, Pumau sent a Wangsa Chief there, and in the next generation the Chief there became a Wangsu and since then a line of Wangsus.

Lonkhau, Pumau and Chating are on the border between Tirap district of NEFA and Tuensang district of Nagaland. In past, these and other neighbouring villages always indulged in inter-village feuds. The whole area without any regard to geographical or political boundary, which, however, did not exit in the true sense of the term at time, resorted to head-hunting in order to take revenge or settle other disputes. The villages were never secured. Living very close to a powerful hostile village was fraught with grave danger and, as such, a strong and powerful neighbour was always a threat to the peace and security of a weak village, and also living away from a powerful friendly or related village was equally dangerous. The cultivation field of an adjoining weak village was the best place for an ambusucade and head-taking. To counteract such surprise attacks, youngmen of the village were sent as vanguard. The working women followed them when all-clear signal was passed to them. A village was not safe, the cultivation fields were not safe, the tracks to game reserve and fishing streams were not safe. Nothing was safe. Peace was elusive and dear to obtain. People had no mental peace. They worked with frayed nerves, with fear lurking all around. Nobody was sure as to who would be the next man from the village to fall to the enemy and thus increase the number of heads in his morung.

The reason and purpose of head-hunting, it appears were varied and numerous. Fear of the intention of the enemy often induced a a man to take initiative by taking a head. If he did not strike first, he thought, the enemy would not hesitate in striking him and taking his head. So to take another's head was always safer and better than to lose one's own. No village wanted to be numerically a loser in head-hunting. If a village lost a head tried its best to see that it captured a head from the enemy village in return. In a bid to accomplish this the village either took a toll of more heads than it had lost or lost a few more. The losing village thus tried to maintain an equilibrium over heads lost and heads gained. And this created an endless chain reaction between the villages as the balance was hard to maintain nay, it was never maintianed. The importance of human or animal heads has always been emphasized by the people. The head of an animal killed was a trophy and a mark of bravery and chivalry. Hunting expeditions which took place over the territories of two villages, or a game from the territory of one village killed in another often caused dissensions. Both claimed the right of possession of the head of the quarry. Since two enemy villages were not under the control of a third village, it was always difficult for another village to intervene and adjudicate. The village which took the animal's head away by sheer force at that time, had in all liklihood, to compensate it later with a human head taken in retaliation. Disputes over territorial rights were often decided by daos of the two contending villages. To yield a certain point or to grant a concession was taken as a sign of weakness and cowardice, and once a village accepted inferior fighting position or dictates of another village it faced constant harrassment and danger of attacks. The best way was to keep one's head high; to rejoice when a head was taken and forget when one was lost.

Women, however were rarely the cause of head-hunting. As already told, excepting the village Chief, no one took a wife from another village and since intercourse between two rival villages was almost impossible, cases of dispartable relations with women of another village rarely, if ever, occurred.'But by this it should not be understood that women were shown any regard or mercy when two villages came into conflict with each other. If sommeone came across a woman from the enemy village he would not hesitate to take her head.'

None of the villages involved in this chain of vendetta could hope to stand alone surrounded on all sides by enemy or unfriendly villages. Each village had either its parent village or dependent villages. Stronger and powerful villages often went to the help of the weaker and smaller villages, partly because they were related or friendly, and partly because the smaller and weaker villages wanted their help for considerations such as tribute of human heads, grain, cattle or other things. The helping villages,besides receiving tributes, had also the advantage of getting a head or two. Heads obtained in this way were retained by them, the village which sought their help having no right over them.

'The Chief never took part in an attack on any enemy village partly because the loss of a Chief's head was a great humiliation and partly because the Chief's fall might cause the rout of the fighters. But the Chief was a good strategist, and he planned the attack with meticulous details.'

At times, the Chief's indiscretion and bad handling of a raid led to serious conflicts between him and his people, particularly the

Wangpen who were always in majority in the village and were always the worst sufferers. It was all right if the village indulged in head-hunting once in a while, but the villagers were rarely prepared for a constant or a large scale feud which might lead to their extermination. The Chief, nevertheless, had unlimited power, and at times, he almost became tyrant. He had the power to impose fines, levy taxes, confiscate and dispose of the property of any recalcitrant man in the village, marry any number of Wangpen girls and drive away anyone from the village. In extreme cases he could also inflict capital punishment.

The decision to launch an attack was taken after properdivination. the official diviner of the village was called and asked to find out the result expected of it. A banana leaf was cut into several pieces and knots were tied in them. The positions of the knots indicated the outcome and the raid was undertaken only when the diviner assured that it would be successful. It was not possible for the whole village to take part in a raid. The responsibility was assigned to certain morungs. Here it need not lead us to infer that a morung could act independently without any regard to the opinion and decision of the whole village. only when the Chief and the village approved a morung could take upon itself the responsibility of organizing and launching a raid.

I was shown once or twice the mimic show of a head-hunting raid which gave an idea of the process which must have been followed in the past. The youngen taking part in the raid were all in their war dress – a helmet studded with boar's tusks and pig's hair and goat's horns in the ear lobes and were equipped with whatever weapons gun, spear, dao- one possessed. They marched in single file, feet moving noiselessly and gripping the hilt of the dao, gun poised on the shoulder and expression of tension apparent on their faces. The party took over behind the bushes and each took position. When the time came the first man in the line plucked a leaf from the bush and passed it to the man next to him and he passed it on to the third man and so it went down the line to the last. This was a silent signal that the time had come and every one should maintain absolute silence. It also enjoined upon them the responsibility of remaining loyal to the cause. No one spoke, none made the slightest movement, suppressed breathing could be faintly heard. Absolute calm prevailed as if no living being existed in the vicinity. All on a sudden at a given signal the party emerged from behind the bushes and charged on a bush in front as a at the pitch of their voices, and attacked the bush, the imaginary enemy. Guns were fired at it, spears thrust into it, and daos cut it up symbolizing the cutting of an enemy. The participants heaved a sigh of relief, apparent satisfaction beaming on their faces. All of them then enganged themselves in cutting the head, hands and feet of the 'enemy'. One cut 'head' and put it in his basket; others took possession of the hands and feet. All were happy. The mission was accomplished. They would be welcone as heroes in the village. Tubes of beer would flow in their honour, a feast would be thrown. The party then came back – not the same tense, silent and orderly, but a rowdy, jubilant and madly joyous party, shouting and singing on the great achievement .

Since the Wanchos no longer resnsrt to head-hunting now, the mimic show was the best one could have to have an idea of the operation involved and the procedures adopted. The one described above conforms to a general pattern of operation involoved. It will, however, not be correct to assume that head-hunting was resorted to quite often on a large scale. It was a periodical occurrence and a village considered it a good harvest if it added to its stock three or four heads in a year. In most of the morungs I saw the heads huddled together in such a way that it was difficult to count them; and nobody could touch them except the village Gampa and Wangsam Pa . Later, during my tour, I found in Khanu village, the heads systematically tied with bamboo ropes and suspended in rows on the wall of the morung. It was easy to count. There were 106 heads. The Chief of Khanu told me that during the head-hunting days heads were also sent from Khanu to Ninu as tribute and that the morung was twice gutted by fire and many heads were burnt. Since nobody maintained an account of the heads, he could not tell me how many were sent to Ninu and how many year burnt down. The rule of sending heads to Ninu as tribute was very simple. If Khanu took two heads at time one was sent to Ninu and one retained in the village. But if only one head was taken it was retained in the village and a hand or a foot was sent to Ninu. It is not possible to get the number of occasions when two heads were taken at a time so that we could arrive at the number of heads sent to Ninu. Similarly how many heads were burnt in the fire was anybody's guess. But perhaps it can be assumed that the total number of heads taken by Khanu village could be anything from 300 to 400 in all. Khanu village has been in existence for about 400 years. So the average number of heads taken by Khanu is about one every year. In case of the smaller and weaker villages the number must be less than that. The number might vary on several considerations. A bigger and powerful village indulged in head-hunting with several villages and consequently took heads from all of them, while a smaller village could hardly afford to go much beyond five to ten miles from its boundary and it was not always that it met with success. Ninu and Niaunu were eternal enemies since the day these villages were founded. It is said that Niaunu declared enemity with Ninu even before it had settled at its present site. When it migrated from Tsangnu it came al the way to its present site telling all the time that it would stop its migratory marches only when Ninu came in sight, and would found the village just in front of Ninu so that there would be comparative ease and convenience in taking heads from Ninu. And so even today Niaunu and Ninu face each other separated by the Tisa river. It can be presumed that the average number of heads taken and lost by these two most powerful and old villages of the Wancho might have been more than one a year.

From among all the participants in a raid it was possible only for one or two to take heads. Taking a head required agility, quickness and daring. The possibility of the raided village charging back was always there. So only he who dared to go right in the midst of the enemy risking his life, could take a head at the first opportunity and run as fast as his legs could carry him back to the village. Such a man became the hero of the day. A man who could risk his own head could get another's. The trophy of a head was so great a prestige-booster that the risk involved was worth taking and amply justified. The others, neverthless, were honoured for their bravery in taking part in the head-hunting and the society sanctioned them the privilege of tattoo. A tattoo mark on the face was an indication of the fact that the man had taken part in head-hunting and not necessarily, as is the common belief, of his having taken heads.

On the return of the party, men and women went down to the village boundary to receive the fighters. Rice, meat and tubes of *zu* (locally brewed beer) were taken from each family to celebrate their safe return. Each woman present there conti- nued to offer *zu* from her tube till it was empty. They were received with a great pomp and eclat. They had raised the prestige of the village; one more head was added to the stock of the village; a pledge to take revenge of an earlier loss of head was redeemed; an occasion of festivity and rejoicing was offered by them to the village and no reception was adequate for their bravery and achievement.

The party then formally reported the success to the village Chief. The head, palm and feet were placed before him. The Gampa was then called and asked to take charge of the trophies. From then onwards it was primarily his duty to clean the head, dry it and finally keep it in the morung. He took the head and the limbs and busied himself with the preparations. A long bamboo was cut and its top was split and made into a funnel into which the head and hands and feet were kept. The bamboo pole was then fixed at one end of the village. From now on the head because a tabooed thing and nobody except the Gampa, who, the Wanchos say, is in charge of all the 'dirty' rituals, could touch it. After a lapse of certain time, when the flesh had rotted away, the head was taken out and the Gampa carefully removed all traces of rotten flesh and skin from it and offered these scrapings to the pigs. A Gampa whom I interviewed later told me humorously that the pigs who ate those tasted sweeter than others. Then the head was placed in the morung along with other heads. The hair was cut from the head and was equally divided between the village Chief and the head-hunter. It formed an important item in the adornment of one's body. It was tied to the headgear and worn in the earholes in various ways. It was a precious thing and none except a Chief or a head-hunter could possess it. Nothing could induce either of them to part with it as it mean parting with a trophy which had been obtained at the risk of one's life.

The head-hunter was held in high esteem. Wherever, he went he was respected. He could appear with the insignia of a head-hunter on festive occassions. These insignia mainly consisted in tying monkey heads on his decorated basket and a locket of human heads made of wood or brass. The girls liked those men whose faces were tattooed, that is, who had taken part in head-hunting . 'How can a girl fall for a face which is not tattooed?' asked head-hunter. A head-hunter was the beau of the village. Girls vied with one another in offering themselves to him. Wangchun, the Wangsa son of Votnu Chief had said, 'Girls would be mad after him and whenever they got opportunity they offered themsleves to him.'

'But what is so extraordinary about a head-hunter to fall so madly for him?' I asked.

'Why not? He is brave and who is that girl who does not want to have a brave lover?'

But gone are those days of head-hunting and gone are the spirit of chivalry and enthusiasm. Equally gone are the accompanying ritual which formed an essential part of their cultural life. The village life is dull, morose and monotonous. No new and exciting event takes place. That dance which followed a head-hunting, that which gave them occasions to flaunt their dress and beauty, and to woo has disappeared. The dress and songs have become meaningless. They were ritual songs and could not be sung on ordinary days. Faces are no more tattooed. An art has died unmourned. A beauty aid which stole the heart of girls has vanished. All untattooed faces are equally 'repulsive' to the girls now. And, over and above all these, the heads in the morung are starving and will continue to starve. Since no new heads can be added and the old ones do not now get fresh companions, occasions when they were fed amd cared for are also no more.

The people are worried about this. How long will the heads like unfed? Something has got to be done. If real head cannot be taken at least a symbolic head-hunting can be performed. Pumau had decided to take care of its heads after they had starved for more than a dozen years. Further, the Chief's son has to know all the ritual connected with head-hunting even though head-hunting is not in vogue now. All these consiederations compelled them to set out in quest of a 'head'. The youngmen of the village got ready. The Gampa led and the Chief's son accompanied. At a little distance from the village, near a banana plantation, the party halted. All operational tactics of head-hunting were followed. At the given signal the party fell upon the banana trees and cut the symbolic enemy into pieces. The operation was over, the 'head', a round stone, was taken and the party returned home. The 'head' after undergoing all the rituals was kept in the morung. It was a day when the other heads in their morung got a companion. Rice and meat were offered to them, libation of beer was made. They were satisfied and no longer was there any cause of alarm. They would not cause any harm to the living beings now.

I had occasions to ask the village Chiefs and commoners individually and collectively, directly and indirectly about their reaction to the stoppage of head-hunting. They did not express their opinions very clearly on this subject, and gave vague and evasive replies. They seemed to give a tacit approval to the decision of the Administration to do away wiht the practice of head-hunting. They said, 'Surely, it is true that with the stoppage of head-hunting we can now live in peace, there is no danger of our being killed. We can go to our haram and trading expeditions unmolested.' 'But,'everyone said, 'this is what now I feel. I do not know how others think about it. I cannot vouch for everyone in the village.' Did it mean that each thought while talking to me that his fellow villagers might be thinking in a different way? Was this opinion of approval only superfical and something else lay hidden in thier hearts which they did not wish to disclose? These are the questions which they did not wish to disclose? These are the questions which are difficult to answer as the people never talk openly and clearly about this or any related matter. But on certain occasions when a village is involved in a land dispute with another and feels that its claim is justified, it makes no secret of its anger, and I have often heard people saying: 'This is the time when such-and-such village should have been wiped out.' Whether they could have wiped out the village in question or not is a question which could have been answered in the past, but when their grievances are not redressed they feel that they should have decided the case in their own traditional manner. They often say,' We also are men, and if we could not have done such and a thing, we would have stopped hearing our loin clothes.' This shows the pent-up anger that is generated when someone's lad is invoved. 'Land is life, 'the Wanchos say, 'when there is no land, how can a men survive, and what is the use of living without land?' In past, we must not forget, land disputes had caused endless feuds and much blood was shed, heads lost and taken. But this did not deter the loser or encourage the gainer because no land could be surrendered to another village come what may. And undess a village was very sure it did not by its claim on any particular piece of land. But surely they cannot decide their land disputes with their daos as they used to do in past. The days of 'might is right' are gone but, it is necessary that such disputes should not be allowed to arise between villages. It is better not to let themk occur than to force a decision. A Wancho can do anything for his land where he was born and where he will die.

It was good to talk about head-hunting with the people. They took interest in describing the acts of their past glory and achievements.

Old man who had been through a period of widespread strife looked back nostalgically to those days of their youth when they ground risks, professed a cult and were proud of it. They look with contempt on the young man of today who have grown 'soft', who are leading a secured life and who have nothing to be afraid of. Within the next forty or fifty years when all these men who have taken part in head-hunting would be dead, a new generation will emerge – a generation which is born and brought up in an atmosphere of comparative calm and quietude. The village elders of today are trying to keep the rituals of head-hunting alive and allow them to be transmitted from generation to generation; the heir, apparant to the village chieftainship is initiated in functions and significance of these rituals. These have been handed down to them from their *apu- apa*, who were wiser. Who are they to abolish them ? No none wants to share the responsibility of doing away with them as they are unaware of consequences of the non-performance of the rituals. Naturally, they are more concerned with keeping a custom alive rather than with breaking it. If they cannot get a human head to perform these rituals, nothing can prevent them from getting a symbolic 'head' and they will base their rituals on this 'head'. Their *apu-apa* are not unaware of the changed circumstances, the impossibility of taking heads now and so will understand their difficulties and forget them. The art of tattooing will vanish with them.

Men of the present generation are not tattooing themselves which is because they are not taking part in head-hunting. The girls have perforce to look for some other physical attractiveness in their lovers. Tattooing among the girls, however, continues. The present generation, at least, is expected to follow the rituals. Men will die but the spirit will remain.

8

EMANCIPATION THROUGH THE DORMITORY

A great deal has been written about the origin of the tribal dormitory systems and many theories have been advanced. On the lines of Freudian thought Dr. Verrier Elwin has suggested avoidance of the "Primal Scene" as the most probable explanation. There are, however, certain overriding considerations which make it impossible to accept this view. Among simple primitive folks the sexual act is looked upon as a natural and normal event without any inhibition from religious and ethical ideologies which give it a secretive character and forbid its discussion. Be it said to the primitive man's credit that his general healthy outlook has prevented the occurrence of abnormal practices like organism, homosexuality and erotic exhibitionism so common in civilized societies. The aboriginal inhabitants of the Andaman Islands live in a single collective hut each pair occupying a separate cot. It is not an uncommon right to find, for instance among the Onges of the Little Andaman, several pairs indulging in the act after the midday meal without any feeling of shame or delicacy. They did not, however, develop the dormitory and there is no parental segregation whatever. The dormitory system has developed among hunting tribes either in the food-gathering stage or in the beginning of shifting cultivation. It is not, however, a uniform or general occurrence. While some have developed it, others of the same region under identical living conditions have not. Among the primitive tribes of the Travancore hills, while the Kanikkars, Malapantarams and Malapulayans possess the dormitory, the Irulas do not have it. Similarly in Chotanagpur the Santals are without the Dhumkuria, while it is in a rudimentary form among the Mundas and Hos. It is among the Oraons and Paharia tribes that it occurs as fully-grown active institution. In Assam while the dormitory formed an important part of the culture of the Kacharis, Garos, Mikirs and Lushais, the Khasi- Pnars show no sign of it. Similarly the Morang is absent or present only in a rudimentary form among the Anagamis but constitutes an integral part of the life of the Sema, Lhota, Ao and Konyak Nagas. Incidentaly, the dormitory is not linked with the culture of the Austric-speaking people as some have supposed. Its absence among the Khasis, Nicobarese and the Santals clearly indicate its non-relationship with the Austric cultural milieu. We do not have adequate evidence of the original linguistic affinities of the tribes of South-West India but in Central India it certainly flourished among Dravidian speaking tribes like the Oraons and Paharia and not among the Austro-Asiatic tribes. In North-East India it occurs among tribes speaking Tibeto-Burmese languages like the Garo, Lushai, Naga and Abor groups. If the avoidance of the primal scene was really the determining cause it is inconceivable why it is totally absent among the Santals but present among their Paharia and Oraon neighbours with very similar living conditions. Similarly, it is difficult to account for its non-existence among the Angamis although their cultural pattern with the pursuit of head-hunting as the central cult is the same as that of other Naga tribes. Finally, while the Moshup forms the most distinguishing feature of the Abor culture of the Siang Frontier Division, it is entirely absent among the Mishmis of the Lohit Valley and the Daflas, Hills Miris, Apatanis and kindered tribes of the neighbouring regions. Among the Gallongs, children sleep in the house with their parents without any segregation. If avoidance of the primal scene were really the objective, how is it that in the Abor ekums, married daughters with their magbos sleep on one side of the family hearth with the girls' parents occupying another side but within close observation? It has been shown before that the dormitory came into existence for the purpose of successful hunting, for provision of training in the science of the chase and for propitiation of the hunting gods. This is true equally of the Ghotul, the Dhumkuria and the Morang. The close association of these instituation with hunting and rites connected with it, or the periodical ceremonial under-taking of chase during the year leaves no room for doubt about the true cause of its origin. As far as the Moshup is concerned, the Abang puts it beyond the sphere of conjecture—the organization of the Moshup into hunting units, the storage of animal skulls and the performance of fesivities like Ampi and Gine unmistakably demonstrate the underlying philosophy.

The dormitory system then owes its origin to the hunting stage of the society and cannot last in its old form with the changes that are rapidly taking place in the modern society with the introduction of intensive cultivation and development of industries. The abolition of head-hunting and gradual abandonment of hunting for procurement of food are undermining the basis of its existence. Yet in the training that it gives the young and adolescents it amply provides for discipline and corporate existence which are the real ingredients of character building. The comradeship between the adolescents and youths of both sexes and its gaiety and fun give the inmates the joy of living and help in the fulfilment of the much needed emotional demands.

The Moshup is the most distinguishing feature in the life of the group of the tribes of the Siang Frontier Division who come under the orbit of Abor culture, namely Shimong, Milang, Karko, Konkar, Panggi, Minyong, Padam and Pasi, extending from the proximity of the northern snow-ranges along the MacMahon line to the foothills below Pasighat and from the Sissiri in the Lohit Frontier Division in the east to the valleys of the Siyom and simen on the west. Although our information on the tribes living in the norhtern and north-western territories like the Bori, Bokar, Pailibos, and Ashings is not complete yet what we do know about them shows that the Moshup, known among them as Bange, exists. Its northernmost extension can be traced up to the influence of the Abors who inhabited this tract and still comprise a considerable portion of the population, for the dormitory system is absent among the Membas as well as among the Hill Miri, Apatani and Dafla tribes west of the Subansiri river. Similarly in the east the Mishmis of the Lohit valley do not posses the dormitory. Even among the Gallongs who live in the valleys of the Siyom and Simen although the Dere(as they call the Moshup), is present, its scope and function are limited to the holding of the tribal council and entertainment of guests. The dere does not provide sleeping accommodation for the young men nor is there any corres-ponfing arrangement for the girls. The zone of the Moshup institution is, therefore, limited to the tribes belonging to the Abor group proper. Among them, however, there is a close similarity in the structure and organisation with only minor variations reflecting the topographical and institutional differnces that have subsequently arisen, but indicating the basic uniformity of the Moshup as enjoyed by the Abang. It is my intention, therefore, to discuss them as a whole and then to indicate inwhat particular respects the inter-group and regional differences have developed.

The earliest account of the Abor Moshupwas given by Lt R. Wilcox in his "Memoir of a Survey of Assam and the Neighbouring Countries" published in *Asiatic Researches* in 1832, although reference to the Abor occurs in an Account of Assam, compiled in 1807-14 by Francis Buchnan who later came to be known as Francis Hamilton. In pages 76-77 of his account the Abors are mentioned as a wild tribe living immediately beyond the Dikrong River just north of the Chingpos. There is some confusion, however, about the exact position of the Abors and even their relation with the Khamptis. As an officer of the Revenue Survey, Wilcox was appointed Assistant to Capt Bedford to survey the sources of the Dihang or Brahmaputra. Bedford preceded Wilcox and arrived in the Abor Hills in November 1825, but was not allowed to go beyond Pasial(Pasighat). In the account of his journey published in the Government Gazette dated Feb. 2,1826 he mentioned his meeting Pasial and Minyong Abors of the villages of Pedu, Sibu and Membu but did not write anything about the Moshup or Abor dormitory system. Lt Wilcox came by boat from Singharughat to Sikughat accompanied by Lt Burlton and visited Membu (Mebo) which was then situated on a range of hills across the river Siku somewhat east of the present site of the Mebo village. Mebo was then the largest settlement of the Padam Abors in the lower region, consisting of about 100 houses on the centre of which was the dormitory. Wilcox called it by the Naga name of "Morang," and described it as a large building which serves as a hall of audience and debate, a place of reception of strangers and a house for the bachelors of the village. Accomodation was provided for him in it but he preferred to camp outside. In the Kebang or meeting of the village elders that was held in the Morang, people from the surrounding villages including Shilluk attended. Wilcox saw young bachelors gathered in the Morang at night and warming themselves by the wood-fire, and found that the decisions of the council made in the Morang were described as those of the Raj with the full authority of the village behind. The farthest point reached by him was the left bank of the Dihang oposite the village of Padu beyond which he was not permitted to go. Capt Neufville, the Political Agent visited Membu in

1827, to discuss with the Abors about the settlement of the Miris and according to the Abors considered the Morang to be a fine building. The next visitor was Dr. John M'Cosh, Lecturer in the Medical College of Calcutta who came to the Abor and Mishmi hill in 1837 and referred to the Moshup as the hall of the entertainer where animal skulls were hung. He was followed by Major V.Vetch, political Agent of Upper Assam, who came to the Abor villages in 1847 and 1848 regarding the amount of 'Posa' to be paid to the Abor tribe but his attempt to penetrate into the parent villages of the Bor-Abor (Padam) did not succeed. He spoke of the Bor-Abors as blunt, independent and warlike but furnished no particulars about the dormitory. Incidentally the Assamese word "Abor" means non-tributory or independent people and was applied in a general sense to the wild inde- pendent tribes of the North-Eastern Frontier irrespective of whether they were Abor, Mishmi, Dafla, Naga, (such as Abor Mishmi, Abor Dafla, Abor Naga etc.). It has no derogatory meaning and implies truculence rather than savagery. Father Nicholas Michael Krick, a French priest who crossed into the Tibetan village of Samety twice between 1852 and 1854 to spread the Gospel was murdered treacherously by the Mishmi Chief Kaissa, visited the Abor village of Membu in 1853 and published an account of his visit to the Abor territory in pages 169-201 of his book entitled "Relation d'un Voyage au Tibet en Tibetet d'un Voyage chez les Abors en 1853". The portion containing his account of the Abors was published in English by the *Rev A. Gille S.J.* in the *Journal of the Asiatic Society of Bengal* in 1913. Father Kricks first encounter with the Abors occurred in November 19, 1851 when he visited them with Captain Smith on the back of an elephant with an escort of 200 soldiers. In 1853, however, he went as far as Membu which apparently was at the same place as Wilcox found it, "on the curved flanks of a mountain" 600 ft above the plain. He was provided shelter at the Moshup which he called "the common building" and "guard-house where huntsmen gathered for hunting meet." He also called the Moshup a council house in which all political questions and topics of the day were discussed. According to him the Moshup served the purposes of extraordinary gatherings and young unmarried men slept there. Among other things, Father Krick found it to be the meeting place of old men who could no longer work but were treated with respect and consideration. We owe for a more detailed account of the Moshup to E.T. Dalton who visited the Abor

Hills accompanied by Lt E.G. Eden of the Assam Light Infantry in 1855, in his capacity as Principal Assistant to the Governor General's Agent in Assam. Before he became the Commissioner of Chotanagpur he spent a considerable time in visiting the country between the Lohit and the Dihang and came to Membu in 1855 and like his predecessors was given shelter in the Morang as he called the Moshup but he preferred to camp outside. The Morang was situated in the most commanding part of the village and Membu was found by him to have doubled in size from the time of Lt Wilcox. In the lower and most compact part of the village he counted as 150 houses. He found the Morang built in the same style as private houses but much bigger, about 200 ft long, consisting of 16 or 17 hearths. He mentioned a central fireplace (Radang) where he was seated along with the Gams. In the Kebang held during his visit at the Morang there were not less than 300 persons present. Dalton found that it was occupied at night by the unmarried young men of the village, both freemen and slaves. A certain portion of the married men, also according to his information kept guard at night to forestall any surprise enemy attack. The Morang functioned as the council house where the Gams and all adult men assembled and issued orders to the village, such as the declaration of genna or holiday on the occasion of his visit. According to him the Morang was the common treasury of the village and had certain property of its own such as pigs, poultry etc., which were kept for public use. Like Fr Krick he found the superannuated men of the village living in the Morang at public expense. Following Dalton, J.F. Needham, Political Agent of Sadiya visited Mambu in 1884 but he was not allowed to proceed beyond the Balek group of villages. He, however, was the first man to use the Abor expression '*Moshup*' for the dormitory instead of '*Morang*' as had been done by previous visitors. He found the Abors to be exceedingly proud of their Moshup in which all important topics were discussed and disposed of.

The accounts of the Abor Moshup from Wilcox down to Needham were confined to the villages of the lower regions. They show certain variations in the size of the village and the Moshup building that had taken place during the intervals, indicating the growth of villages like Membu due to the influx of people from other parts as well as the fact that the Moshup building had no fixed dimensions but varied in length and number of hearths to meet the needs of the changing situations at the time of its periodical reconstructions.

During the period following Dalton's visit from 1859 to 1909 several visits were made including that of Williamson in 1909 and not less than 10 military expeditions were sent to the Abor Hills for reprisals of murders and raids perpetrated by the tribe on friendly people of the neighbouring villages. The last and biggest of these was the Abor Expedition of 1911-12 sent for punishment of the murderers of Dr. Gregorson and Mr. Williamson, Political Agent, on 30th and 31st March, 1911 respectively at Renging and Komsing and for establishing administrative control over the territory. The expedetion was under the command of Major-General Bower with Capt W. B. Hore as Field Intelligence Officer and Sir George Dunbar as Commandant of the Lakhimpur Battalion of police as one of the officers. The expedition, starting from Kobo on October, 1911 traversed the Gallong and Abor territories on both banks of the Dihang (Siang) reaching as far north as Singing on latitude 28.45° north. We are indebted to Capt Hore for the most authentic account of the Abor village structures and Moshup organizations of the upper regions. Capt Hore travelled with the expedition all through the Abor territory and disclosed many hitherto unknown facts about their customs and rites with particular reference to the dormitories. He found that the Moshup varied according to the size and condition of the village. In the Minyong country for instance on the right bank of the Dihang, the Moshup at Komsing was as long as 250 ft with nine fireplaces. On the other hand in the northern villages such as those of Riga, Dimroh etc., each clan lived sparately under its own Gam and had its own Moshup. There was no common village Moshup as in the lower regions. Hore corroborated the earlier findings of Wilcox and Dalton that the Moshup served not only as the sleeping place of the unmarried men but also as the council house where all matters pertaining to the village were discussed and decided. He was also the first to call attention to the existence of the Rasheng or dorminatory for unmarried women which he found prevalent in the upper regions particulary on the eastern section of the Dihang valley. In the Memoir published by Dunbar, the word Moshup is spelt as "Moshup" and described as a barrack for unmarried men. The Moshup acording to him was situated in the central part of the village and was a big building with numerous exits, built on the same pattern as the private houses. It was the place where guests were entertained and councils held. Dunbar noticed that women were prohibited from entering the

Moshup. With regard to the Rasheng, however, he found that men had free entrance. He described the Moshup in the Minyong village of Kombong as a fine building outside the village itself. He was mistaken, however, in thinking that the Dere (Moshup) of the Gallong was also a bachelors' dormitory. But he was right in stating that the Gallongs had no house corresponding to the Rasheng and girls slept in their parents' houses. After Dunbar no trustworthy account of the Abor life and dormitory customs appeared nor was any systematic survey undertaken till our investigation from 1948 when a serious attempt was made to assess the true significance of the institution.

The Moshup is built in a prominent part of the village suitable as the centre of community life. In the olden days it acted also as an outpost from where the different approaches to the village could be watched. The Abors were a fighting people like the Nagas and until a Few decades ago were engaged in constant tribal and inter-tribal feuds. Not only did the village units fight against one another but there were often confederations of tribes such as those of the Padams and Milangs against the Mishmis in 1894, of the Shimongs and Karkos against the Minyongs of Riga against the Panggis to prevent them from trading with the plains in the south and through the Shimongs with the Tibetans in the north. As a measure of protection, the villages were built on the spurs of hills overlooking the valley and were well stockaded and flanked by rock-chutes. The paths leading to the village were often panjeed. Well-known stockades such as those of Igar two miles from Rotung and Kekkar Monnying near Kebang were not taken without difficulty by the Abor Expedition of 1911-12.

The Moshup served like the Naga Morang as the centre from which raids were undertaken and which could also function as the village defensive organization. With the disappearance of interibal fighting and the gradual establishment of peace this aspect of Moshup life has also disappeared but its position in a commanding part of the village still remains. Wilcox found the Moshup of Mebo in 1826 in the middle of the village. At the time of the Abor Expedition eighty-five years after, the location of the Mebo Moshup had shifted to its north-western entrance. When we visited Mebo in 1948-49 the position was unchanged. The Moshups at Bodak and Lekko (at the old sites before the earth-quake) and villages like Ayeng, Balek and Jero were also at the entrance, but the Kalek, Ledung and Sibbum Moshups were in the centre. The Memosepo Moshup was at the extreme eastern outskirts of the village giving a commanding view of the valley. There is, therefore, no precise canon for the location of the Moshup but it depends on the topography as well as the suitability as an observation post and as a centre of community life with some open ground in front, convenient for a Ponung Ingkong i.e., an open dancing ground for the ponungs.

Unlike the dwelling houses, the Moshup is a single rectangular hall divided into a number of meroms or hearths made in the shape of a wooden square 4 ft × 4 ft or more sunk in the floor of the house to a depth of one foot or so and rammed with gravel and earth with a stone fireplace in the centre called letik. Unlike the Nocte chief's Morang the floor of the Abor Moshup has no special design. It is made of split bamboo in chequered pattern as in the dwelling houses. Over the merom there is a square wooden frame called kumbang or bare where the heads of the animals killed by the members of the merom are hung. Below this there is a platform called perek, made of split bamboo on which articles belonging to the members of the merom may be kept. In the villages of the lower foothills, however, such as those of Ayeng, Mebo, Kalak and Ledung, the perek is often dispensed with only the kumbang or the bare remaining. Around the kumbang there is a square frame of a thorny creeper called tatkiye forming a sort of overhead boundary to act as a protective shield. The Abors believe that just as the thorns of tatkiye entangle a man, so would setting up of a tatkiye frame immoblize animals during hunting. The tatkiye frame is considered symbolic of the obstacles put in the path of animals and is considered to be of good import.

The Moshup was originally conceived on a clan basis each clan having one. For instance there are ten clans at Damroh and there are ten Moshups, one for each of the opiuns (clans) such as Orang Moshup, Borang Moshup, Lego Moshup, Pertin Moshup, Tayeng Moshup etc. The same is true of the Moshups of the upper regions, in Shimong, Milang, Karko, Riga, Gekko etc. In these parts there are no common village Moshups as each of the opiuns lives separately with its Gams and Kebangs (councils) as onserved by Hore in Damroh in 1911-12. It appears, therefore, that on ancient times, as illustrated in the pattern of village organization in the parent villages of the upper regions, for defensive purposes and for the common interests of the village only, the opiuns combined and acted together, but for their own socio-economic life, such as hunting and festivities connected with it they functioned independently through their own Moshups. These clan or opium Moshups are called Retek or Suptek as distinct from the central organisation belonging to the whole village which is called Moshup.

When, with the pressure of population and shortage of tillable land, people began to move to the southern virgin lands, they at first followed the pattern of their parent villages and each clan led its socio-economic life separately with its own Retek and Gam. Continued immigration of new groups of people causing sudden increase in certain clans which could not be accommodated in the exisiting Reteks led gradually to the growth of a central Moshups where the surplus huntsmen could be housed. Sibbum offers an example of this transistional state. When the Panggis first settled here from their parent village of Gekko, the nine clans that moved, namely Taying, Pange, Tage, Gate, Tateng, Tengu, Taku, Padung and Age set up their independent Reteks, and, although members of a common village organization for political and defensive purposes, pursued their independent socio-economic clan life. Soon, however, the rise in number in some clans such as the Pange and Padung, who could not be taken in the clan Retek and who belonged to none of the already settled clans, made it necessary to have an organization which could accomodate them irrespective of their clan affiliations. In this way a central village Moshup grew up. The different exisiting Reteks were retained in the beginning but the concept of clanwise membership of Retek was transferred to the meroms of the central Moshup which finally replaced them. Not all the meroms, however, were filled up on the clan basis; professional and other heterogenous groups were taken on topographical and other considerations and the Moshups came to represent a true cross section of the community. Thus out of the nine meroms in the central Sibbum Moshup, two, namely Pange and Padung are clan meroms, two others like Keku and Kebuk signify the chronological orders of their establishment. Sange has reference to the elevated nature of its hunting ground etc., and Bari is constituted of the singers of Bari sung at the construction of houses, namely "Ge-ey-ey Abonane Kape Mone-ey etc.." During this transitional stage the clan Reteks were retained along with the central Moshup whose meroms were formed partly on clan basis and partly on other considerations.

A further development occurred with increased colonization as shown in the Moshup organization of Jero where the Panggis moved from Sibbum in their drive southwards towards the Yammer valley. As the number of colonists was small there was no scope for separate Reteks. Accordingly only one village Moshup was set up with four meroms namely Sange, Paran, Riang and Romkeya of which Paran and Romkeya were clan meroms and Sange took the name of Sange merom of Sibbum whose members had moved into Jero. In the third phase of development seen mostly in the villages of the foothills whether Padam, Pasi or Minyong, the clan Moshups or Retecks have completely disappeared, replaced by a central village Moshup. Where the villages are large as at Komsing, Ayeng and Mebo, the meroms are many but formed chiefly on topographical position of the houses of the memebers or other factors. The clan membership of the meroms as transferred fronm the Reteks found little scope in the Moshup. It became represenlive of the total village rather than a federation of different clans e.g., in the Ayeng Moshup there are altogether nine meroms divided into the Ango-Sango sections. The names of the meroms have reference to their position in the Moshup such as Gidum meaning one end, Gingkong the other end and Radung the centre of the Moshup.

A still further stage of development is illustrated in the village of Bordak. This village was founded about 1915-16 by some of the Padam families moving from Padu and Silli belonging chiefly to the Taying, Megu, and Perme clans totalling altogether about 40 houses, not sufficient for forming meroms either on the basis of clan or topography. The three meroms called Romdang, Romtak and Romsam were formed on age basus i.e. Romdam for old men, Romdang for young men and Romtak for adolescents.

The merom division of the Moshup is basic in Abor society, each merom being considered a social unit such as it occurs in the ordinary family dwellings. This idea of a single unit of the merom was, therefore, a transference from the family to the Moshup. The number of meroms in a Moshup, although it varies in different villages, is made primarily with the idea of their forming viable hunting units i.e., neither too small nor too large for the purposes of successful hunting. In the Reteks of the upper villages there are often more than one owing to the large number of members; as for example, in the Irang Retek at Damroh, where our party stayed in 1949 there were two meroms. The same is true of some of the other Reteks which have large membership. In the Sibbum Moshup we found nine meroms; similarly Hore found nine in the Komsing Moshup. Wilcox found as many as 17 or 18 in the Mebo Moshup which increased to 24 at the time of Dalton's visit, but at the time of our visit the number of meroms did not exceed nine. It is possible that the large number of meroms mentioned by Wilcox and Dalton is due to the inclusion of Romsams made for the use of mijjims (old men). At Sibbum, for instance, there were nine Romsams for nine meroms during our visit in 1950. These Romsams are without kumbang and perek and are really extensions of meroms functioning only during the day and not true meroms. At the present time in the lower Abor villages separate Romsams do not exist but old men or mijjims sit and work together in any part of the Moshup during the day.

The membership of the merom does not depend on the individual but is hereditary. Children of the families belonging to particular meroms whether constituted on clan or other basis become automatically members of these meroms and cannot change to any other merom according to their wishes. When new people move into particular villages it is the Kebang which decides in which particular merom or meroms they should be placed. They are usually assigned to those meroms whose membership has declined due to depletion caused by death or migration, with an eye to the position of their houses. In the case of people belonging to particular clans where clan meroms still exist the newcomers automatically become members of their clan meroms. In some cases, as for example at Jero, if Minyongs and Padmas instead of Panggis come and settle in the village, those of the former tribe who belong to Jammu and the Iring clans will automatically become members of the Riang and Ronkeya clans and the Taying, Porting and Parmeya of the Padams will also become members of the Ronkeya clan. These clans are accepted as affiliated to the Riang and Tonkeya clans of the Panggis and can, therefore, partake of their privileges and obligations.

The basis of the Moshup organization is the Ango-Sango division, a feature which distinguish it from the dormitory systems of other tribes. The social structure of the Abor tribes is founded on dual organisation which not only regulates marriage but runs through the entire tribal life. Among the Minyongs, for instance, the marriage division is called Kuri Kuming and among the Padam it is known as

Nguda, and Nguping among the Panggis. All the clans of the tribes belong to either of these two divisions and marriage within them is not permitted but must take place between the clans of the two divisions. Any infringement of this rule entails heavy fine and even expulsion. Although this system is no longer rigidly followed, for all practical purposes it still hold good. For purposes of war and control of trade, there was a similar division between the northern and the southern villages. The Minyongs of the villages above Kebang to Riga came under a confederation known as Ngorang and from Kebang down to the foothills it was known as Ngango. The equivalent Padam divisions were Gingkong Magbo and Gidewe Magbo. The use of the word Magbo (bridegroom) signifies their subsequent development into exogamous divisions. With the disappearance of war and enforcement of free-communication between the north and the south, the divisions have ceased to exist. There can, however, be no doubt that the territorial divisions between the north and the south were of later growth but the Kuri Kuming, Nguda and Nguping divisions for the regulation of marriage are certainly of an early epoch. These dual divisions, however, cannot be integrated with the Ango-Sango division which must be considered as a separate organization regulating a different sphere of Abor life. At the present time its importance is much greater than that of the former. The sphere of Ango-Sango division embraces the set-up of the whole village, the political organization, Moshup, hunting, as well as the ponung. Accordingly, all villages in the Abor territory are divided into an Ango and Sango section with a pathway running between the two. The eastern portion is known as the Sango and the western Ango. For instance in the village of Ayeng the Sango section lies east of the central village pathway towards the Sibbum korong and the Ango section towards the Siku korong. At the start the sections were of equal or of very nearly equal size but the equilibrium is often disturbed with the migration of some families to other villages or their movement from one part to the other. As for example, the chief Gam of the village, Talo Borang, moved from Sango to Ango ssection and Lego Gam similarly came over from Ango to Sango section in the village of Kalek. While change of habitation from one to the other section is permitted, the affiliation of the person to his original division remains true. During kiruk or ceremonial hunting and Moshup feast he must go with his original group though at that time he may live on the other side.

Among the Abors, before the extension of the administration, each tribe had its own land recognized by convention; the whole of the area fron Damroh to Dambuk belonged to the Padam tribe. Within this territory the Padam villages had their territorial boundaries well recognized and no poach·ng on the hunting ground of one village by another was tolerated. If such a thing happened then there would be troubole. This as a matter of fact was one of the reasons of inter-village warfare. Within the village itself the hunting ground of the Ango and the Sango sections are sharply demarcated by the Kebang. The meroms of each section similarly had their respective allotted shares within these grounds. No poaching either by the Ango on the Sango sections or *vice vera* or by one merom on the hunting ground of another was permitted. This is probably due to the original independent life led by each clan with its separate Moshup and Kebang, as it still found in the upper villages like Damroh, Karko, Shimong, Milang and Gekko. The meroms developing subsequently on clan basis when a central village Moshup first took shape retained their separate hunting grounds even when at a still later stage the meroms ceased to be formed altogether of a single clan membership. Should, however, the violation by one of the Ango-Sango sections of the well-defined hunting ground of the other take place there is likely tobe serious trouble not unoften ending in fighting. In the case of poaching by one merom on the hunting ground of another, a fine is imposed depending on the nature of the game killed; usually a perok (an earthen jar) of apong has to be given to the aggrieved merom. When, however, large game, such as a wild boar is killed, a pig is the penatly. In case of samll game a fine of four annas is the usual compensation. The proceeds of these fines would not, however, go to the fund of the whole Moshup but to the aggrieved merom.

The division of work between the Ango-Sango divisions though primarily concerned with hunting is also extendd to other spheres excepting agriculture: ariks are distributed not on Ango-Sango basis but indiscriminately. In all cases of ritual hunting or kiruks such as Ampi-Dorung which takes place between December and January when the granary is exhausted and in Gine- Dorung between October and November at the time of harvesting, the Sango section will do the kiruk on the eastern side of the territory and the Ango section on the western side; but the game when brought to the Moshup is not separately distributed but is made on a joint basis as the game bagged may not be equal in the two sections. In all other important activities like Etar i.e. construction of the fence for the mithum, Aran and other Dorungs, the two sections are assigned separate tasks; but the interest of the village as a whole is never forgotton although the explanation now offered—that the assignment of separate tasks brings in competition and each group tries to do better than the other with the result that the work is most efficiently accomplished—is certainly a rationalization. The basis of separation must have been due to the existence of the dual division from a remote past. Before building the Moshup or before its annual reconstruction the two sections collect the materials and store them separately in their own sections, but at the time of the actual they work together.

The dances performed during Aran by men is on a village basis led by a Miri; for instance at Kalek, Mutsang who is the undisputed Miri of the village leads it for the entire village. In very small villages like the Padam village of Bordak where there are only 40 houses, the Moshup although divided on the Ango-Sango basis has no separate hunting grounds alloted to the two sections but in kiruks and in ordinary hunting the three meroms go together and the game is distributed to the entire Moshup. This deviation has taken place due to the exigencies of circumstances and is a foreboding of what is going to take place in small settlements in the future. In all the old villages of both the upper and the lower regions, however, the original pattern of Ango-Sango division still holds good and is the most important factor in the Moshup and the village organization of the tribe.

The inmates of the Moshup are called Moshup-ka. There is no definite age for entry to the Mishup. The ususal practice is that when a boy is able to sleep away from his parents he must come to the Moshup and sleep there. In the case of the Padams and Pasis the entry to the Moshup begins from the time the boy starts wearing the ugon or the piece of cloth hung in front to cover the genitals, but among the Minyongs and Panggis the boy is sent to the Moshup when he is able to take care of himself. He must come and sleep in the merom to which members of his family belong. Membership of the merom cannot be changed. Even if for some reason a family moves from one section, say Sango, to the other section (Ango), his membership to the original merom would still remain binding. In the merom there is no scramble for places for which there is no special rule or procedure but once a boy sleeps in a particular spot his place is not taken by any other even if he may come late. The Moshup-ka are further divided into distinct age groups namely Anyengs or novices, Radang the next age group and the senior group known as the Abuing. Each merom has a proportion though not necessarily equal of these three age groups. The Anyengs or the novices usually come to sleep in the Moshup after their evening meals and are expected to bring firewood and light the fire. If there is any neglect they are taken to task by the Abuing. From the Abuing one member is selected not on seniority alone but on ability also, to act as the leader of the merom and is known as Abuiyana. In addition to the Abuiyana, in some Moshups, there is a Moshup Rotung who is in charge of the entire Moshup-ka. Abom Tayeng was a Moshup-ka of the time of our visit in 1954.

Besides the fagging duties, the primary function of the Moshup being training in hunting, the Anyengs are slowly initiated in that art by the two senior groups. When a merom goes out on a hunt they advance in a converging line shouting "Ho Ho" with the Anyengs between the older boys so that they are not exposed to sudden danger or attacks from animals. The boy who first spots the game has the right to shoot it first. If he misses he does not get a second chance. If and when the animal is killed, he is, however, given the front part as he has first sighted the animal. The members of the merom, both Anyengs and Abuings, must carry out the instructions of the Abuiyana or the leader of the merom. If any one absents himself from the Moshup excepting when ill or disobeys, he is first reprimanded; if he persistently does so or fails to carry out the orders he is beaten with a stick. Among the Panggis he is only scolded but not beaten. In the case of a serious offence, however, e.g., the failure to carry out the orders of the Kebang, he is to pay an ajeng or fine. As an extreme case among the Padams and Panggis, but not the Minyongs among whom only physical punishment is given, rice may be forcibly taken from his kumsum and fruits of his jackfruit tree destroyed. The parents do not and cannot interfere as they consider it a just punishment. The proceeds of the ajeng are given to the injured merom and not to the Moshup as a whole or the Bango.

As hunting takes place on the Ango-Sango and merom basis the hunters belonging to each of these sections gather at their respective dumbangs and do not start from one and the same. Each village has well marked dumbangs separately for the Ango and Sango sections e.g., the Sango dumbang of the village Ledung is known as Dekan dumbang and that of the Ango is called the Sille dumbang from the name of the Sille korong or stream. The position of a dumbang in hunting among the Abor tribes as enjoyed in the Abang is very important. It is here that the hunters gather, as well as the mijjims or the old men who can no longer actually hunt. In small hunts this is not usually done but in all major operations like the Ampi-Dorung or Gine-dorung and other important kiruks this practice is followed. The animals killed by members of each of these two sections are brought to their respective dumbangs and there they are cut into peices by the mijjims. Smaller animals, like rats, or small birds are consumed at the dumbang but portions of large animals are brought to the Moshup and there distributed among the mijjims. The hunters do not take any share except sometimes a little of the portions given to the mijjims of their families. The meat must be cooked in the Moshup. Formely the Ango-Sango sections used to eat their shares separately but nowdays they all sit together and eat. At the end of each of these kiruks, the patar mijjim, the oldest man of the village gives a feast. Rice and apong are prepared in his house and brought to the Moshup but the meat has to be cooked in the Moshup itself. Women, however, cannot take part in the mijjim's feast either in the Moshup or in the houses of the mijjims. These feasts to celebrate successful hunts or Dorungs is a purely men's affair. When the hunt is undertaken not on the merom basis but on the initiative of one or two members, the game need not be given to the mijjims but the hunters take it all. Even in the case of kiruks while the front part of the animal is given to the hunters the rest goes to the mijjims.

The skulls of the animals killed are hung on the kumbang of the respective meroms of the hunters. A ceremony known as Bango-Bomdum has to be performed before the skulls are hung. This ceremony differs from animal to animal. For a small deer a fixed quantity of ginger and apong is thrown on the skulls but in the case of a large deer such as sambar or a wild boar, a fowl has to be killed and intestines removed. It is then pierced with a stick and is hung on the road leading to the village. In many Moshups, particularly smaller ones as in Jero, Ledung, Bordak etc., the skulls are not hung in the kumbang but in a line along the northern walls of the Moshups called reu or konyang. This is the usual practice nowdays except in the large

Moshups of the upper regions where the older and more orthodox custom of hanging the skulls on the kumbang is still observed. The philospphy behind the preservation of the skulls in the Moshup lies in the Abor belief that the animal souls(monit mono) like human souls(aith) go out at night and being attracted by the smell of apong and ginger come to the Moshup. And when the souls are wandering about, the animals are spiritually blinded by Tori Mono and move about without being able to see and take care of themselves with the result that they become easy preys to hunters. Gaumen Soyen the presiding spirit of the Moshup would then lead the hunters to the animals for a sure and easy bag.

One of the striking feature of the Moshup is the place it provides for the old men or mijjims who can no longer take active part in hunting but still have a part to play in the community life with advice and suggestions they can offer from their experience. It is also to make them feel that they are no longer superfluous to the community but still are useful in their advisory capacity. They may feel also that affection and consideration are still there which are their due from younger members whom they brought up but who are now in control of the activities of the tribe. This aspect of the Moshup life was noticed by early visitors form Wilcox to Dalton. Father Krick was so struck by it that he described it as surpassing even that recorded of old Lacaedemon of ancient Greece. With each merom there is a supplimentary hearth called Romsam where the old and infirm male members of the families belonging to the meroms sit together and chat during the day and may even sleep at night if there is not enough room in the ekum. The system still prevails in the Moshup at Sibbum and those of the upper villages but has disappeared in the lower ones as shown from the fact that Father Krick found the Romsam in the Moshup of Mebo in 1853 but during our visit in 1949 there was no Romsam at the Mebo Moshup. In all the ceremonial hunts or kiruks as well as those undertaken by the joint efforts of the meroms the animals killed are not taken by the hunters. Only in the case of wild boar or gumbong the actual hunter takes the front part, and the trunk is given to the mijjims of the respective Romsams who divide it among themselves. When, however, the game is a large one, a deer or a wild boar, it is given to the village as a whole from whcih the hunters may get a little share. On their own part, the mijjims have to provide feasts on these occasions by giving rice and apong cooked in their houses and brought to the Moshup. The meat, however, has to be cooked in the Moshup itself. All male members of the village participate in these feasts but the patar mijjim does not take part except in providing the stuff. His satisfaction is that the feast given by him has been enjoyed by the members. Women are not allowed to take part in the mijjims feasts. The provision of these feasts by the mijjims at the end of the annual Dorungs is intended to preserve their self-respect that they are not parasites as well as to give them satisfaction that by means of theis feast they are still able to add to the enjoyment and gaiety of the life of the village. In this manner, a sort of two-way traffic is maintained viz. not only is the filial bond kept strong but the feeling is sustained that the mijjims even in their old age when they are unable to hunt still play a useful life. One will observe groups of them on a sunny day sitting in the open courtyard in front of the Moshup engaged in these activites. The mijjims in their turn do not remain idle but spend their time in basketry, wood-work and other handicrafts needed for their families.

In addition to hunting and warfare, the Moshup functions as the centre of the village political life. As observed by Wilcox, Krick, Dalton, Needham and Capt Hore, the Moshup is the meeting place of the Kebang or the village council where all important matters pertaining to the community are discussed. In former times, measures for protecting the village against enemy raids or for attack on other tribes used to be discussed. At the present time, however, with the cessation of inter-tribal warfare the Kebang's activities are confind to village affairs, declaration of genna, accommodation and supply of porters for visitors, the fixing of the date of the kiruks etc. The Kebang assembled in the Moshup is also the chief judiciary of the village where complaints by the villagers can be brought and punishment to offenders meted out. The orders of the Kebang are carried out through the Moshup-ka whose duties are to inform the villagers of the decisions of the Kebang and to act as messengers on urgent work for the Kebang. The orders of the Kebang are conveyed by the chief Gam to the Moshup-ka through the Abuiyana or the leader of the merom. In the absence of the chief Gam the next Gam in seniority is competent to issue the orders. Any reluctance to obey the orders of the Kebang is considered as a serious offence and the punishment is beating or fine. As the Abor saying goes "Lomnan ager gipayada" (for urgent work go). The importance of the Moshup, therefore, is not confined to the training and efficient performance of hunting and festivities associated with it but also in its functioning as the instrument through which the Kebang operates. Without the Moshup the entire village government by the Kebang would collapse.

"Rasheng – Girls' Dormitory"

The women's counterpart of the Moshup is called the Rasheng, literally, a meeting place or rest-house. The Abang gives the reason for its construction as the need for gaiety, amusement and the art and regulation of love-making. The boys are trained in the Moshup in the various spheres of men's activites such as hunting, warfare, administration and rituals connected with these. In the case of women, however, the duties chiefly concern household affairs, such as jhum cultivation, weaving, cooking and taking care of children. But amusement such as dancing, music and the art of love-making cannot be taught by the parents, so Idum Bote or the Doying felt, on the completion of the Moshup, that a similar institution was necessary for women. As, however, love-making cannot be carried on under the observation of Uyus(spiits) their presence was not invoked. Thus, the Rasheng is of a purely secular character and has no sanctity or spiritual significance behind it like the Moshup which is sacred as an abode of the good gods to ensure successful hunting. Unlike the Moshup it has no central institution but is made purely on the basis of clan organization. Like the clan Moshups there are several Rashengs in a village. Here also the Ango-Sango division operates. As usually there is only one, the number of girls being fewer, the merom is not made on an Ango-Sango basis, but those Rashengs on the Sango side of the village are called called Sango Rashengs and those on on the Ango side Ango Rashengs. The Rasheng, being confined to a clan, is a small simple structure about 40ft × 20ft without any porch. The walls are well protected with wooden planks and so is the entrance which is secure and strong to prevent forcible entry and undue liberty being taken by young men. Just as the boys are entitled to be members of the Moshup when they begin to wear an ugon, girls who have reached puberty and whose breasts have developed, can sleep on the Rasheng. There is no Pobang in the Rasheng as no Ipaks are performed in the Rasheng and no Uyus reside there. The Rasheng is generally situated in a secluded corner of the village and its whereabouts are not publicized but are known to the villagers. The chief functions of the Rasheng as enjoined in the Abang are the art of love-making and the organization of ponung or music and dance. Just as Karduk taught Doni the Lutor Delonge so also Karpung showed the girls how to dance the Monam which is done by men and women together in the Rasheng in demonstration of love. Other dances for gaiety and amusement are also performed in the Rasheng, but those which have a bearing on agriculture such as the Solung dance, are not done in the Rasheng itself but in the Ponung Ingkong or the dancing ground in front of the Moshup as this concerns the propitiation of various gods and goddesses connected with agriculture.

Although the Rasheng is not so well organized as the Moshup, it has its own system which is strictly followed. The girls constituting the members of a Rasheng are called Ponung i.e., bevy of girls organized for music and dancing. Discipline is enforced by the leader of the Ponung called "Ponung Rotum" and any disobedience or neglect of duties is punished with reprimand or fine. Younger girls pass through a period of novitiate when they bring firewood, light fire and do other work assigned to them. They come to the Rasheng after their meals and it is their duty to see that the fire is lighted so that when the older girls come they find everything in order. The younger girls or the novitiates sleep on one side of the hearth and the older on the other where they receive their lovers.

There are two kinds of Rashengs girls, namely those who have recognized lovers with whom they consort regularly and must often sleep in the Rasheng and those who do not have recognized boy friends but consort with any of the Moshup boys they please. The older Rasheng girls who are visited by their lovers come late and sometimes, when there is a Miri or dance, after the dances are over. Each pair sleeps side by side under a baḍu(rug). Though the inmates know what is going on, so long as the sexual act is not seen but done under the cover of the badu, deceny and decorum are not considered to be violated. Only unmarried girls can have such relationship with their boy friends. Among the Abor as well as many other tribes, particularly the Naga, such as the Konyaks, Noctes, Aos etc., among whom the girls' dormitory is similarly developed, a considerable amount of premarital freedom and latitude is allowed to young people of both the sexes. Among the Noctes, after the betrothal, the couple are expected to sleep in the Yampo or dormitory and not in the house untill one or two children are born. This is the recognized social practice. Among the Abors who have a similar custom, on the other hand, girls may sleep with their boy friends only in the Rasheng so long as the betrothal has not taken place and the assum or the purchase money has not been paid. But after the nametaddo (Betrothal) they are not permitted to do so. They must sleep in their own houses for three or four years before they go to their husbands' houses. While laxity and freedom exist during the premarital period, after mariage conjugal fidelity is strictly observed. On the occasion of the betrothal the bride's father enjoins upon his daughter that henceforth she must sleep with any other boy but only with her magbo (groom). Any violation leads to heavy fine or divorce and there is no condoning of extra-marital sexual transgression.

In the free life of the Rasheng it is not possible to prevent sexual union between the members of the same clan although this is against the exogamous rules of the tribe. Among the Noctes who are also exogamous, sexual union between the members of the same clan is not entirely unknown. This has led many observers to think that while marriage is not allowed between the members of the same clan there is no bar to sexual union as such between the members of the same clan among these tribes. As Capt Hore has remarked "cohabitation before marriage is university recognized and curiously enough may take place between persons of the same clan without any breach of the tribal law." In reality, however, such action, though it is ignored, is not socially approved and if any child is born out of such union it is considered a serious offence which is liable to heavy ajeng or fine and the couple may even be excommunicated. Should, however, the girl bear a second child to a member of her own clan she is turned out of her parent's house and may be sold as a slave. In this manner the exogamic rules of the tribe are enforced but it cannot prevent altogether in actual practice sexual intercourse within the prohibited groups. In general, conception in premarital life is not liked and steps are taken to ensure against it and Abor girls often resort to certain abortifacient practices such as the oral use of the juice of the bark of the *sitih* tree or the roots of the *rinko* and *oko* plants. This is done in secret without the knowledge of the elders for this is a crime according to the Abang amounting to the destruction of foetal life. In the event of conception taking place no social stigma falls on the girl but the lover is expected to marry her if outside the clan or pay a heavy fine. When a marriage does not take place althrough permissible, it the child happens to be a boy he takes the surname of the father and if a girl that of the mother and resides with the mother.

The Rasheng is built on clan basis as the Moshup. In all the upper villages there are as many Rashengs as there are clans: for instance, in Damroh there are ten Rashengs for the ten clans. At the time of our visit to Sibbum in 1950 in 1950 there were nine Rashengs corresponding to the nine clans Taying, Pange, Tagi, Geteh, Tatung, Tangu, Taku, Padung and Aje. Similarly at Jero there were three Rashnegs, namely Paran Rasheng, Monku Rasheng and Monc Rashengs. The same situation prevails at Riga, Shimong, Milang, Karko, Gekko and other villages of the upper regions. Below Padu, however, in the lower Abor villages, whether Padam, Minyong or Pasi, the Rasheng does not exist. This is attributed to the influence of people from the plains who consider it as a centre of immorality. With increased contact, this notion has gradually been spreading upwards, and at Jero in 1950, following the example of Balek, the Ponungs refused to allow the Moshup boys to sleep with them with the result that the enraged young men, considering it as contrary to the Abor custom, destroyed the Rasheng houses. Subsequently, however, the Rashengs have been re-established at Jero. From the absence of Rashengs in the lower regions, Hore regarded that the Rasheng was a secaying institution; but from the re-establishment of the Rasheng at Jero in 1950 it may still be considered to be active in the upper regions, fulfilling its allotted place in Abor society. Many old- timers consider the absence of the Rasheng in the lower parts as not altogether beneficial to Abor society for one of the reasons for the institution of the Rasheng was the regulation of sexual behaviour within the tribe. In ancient times before the Rasheng was established there was often indiscriminate sexual intercourse and even incestuous relations took place sometimes as illustrated in the well-known story of Karduk and Karpung. The Rasheng was introduced as a means of stopping indiscriminate sexual intercourse and regulating sexual behaviour so that it could only takes place within approved tribal laws and codes of conduct. During our visits to the Minyong and Padam villages of Ledum and Shilluk, elderly men like Tatem Pada of Ledum and prominent Miris like Akom Megu, Mustang and others complained that the abolition of the Rasheng had led to the decay of sexual morality and young people were found to indulge in such practices at all places such as back portions of dwellings, vacant houses, kumsums or granaries, and in the open fields at all times without any check or hindrance, forgetting not only decency but tribal laws of prohibited relationships. It cannot be denied, therefore, that while the Rasheng as an institution of sleeping place for unmarried persons is abhorrent to the notion of the sancity and decorum of sexual life, it certainly acted as a deterrent to promiscuous union and, in the regulation and control of sexual behaviour among free primitive hunters like the Abors, it played a significant role.

Besides the art of love-making and free mixing between the unmarried of both sexes, the other functions of the Rasheng are (1) the organization of dances of the Ponung, and (2) supply of workers for doing various work in the village or in the houses of others during harvesting and entertainment of distinguished visitors or migams.

Among the Abors dancing is very well organized and has developed into a fine art with great variety of rhythm and dignity. It will be no exaggeration to say that, not excluding the much publicized dances of Manipur, no other primitive tribe has so many picturesque dances as the Abor tribes. The dances are all of the folk-dance type and not danced in solo but in a group with the Miri leading and keeping tune with his yoksa or sword. There are some dances where at the end there is a pairing of couples but most often dances are done in a circle or moving in two converging lines meeting each other. The dance can be led either by a male or female Miri and not unoften female Miris are seen leading the dances. For each Rasheng there is a Ponung or a group of dancers. It is one of the functions of the Rasheng to train girls in the dances with only vocal music sung and without any instrumental accompaniment. The Miri leading the dance will sing the whole song and the Ponung only sing the chorus. The Ponung select from amongst themsmelves the seniormost and the ablest girl as their leader who is called "Ponung Rotum." Seniority, however, is not the only criterion but the important factor is intelligence and personality to inspire confidence in the Ponung. As for instance Arane, (born during the Aran festival), the Ponung Rotum of Jero whom we met in 1950 was not the oldest. She was younger than her companion Pepe, but in point of intelligence and attractive personality she was outstanding and could have made her mark in any society. Like the Moshup-leader she supervises the work of the other girls, organize dances and enforces discipline. If her instructions are disregarded or disobeyed the offender is scolded or fined, and the parents do not interfere. It is the duty of the Rotum to organize the Ponung for dance and there is considerable rivalry between the different Ponungs regarding their dancing performances. It is those Ponungs who are pretty and dance well that have a great demand for them on all festive occasions. The Ponung of each Rasheng dances separately and does not combine with other groups. Being formed on the clan basis each is an independent unit with separate organization and its own Miri. The selection of the Miri to lead the dances depends upon the Ponung Rotum who does so in consultation with the other members as to which of the known persons versed in tribal lore would be the most suitable to act as their Miri. Although a woman is permitted to lead the dances on special occasions as a Miri, only a man can be selected as the recognized Miri of a Ponung, as he is expected to know the Abangs and rituals of dances. There is an elaborate procedure for the selection of the Miri and his installation. The Ponungs have an intermediary called Irging selected from among the well-to-do young men of the clan or village who acts as the go-between. It is the duty of the Irging to do all the work for the Ponung and act on their behalf with the Miri. He entertains the Ponung in his house and at the time of festive dances the Ponung are guests at his house along with the Miri. In return the Ponung work in his field for one day and in the field of the Miri for another day. The Miri cannot demand any remuneration from the Ponung but at the time of his installation or the Solung dance they give him a tadok, a red galé and a Miri kiring, a semi-circular garland of beads hung on his neck as the insignia of the Miri. The Ponung also give him a large quantity of meat as a token of appreciation and love. The relation between the Miri and his Ponung is not merely that of teacher and pupils but of attachment and love. Sexual intercourse between the Miri, the Irging and the Ponung is socially condoned and not objected to by their wives. In the well-known song "Boileko boimang babine baimang boileko boimang" the Miri deplores that "as he is no longer young, he has become like their elder brother, and the Ponung will refuse to take him as their Miri" and although consoled by the latter "Boioleko boeka babine boeku boileko boeka," that "though old and like an elder brother they will still take him as their Miri," he knows that the most intimate part of his association with the Ponung is over. The majority of the dances are connected with various rituals and the invocation of gods and goddesses presiding over various phases of agriculture, the welcoming of guests etc. Just as hunting is the special sphere of man's activity, agriculture is woman's. The special dance called monam, which according to the Abang was taught by Karpung to women, is a mixed dance of young men and women in demonstration of love and is danced in the Rasheng. Other dances are usually danced in the Ponung Ingkong or village dancing ground in front of the Moshup, as the space in the Rasheng is limited. During rains and inclement weather dances are also performed in the Moshup which is more spacious.

The festival which concerns the Ponung specially is the Solung Lune, also known as the Mime Solung or women's festival. It takes place in the months of Yil and Tanno (July and August), during weeding time and before the ripening of amo (summer rice). The Solung ceremonies are connected with agriculture and are in propitation of Kine Nane the presiding deity of ariks(fields) and other Uyus. Just as Ampi and Gine Dorungs are connected with kiruks (hunting) similarly Solung is an agricultural festival *par excellence* and therefore, it concerns women who are in charge of agriculture. It is the most important festival among the Abors and lasts for seven days and nights during which the Miri, specially commissioned by the Ponung and called the Solung Miri, sings the entire Benyat Abang or the origin of agriculture. Spirits headed by Kine Nane look after the ariks and are responsible for the success of the crops. Men are not excluded as women are in the Aran, Ampi and Gine Dorungs. They kill mithun and pigs and collect their blood in the kakong (trough) and prepare in the meat for the feast. They, however, do not participate in the dances which go on for most of the day and night but sit and listen to the narration of the Benyat Abang. The third and the fourth days are genna and after the end of the festival two and a half days are also declared genna with complete cessation of work. During this festival people visit their friends and relatives and are feasted with meat and apong. On the fifth and most important day of the festival known as Benyat Edung, the Ponung visit their individual ariks in gala dress in the morning and perform the cermonial planting of trees and offer the blood of the animals sacrified to Kine Nane and after ringing a pair of emol they invoke her blessings for the success of the crops. On the way back from the field the Ponung perform the same ceremony in the kmsums or granaries. The end of the Solung is celebrated in the Moshup with a feast for men given by the mijjims and known as Melo